ROGER SCRUTON:
THE PHILOSOPHER ON DOVER BEACH

T0038790

Roger Scruton:
The Philosopher on Dover Beach

MARK DOOLEY

BLOOMSBURY CONTINUUM
LONDON · OXFORD · NEW YORK · NEW DELHI · SYDNEY

BLOOMSBURY CONTINUUM
Bloomsbury Publishing Plc
50 Bedford Square, London, WC1B 3DP, UK
29 Earlsfort Terrace, Dublin 2, Ireland

BLOOMSBURY, BLOOMSBURY CONTINUUM and the Diana logo are trademarks of
Bloomsbury Publishing Plc

First published in Great Britain 2009
This edition published 2024

A catalogue record for this book is available from the British Library

Library of Congress Cataloguing-in-Publication data has been applied for

ISBN: TPB: 978-1-3994-1419-7; eBook: 978-1-4411-9519-7; ePDF: 978-1-4411-5927-4

2 4 6 8 10 9 7 5 3 1

Typeset by Deanta Global Publishing Services, Chennai, India

Printed and bound in Great Britain by CPI Group (UK) Ltd, Croydon CR0 4YY

To find out more about our authors and books visit www.bloomsbury.com
and sign up for our newsletters

For 'DD'

Praise for *Roger Scruton: The Philosopher on Dover Beach*

'With clarity and grace, Mark Dooley's book fully captures the philosophical achievement of the late Roger Scruton. In its pages, Scruton's evocative account of the "life-world" truly comes alive. The world as Scruton describes it, the real world, the one available to the incarnate persons that we are, is one where free and responsible persons are accountable to each other, where sacred or holy things lift us out of our mundane selves, where beauty is real and not invented, and where politics is marked by law, loyalty, and settlement. As Dooley admirably shows, Scruton's urbane and humane thought dares to say "Yes" to our civilized inheritance, and to look up to what endures. Dooley's account of Scruton's life and thought remains a shining achievement, and one very unlikely to be surpassed in the coming years.'

Daniel J. Mahoney, Professor Emeritus at Assumption University, and author of *Recovering Politics, Civilization, and the Soul: Essays on Pierre Manent and Roger Scruton* (2022)

'In this short, lucid study of Scruton's thought … [Mark Dooley] mounts a powerful defence of an important thinker. Dooley covers all aspects of Scruton's thought, from sex and art to religion, politics and the defence of the nation.'

Alex Moffatt, *Irish Mail on Sunday*

'Dooley's book aims to show that Scruton's ideas are proving more and more true to our current times. This is an important and challenging re-appraisal of an important philosopher.'

Stav Sherez, *Catholic Herald*

'Sets out eloquently Roger [Scruton's] positions on politics and art – and explains why there was no one I ever commissioned to write whose articles provoked more rage.'

Sir Peter Stothard, Editor, *Times Literary Supplement*

'Beautifully written, clear, concise, restrained, *Roger Scruton: The Philosopher on Dover Beach* is a masterpiece of concise exposition, a model of clarification and, above all, a pleasure to read. For anyone who wants a comprehensive overview of Scruton's work, Dooley's book is indispensable. There is no other work of this kind on the market. Short of reading all of Scruton's writings yourself, there can be no better way to gain a clear understanding of this most significant of contemporary philosophers.'

Yearbook of the Irish Philosophical Society

'Dooley makes a strong case for taking [Scruton] seriously and puts to rest the absurd and, thankfully, now less fashionable view that he is the "unthinking man's thinking man".'

The Journal of Philosophy

'Dooley's erudite exposition of Scruton's thought is not only intellectually provoking but genuinely stimulating.'

Serge Grigoriev, Ithaca College, USA, *The European Legacy: Toward New Paradigms, vol. 19*

Contents

Preface to the 2024 Edition

This book was originally published in 2009, a time when Roger Scruton was only just beginning to receive due recognition for his philosophical and literary accomplishments. For many years, he was regarded as a pariah because of his public pronouncements in the press, especially those he published as a columnist for *The Times* during the 1980s, and many of which I republished in *Against the Tide: The Best of Roger Scruton's Columns, Commentaries and Criticism* (Bloomsbury Continuum, 2022). There was, however, no doubting his exceptional ability as a philosopher, someone who had lived out the principles he defended so eloquently in the forty books he had published by the time I wrote this volume. In thus publishing this work, my aim was to provide the first book-length treatment of all aspects of his thinking – from his theory of the person to that of the sacred, sex, politics and aesthetics. Secondly, I wanted to write a book that simply placed before the reader a clear statement of what Roger Scruton believed, and to say why it is not only reasonable but a way of finding fulfilment in the world. Some responded by charging that it lacked sufficient critical analysis of Scruton, that it was, perhaps, too biased in favour of its subject. However, after a lifetime of endless criticism, some of which brought him very close to the edge, my purpose was to correct the misinterpretations and the caricatures of Scruton by showing that he was not only an intellectually brilliant man, but one of exceptional grace, virtue, and vision. That he was knighted to much acclaim in 2016 – and that news of his untimely death in 2020 was received with such reflective and insightful tributes from across the philosophical and cultural divide – suggests that my assessment of Scruton was ultimately shared by most. As I wrote in the original version of this book: 'The world can no longer afford to ignore the message of one who offers love in place of hate, affirmation in place of repudiation and hope in place of nihilism.' My sincere hope is that, in reading this work, people will not only realize that love, affirmation and hope were central to Scruton's message, but that, by embracing his joyful wisdom, we, too, can make those things central to our own outlook.

Apart from a revised Introduction, Afterword and an expanded Bibliography, I have not altered the original structure of this work. Scruton's thought had a striking consistency of theme and purpose that was evidenced in all his writings. Therefore, what I wrote in the 2009 edition was simply reinforced by Scruton's subsequent publications. Finally, I am grateful to my editors Robin Baird-Smith and Sarah Jones for their constant support and encouragement.

Mark Dooley
Dublin, October 2023.

Introduction

Sir Roger Scruton (1944–2020) was a most uncharacteristic contemporary intellectual: a philosopher of deep learning who spent much of his long career at war with the academy; a prolific author who eschewed the city for life on a farm, who hunted to hounds and wrote movingly on wine as that which comes to us wrapped in a 'halo of significance'; a conservative who rejected liberal internationalism, but whose outlook was genuinely cosmopolitan; a courageous activist expelled from Communist Czechoslovakia for daring to speak of hope at a time when none existed; a thinker schooled in the Anglophone tradition of philosophy, yet one who is quintessentially European; someone that 'served a full apprenticeship in atheism', but who, having pondered his loss of faith against the backdrop of advancing secularism, 'steadily regained it'. Scruton was a man who not only thought deeply, but one who gave substance to this thinking. A public intellectual who took risks for freedom and who never sought popularity when truth was at stake. Indeed, he spent a lifetime, as he put it, seeking 'comfort in uncomfortable truths'.

Those truths were enunciated and defended in a corpus comprising sixty books (including four novels and a book of poetry), hundreds of scholarly articles and scores of newspaper columns on topics as diverse as beauty, architecture, music, sex, politics, animal rights, wine, hunting, farming, religion and the environment. Unifying all these works is, however, one underlying conviction, which is that we all long for *the consolation of home* or of *membership*. We all desire to surmount 'natural alienation', to belong 'somewhere' that we recognize as ours. As I wrote in *The Roger Scruton Reader* (Bloomsbury, 2009), in a world where nihilism and estrangement are the norm, Scruton, 'shines a light on our failures, not in order to condemn them, but in order to lead us from despair, loneliness and desecration back home to beauty and its sacred source'. That is why I consider him something of a latter-day Hegel – someone who incorporates the full range of human experience into his thinking, and for whom art, religion and philosophy serve as 'a living endorsement of the human community'.

Scruton was often correctly acclaimed as the greatest conservative philosopher of his generation. However, as he said to me in our book *Conversations with Roger Scruton* (Bloomsbury, 2016): 'All that conservatism ultimately means, in my view, is the disposition to hold on to what you know and love'. Politically, therefore, he was a thinker in the mould of Edmund Burke, one for whom the defence of ancestral institutions was vital to the health of a nation. However, when Scruton writes in defence of conservatism, he does so from a *philosophical* and not merely a political perspective. That is because Scruton's politics emerge from his deeply held philosophical convictions about the human person and the repeated attempts by science and pseudo-science to undermine it. Communism is one such form of pseudo-science, and one that he spent his life opposing, but so too is hard-nosed naturalism, evolutionary biology, neuroscience, or, indeed, any of those academic disciplines that push an ideological agenda while masquerading as a 'science'. To a lesser or greater extent, these tear aside all those 'features of the world which constitute its personal face – rights and duties, laws and values, institutions of membership and religion.' This leads, in turn, to a 'peculiar society, devoid of counsel, in which decisions have the impersonality of a machine'.

Scruton's anti-communist stance, his aesthetic theory, his belief in the sacred and the transcendental, his defence of nationhood and home, his writings on sex, music, wine, architecture, hunting, the environment, culture and animal rights, are all attempts to re-enchant what he called the *Lebenswelt*, or the lived human world. That is why he considers philosophy, not as the 'handmaiden of the sciences', but as the 'seamstress of the *Lebenswelt*'. As such, the primary task of philosophy is not to undermine appearance for the sake of reality, but rather to 'repair the rents made by science in the veil of Maya, through which the wind of nihilism now blows coldly over us.'

Scruton begins his defence of philosophy as the 'seamstress of the *Lebenswelt*' by drawing the familiar Kantian distinction between the subject or the person, and the object. Kant sought to reconcile the world of Newtonian physics with the realm of reason and faith, and he did so by arguing that, like all creatures, we are objects in nature determined, no less than the animals, by its laws. However, we are also subjects that can exercise freedom in defiance of our natural impulses. The subject that says 'I' demonstrates that he or she is a unique individual, the bearer of rights, responsibilities, duties and claims. The 'I' is the defining feature of the human being. As a locus of liberty, it permits us to stand back from our immediate condition so as to exercise self-control, self-sacrifice and love.

To say that the human being is both a subject and an object, is not to suggest that it is comprised of two things. The 'I' or the subject is not a separate entity that is somehow trapped inside a body. The effects of our freedom and self-conscious awareness are everywhere apparent, and yet where is the subject that exercises that freedom? Subjectivity, the soul, the 'I' are nowhere to be found inside the object. Put simply, we are not two things but one that can be described or understood in two distinct ways.

The example used most often by Scruton to explain this theory is that of a painting. From the perspective of science, the painting is nothing but the materials of which it is comprised. That is certainly true, in as much as the figure depicted in the painting cannot be separated from the materials which constitute it. There are not two things here but one. And yet the scientific understanding of the painting is not the only one, and certainly not the most important. There is also intentional understanding, which is captivated, not by the canvas or the pigments, but by the subject of the painting: *the painted saint*. Intentional understanding looks for the meaning in the painting and is open to being transformed by it. It does not deny that the painting is only one thing, that the saint cannot be detached from the stuff of which it is composed. It insists, nevertheless, that there are two ways of understanding this same thing, one of which transcends the material composition in the direction of the transcendental.

The radical and revolutionary mindset seeks to de-personalize or deface the world. That is why the experience of communism is that of alienation and despair. When the *Lebenswelt* is torn away, we 'see the world under one aspect alone, as a world of objects.' We are told the subject is a fiction and that 'beyond death there is nothing'. We all know, however, that when we gaze at a painting, a landscape or the community in which we are at home, we cannot help but encounter the subjectivity of the world. That is, we encounter the very same type of thing we experience when beholding another person. It is as though the world smiles back at us from a place beyond time. Kant called this experience of the subject 'the transcendental', a term which Scruton also uses synonymously with 'the sacred'.

We catch sight of the subject in a painting, or a landscape, in a sonata, a glass of wine, or, indeed, in a building that we love. It is as though all these things shine with a personality of their own and smile back at us with a human face. 'In the sentiment of beauty,' Scruton says, 'we feel the purposiveness and intelligibility of everything that surrounds us.' Human beauty, he tells us, 'places the transcendental subject before our eyes and within our grasp'. We will not discover the subject in the anatomical substructure, but only in what I see on the surface – in the appearance or facade which comes to us wrapped in a halo of beauty. In this I am confronted with a sacred thing, in as much as it is not a means to an end but an end-in-itself.

That is why, as Scruton provocatively put it, the Devil consistently wages war against art and culture. He does so because the culture of a nation – expressed in its literature, music, artworks, political institutions and religious rites – is the fabric of our common home. Through them, we connect, not only with the living, but with the dead and the unborn. They root us to place, time, history and to that homeland of the soul that we all crave as a remedy to our existential isolation. They speak of somewhere rather than nowhere, of settlement and belonging rather than estrangement and alienation. They reflect how 'we' see the world, something which is obvious to anyone who observes the character or personality of any nation in old Europe.

In attaching us to our common home, in giving it a face that can be known and loved, culture is a source of what Scruton called '*oikophilia*' or love of home. This he contrasted with *oikophobia* or hatred of home, something which goes hand in hand with a repudiation of subjectivity, transcendence, the sacred, first-person freedom and the 'we' of membership. This culture of repudiation is equivalent in many ways to what Burke meant when he spoke of 'Jacobinism by establishment', something that Western society as a whole is now experiencing. In denying students access to their history; in dumbing down art, music, literature and even the sacred liturgy; in redesigning the social space so that it no longer has a face; in promoting a form of sexual liberty that makes no room for the human person as that which animates the body; and in celebrating obscenity over beauty, you detach people from their past, their home, and the transcendental dimension of the human experience. You make them strangers to themselves, to the soul and the soil alike. In denying that there are objective values of taste, you ensure that art becomes kitsch, thus glorifying the profane above the sacred.

In sum, Roger Scruton defended a Hegelian and Burkean view of human nature, one founded on allegiance to institutions as the guarantee of tangible freedom. As such, he opposed any and all variations of the social contract theory, liberal individualism, or philosophical theories of the 'authentic' self in isolation from its kind. Hence his rich defence of Western culture and the religious and philosophical concepts of personhood upon which it depends. That is why understanding Scruton and his substantial contribution, demands studying all the elements of his work at once. You cannot, in other words, consider his philosophical theories of conservatism in isolation from his work on aesthetics, the religious origins of culture, sexual ethics, animal rights and his powerful defence of the nation state. Each dimension of his *oeuvre* is, I maintain, a restatement of the following insight from his 1990 collection of essays, *The Philosopher on Dover Beach*:

There is an attitude that we direct to the human person, and which leads us to see, in the human form, a perspective on the world that reaches from a point outside it. We may direct this very attitude on occasion, to the whole of nature, and in particular to those places, things, events and artefacts where freedom has been real. The experience of the sacred is the sudden encounter with freedom; it is the recognition of personality and purposefulness in that which contains no human will... It is difficult, however, to retain the sense of the sacred without the collective ritual which compels us to listen to the voice of the species. For the modern intellectual, who stands outside the crowd, the memory of enchantment may be awakened more easily by art than by prayer; it is an attempt to call the timeless and the transcendental to the scene of some human incident... The point of intersection of the timeless with time may not be an occupation for the saint; but for those who are not in some measure saintly, it demands the willing co-operation of the whole community. And without the sacred, man lives in a depersonalised world: a world where all is permitted, and where nothing has absolute value. That, I believe, is the principal lesson of modern history, and if we tremble before it, it is because it contains a judgment on us. The hubris which leads us to believe that science has the answer to all our questions, that we are nothing but dying animals and that the meaning of life is merely self-affirmation, or at best the pursuit of some collective, all embracing and all-too-human goal – this reckless superstition contains already the punishment of those who succumb to it.

If, in other words, man is to find a place in the world that, following Hegel, he can truly call 'home', it will not be through the scientific worldview, irrespective of how essential that is. Neither will it be through political or philosophical theories that drive at a universal or abstract view

6

of 'liberty, equality or fraternity'. For such schemes undermine 'the humble forms of ordinary love…on behalf of an earthly idol whose sole reality is to destroy human relations, by measuring them against a standard which they cannot attain'. Rather, Scruton's sense of the sacred is predicated on a notion of the person that is at once free, and yet fully bound by communal attachments and local loyalties.

Stated otherwise, it is in and through a 'shared language, shared associations, shared history', or what he calls a 'common culture', that man realizes himself and acquires a form of liberty worth the name. Such is the 'core experience of membership', which involves 'a recognition of a shared identity'. This is to say, following Burke, that the 'self-consciousness of a nation is part of its moral character. It endows nations with a life of their own, a destiny, even a personality. People who think of themselves as a collective "we" understand their success and failures as "ours", and apportion collective praise and blame for the common outcome'.

This book will attempt to give coherence and shape to a much-misunderstood yet powerful intellectual, whose controversial public image often belied the depth, sincerity and profundity of his writings. I shall suggest that Roger Scruton's vision derived from a deep wish to preserve the best of the West, thereby experiencing 'in reward, the experience of belonging'. That is a highly unfashionable and contrarian position to adopt in our times, but it is one that Scruton defends, not only polemically, but also philosophically. Like Matthew Arnold, he stands on Dover Beach listening to 'the turbid ebb and flow of human misery'. For now, the 'Sea of Faith' has withdrawn, leaving in its wake 'neither joy, nor love, nor light'. Scruton's work is an attempt to restore some joy, love and light to a world 'lost in a morass of addictive pleasures'. It is an attempt to 'paint ideal portraits of the human condition', that will console and comfort those stranded, as Arnold puts it, 'on a darkling plain swept with confused alarms of struggle and flight'. And therein can be found the originality of his position: Scruton has given us a way of philosophically affirming traditional institutions and forms of life, in a world dedicated to their extinction.

My principal aim in this work is simply to provide the reader with synoptic snapshots of the major themes that preoccupied this intriguing thinker throughout his long career. Hence in Chapter 1, I outline the philosophical origins of Scruton's thought, his theory of the sacred and his views on religion. In Chapter 2, I focus on his notion of personhood, his controversial stance on animal rights and fox-hunting, and on his equally contentious theory of sexual desire. Chapter 3 is devoted to Scruton's aesthetics. It begins by distinguishing 'common' from 'high' culture, and proceeds by analysing his views on education, music and architecture. Chapter 4 deals with Scruton's conservatism, and the implications of his political theory for economics, the law and the environment. Finally, in Chapter 5, I chart Scruton's rough ride in defence of the nation state as an alternative to the dangers of liberal internationalism.

The big problem faced by someone trying to write a book about Scruton, is that he was himself a masterful writer. His astonishingly beautiful prose is so clear and cogent that it requires no further elucidation. Hence, where possible, I let him speak for himself in the hope that those coming to him for the first time will be inspired to delve deeper into his work, while those already acquainted with him may once again relish his extraordinary artistry. As he said in one interview: 'I get a tremendous benefit, but also I lead a studious life and work extremely hard at getting the right word, the right sentence and so on, which I needn't bother with if I didn't have that sense that this is of intrinsic value. And if I didn't do that but just wrote sloppily I wouldn't be able to propagate any message and maybe that would have negative impacts on others'. I hope this book proves that Scruton's writings are indeed of intrinsic value, and that those who engage seriously with them can look forward to a life of happiness and consolation in a world gone mad.

In sum, this is a modest attempt to shed light on the work of a profoundly accomplished thinker, who not only challenged our conception of the aesthetic and its relation to everyday experience, but who helped his readers 'to re-discover the world which made us, to see ourselves as part of something greater, which depends upon us for its survival, and which can still live in us' – if we are willing. As such, Scruton's thought cannot be easily dismissed. If anything, it should be judged, by friend and foe alike, as 'the conservative message for our times, ... a message beyond politics, a message of liturgical weight and authority – but a message that must be received, if humane and moderate politics is to remain a possibility'.

1

Philosophy: The Seamstress of the Lebenswelt

But that is precisely what is wrong with the search for the really real: it peels away the personality of the world, and then complains that what it finds is meaningless. In things that matter it is only a superficial person who does not judge by appearances.[1]

So says Xanthippe, wife of Socrates, and star of Roger Scruton's satirical send-up of Platonic philosophy in the *Xanthippic Dialogues*. For Scruton, the predicament of modernity is one of 'disenchantment', where the personality of the world has been peeled away in favour of a plethora of pseudo-sciences. War has been declared on the old certainties that once bound communities and societies together. In politics, culture, religion and philosophy the new objective is to see man, not as the summit of creation, but merely as an object amongst objects. For that is the temptation of liberalism in all its variations: to wipe clean the slate of history, thereby eradicating from the world all vestiges of personhood and subjectivity. Put simply, the search for the 'really real' extinguishes the sacred light of humanity. Listen again to Xanthippe:

When I encounter another person, I am granted a strange experience – though so familiar that its strangeness is lost to all but the philosopher. The encounter with the other is like a revelation. And the meaning of the revelation is expressed in action, not in thought. The other is sacred for me. He is not to be treated as things are treated: he is not a means to my purposes, but an end in himself. The calculation of my own advantage, which runs riot through the world of objects, ceases abruptly at the threshold of the other, awaiting his consent. In this way the world of nature is filled with meaning. Everywhere I encounter value, not as an abstract idea, but as a host of incarnate individuals, each of whom is unique and irreplaceable.[2]

11

That beautiful citation is, in a nutshell, the centrepiece of Roger Scruton's moral philosophy. Following Immanuel Kant, Scruton contends that human beings possess a 'transcendental' dimension, or a sacred core that is exhibited in their capacity for self-reflection. Unlike animals, humans are *self-conscious* creatures. We are moral beings who dwell in the sphere of freedom – freedom to act, praise and blame. In so doing, man stands as the origin of value and meaning in a world otherwise devoid of such things. This ability to fill the world with meaning is what renders man sacred or 'an end in himself'. It is what makes each individual 'unique and irreplaceable'.

In his magisterial account of Richard Wagner's opera *Tristan and Isolde*, *Death-Devoted Heart*, Scruton expands upon Xanthippe's Kantian picture of the human being as follows:

According to Kant, human beings stand in a peculiar metaphysical predicament – one not shared by any other entity in the natural world. We see ourselves, he argued, in two contrasting ways – both as objects, bound by natural laws; and as subjects, who can lay down laws for themselves. The human object is an organism like any other; the human subject is in some way 'transcendental', observing the world from a point of view on its perimeter, pursuing not what is but what ought to be, and enjoying the privileged knowledge of its own mental states that Kant summarized in his theory of the 'transcendental unity of apperception'. It is not religious belief that forces us to see ourselves in this dualistic way. The need to do so is presupposed in language, in self-consciousness, and in the 'practical reason' that is the source of all human action and moral worth.[3]

We are, as such, both in the world as organic beings, and yet not fully constrained by it. We are determined by our physical incarnation, and yet we can freely transcend those circumstances through self-conscious deliberation, moral evaluation and cultural creativity. Man is, at one and the same time, object *and* subject. To treat him merely as an object is, therefore, an act of *desecration* – a squandering of his personhood and a denial of his subjectivity. But that, suggests Scruton, is what happens whenever we search for the so-called 'really real' in defiance of the 'personality of the world'. To reach the really real would require us to scrape away all the marks of human subjectivity that lie across the surface of our world. Human beings express their subjectivity through creative acts that make the world intelligible and meaningful. These are the so-called 'appearances' of which Xanthippe speaks. The appearances, as we shall see, are certainly meaningless for the scientist, but for the philosopher the world is senseless without them. Peel them away and you get causal explanations. In so doing, however, you will destroy human meanings and reasons, without which the world is devoid of true sense.

The upshot of Xanthippe's claim that 'in things that matter it is only a superficial person who does not judge by appearances', is this:

... human freedom, selfhood, subjectivity, and personality: all these terms point to a way of seeing our fellow human beings, which both distinguishes them from the rest of nature and creates the basis for those moral, legal, and political relations in which our freedom is exercised and fulfilled. We see each other as engaged in a common dialogue, each characterised by his own indescribable ('transcendental') perspective and each responding freely to the free acts and words of others. And it is reason itself that leads us to see each other in this way. If we could not do so, then we could not reason either with others or with ourselves about what to do, what to think, or what to feel. We would be as blind to the human world as the person who could see only lines, shapes, and colours would be blind to the world of pictures. And being blind to the human world, we would also cease to belong to it.[4]

It is Scruton's principal belief that we have indeed become blind to the human world. Hence, if you want to identify a single theme that unites his philosophy, politics, aesthetics and cultural criticism, the rootlessness and alienation of modern man is it.

THE CULTURE OF REPUDIATION

The attempt to peel away the personality of the world, to extinguish the flame of human subjectivity and freedom, thereby making man blind to his own condition, began for Scruton in the 1960s, culminating in the Paris riots of May 1968. At the heart of that conflagration stood an angry 24-year-old English philosopher. Scruton recalls:

In the narrow street below my window the students were shouting and smashing. The plate-glass windows of the shops appeared to step back, shudder for a second, and then give up the ghost, as the reflections suddenly left them and they slid in jagged fragments to the ground. Cars rose into the air and landed on their sides, their juices flowing from unseen wounds. The air was filled with triumphant shouts, as one by one lamp-posts and bollards were uprooted and piled on tarmac, to form a barricade against the next van-load of policemen. ... Great victories had been scored: policemen injured, cars set alight, slogans chanted, graffiti daubed. The bourgeoisie were on the run and soon the Old Fascist and his regime would be begging for mercy.[5]

The 'Old Fascist', he tells us, was Charles de Gaulle, 'whose *Mémoires de Guerre* I had been reading that day'. What Scruton gleaned from the General's memoirs was that 'a nation is defined not by institutions or borders but by language, religion and high culture; in times of turmoil and conquest it is those spiritual things that must be protected and reaffirmed'.[6] During times of political unrest, in other words, it is to the personality of the world that we must inevitably turn for answers. But it is precisely those 'sacred' things that the *soixante-huitards* sought to shatter as they stormed the barricades. One of those fiery iconoclasts was a friend of Scruton. That same night, he confronted her with these questions: What, he demanded to know, did she 'propose to put in the place of this "bourgeoisie" whom you so despise, and to whom you owe the freedom and prosperity that enable you to play on your toy barricades? What vision of France and its culture compels you? And are you prepared to die for your beliefs, or merely to put others at risk in order to display them?' I was, writes the young Scruton, 'obnoxiously pompous: but for the first time in my life I felt a surge of political anger, finding myself on the other side of the barricades from all the people I knew.'[7]

Thus began a lifetime defending the sacred from the poison of the profane, the beautiful from the ugly and the good from the wicked. Unlike his Parisian friend, who worshipped at the altar of the French post-structuralist philosopher Michel Foucault, Scruton took refuge in the writings of Edmund Burke, Kant, Hegel, T. S. Eliot, F. R. Leavis and Ludwig Wittgenstein. What distinguished those authors from the likes of Foucault is that they never 'tended to adopt the ways and manners of the Jacobins'. But Foucault certainly did, which is why his system is one of mere destruction:

He knows the illusoriness of values, and finds his identity in a life lived without the easy deceptions which rule the lives of others. Since he has no values, his thought and action can be given only a negative guarantee. He must fortify himself by unmasking the deceptions of others. Moreover, this unmasking cannot be done once and for all. It must be perpetually renewed, so as to fill the moral vacuum which lies at the heart of existence. Only if there is some readily identifiable and, so to speak, renewable opponent, can this struggle for authenticity – which is in fact the most acute struggle for existence – be sustained. The enemy must be a fount of humbug and deception; he must also possess elaborate and secret power, power sustained through the very system of lies which underscores his values. Such an enemy deserves unmasking, and there is a kind of heroic virtue in his assailant, who frees the world from the stranglehold of secret influence.[8]

Foucault and his allies saw it as their main mission to 'de-sacralise' the human world by 'unmasking' its institutions and values, thus revealing them for what they essentially are – an arbitrary 'system of lies'. This implies that the leftist intellectual advocates 'the old idea of justice, but believes justice to involve his own emancipation from every system, every "structure", every inner constraint'.[9] Rather than identify prevailing injustices and respond to them with practical reforms, the high priests of what Scruton calls 'the new Left' seek to tear down the existing system so as to make it wonderfully and utterly new. Unlike Scruton's conservatism, which urges a 'politics of custom, compromise and settled indecision', one that 'has no overriding purpose, but changes from day to day, in accordance with the unforeseeable logic of human intercourse', the politics of the new Left is one of fanaticism.[10] Its mantra is simple: 'All power in the world is oppressive, and all power is usurped. Abolish that power and we achieve justice and liberation together.'[11]

For Roger Scruton, the consequences of this 'revolutionary sentiment' for future generations were perfectly obvious. By opting for 'the easy holiday of destruction', people like Foucault 'made fury respectable and gobbledegook the mark of academic success. With the hasty expansion of the universities and polytechnics, and the massive recruitment of teachers from this over-fished and under-nourished generation, the status of the New Left was assured. Suddenly whole institutions of learning were in the hands of people who had identified the rewards of intellectual life through fantasies of collective action, and who had seen the principal use of theory in its ability to smother the questions that would provide too sturdy an impediment to [revolutionary] *praxis*. For such people the new

Left was the paradigm of successful intellectual endeavour'.[12] What resulted from this was a 'culture of repudiation', or a movement that strives 'to cleanse and liberate the world'.[13] It does so by driving 'the heretics and half-believers from its ranks with a zeal that is the other side of the inclusive warmth with which it welcomes the submissive and the orthodox. And it stands implacably opposed to the old order, in something like the way that Protestantism stood opposed to the Roman Catholic Church during the Renaissance.'[14]

Those who inaugurated the culture of repudiation did so with a view to polluting the personality of the world. For them, that personality was mere ideological topsoil which, once uprooted, would reveal man in his purity, devoid of all 'masks or camouflage'. Karl Marx identified that ideological topsoil as the 'bourgeoisie', and he was followed in that assessment by Foucault and his followers. The result was a visceral and sustained attack on the very political, moral and aesthetic foundations of Western civilisation. But Western civilisation is in essence bourgeois civilisation, and it contains, according to Scruton,

... features which are or ought to be the envy of the world: a rule of law, which stands sovereign over the actions of the state; rights and freedoms which are defended by the state against all-comers, including itself; the right of private property, which enable me not only to close a door on enemies, but also to open a door to friends; the monogamous marriage and property-owning family, by which the material and cultural capital of one generation can be passed without trouble to the next; a system of universal education, formed by the aesthetic and scientific vision of Enlightenment; and – last but not least – the prosperity and security provided by science and the market, the two inevitable by-products of individual freedom.[15]

Unlike socialism, bourgeois society has no overarching goal or *telos*. It is, if anything, a spontaneous order that arose from 'the gift of human freedom'. Such freedom is one in which 'the old experiences of sanctity and redemption' are sustained in spite of science. For Foucault, however, human freedom is simply an illusion maintained by the ruling bourgeois class. Hence, for him there is 'nothing sacred or inviolable in the existing order, nothing that justifies our veneration ...' If everything that we in the West call 'sacred' is but the product of pernicious power-relations, then why, he asks, should we genuflect before anything? Due to the fact that he believed power was ubiquitous, 'it became impossible for Foucault to accept that power is sometimes decent and benign, like the power of a loving parent, conferred by the object of love. The social world, subject to Foucault's searing condemnation, was cleared of everything that redeems its ordinariness.'[16] The culture of repudiation is, thus, a full-frontal assault on the phenomenon of the sacred as it appears in the ordinary human world. Consequently, it 'abhors nothing so much as the bourgeois family – the institution of social reproduction, which involves a voluntary surrender to loyalties that bind you for life, and bind you most of all when you discard them'. And then, having cast aside 'the charming images of that former life', we are left to wander alone in a desiccated world 'devoid of sacred and sacrificial moments, in which the effort of social reproduction is no longer made'.[17]

SAVING THE SACRED

Modern life is, therefore, one in which the old 'idea of human distinction, of the sacred nature of our form and the consecration of our loves, has been driven away'.[18] But for Scruton, there is a way of saving the sacredness of our form from the deadly grip of the culture of repudiation, thereby giving renewed life and substance to the charming images of our former life. And what exactly is that way? The answer is simple: the study and practice of philosophy – but not, it must be added, as traditionally conceived. Scruton's originality derives from his belief that philosophy's traditional vocation is ill-suited to the particular problems of contemporary life. Whereas 'Plato and Socrates were citizens of a small and intimate city state, with publicly accepted standards of virtue and taste, in which the educated class derived its outlook from a single collection of incomparable poetry', we live in 'a crowded world of strangers, from which standards of taste have all but disappeared, in which the educated class retains no common culture, and in which knowledge has been parcelled out into specialisms, each asserting its monopoly interest against the waves of migrant ideas'.[19] Having been ravaged by the culture of repudiation and disenchantment, having lost sight of the sacred and having plundered the personality of the world, we are left without the certainties once provided by our common culture. This means that philosophy 'has been deprived of its traditional starting point in the faith of a stable community'. For Plato, the object of philosophy was to undermine the prejudices of the common culture in order to access 'Truth'. But when the common culture is no more, traditional scepticism as practised by the likes of Plato, 'runs the risk of being disengaged from the life surrounding it, and of forswearing the ancient promise of philosophy, which is to help us, however indirectly, to live wisely and well'.[20]

If traditional philosophy sought to liberate man from 'custom, prejudice, and the here and now', the form of philosophical reflection advanced by Roger Scruton is not one that strives to obtain that 'God's-eye standpoint'. Rather, if modern philosophy is to help us live wisely and well, it must follow Ludwig Wittgenstein by returning us 'to our shared "form of life" as the only thing we have'.[21] And if, for Plato, the object of wisdom is to free the self from the everyday world of illusion, for Scruton it is to thoughtfully 'restore what has been thoughtlessly damaged' – that is, 'the ordinary human world: the world in its innocence, the world in spite of science'.[22] We might say, therefore, that if philosophers like Plato, Marx and Foucault wish to prioritise the 'really real' at the expense of 'appearance', Roger Scruton seeks to emphasise the appearances at the expense of the really real. In other words, philosophy's task in the contemporary context is not to reveal the reality behind appearances. For that, to repeat, is not a job for philosophy but for science, whose 'concepts and theories describe a reality so remote from the world of appearance that we can hardly envisage it, and while its findings are tested through observation, this is no more than a trivial consequence of the fact that observation is what "testing" means. Science explains the appearance of the world, but does not describe it.' This is not to say, of course, that Scruton follows the pragmatist philosopher Richard Rorty in contending that the 'appearance-reality' distinction is a redundant dualism that should be discarded. It is simply to note that, for Scruton, 'the claim so often made on behalf of philosophy, that it shows the *reality* behind *appearances*, could equally, and more plausibly, be made on behalf of science'.[23]

The upshot of this is that, for Scruton, the world should be viewed as much more that an 'object of scientific curiosity'. It is an enormously rich and variegated entity, one that feeds our desires while simultaneously placing obstacles in the way of our will. And in striving to understand the world, 'we are often more interested in the relation of objects to ourselves than in their causality and constitution'. That is because, as rational beings, we are more interested in looking for the *meaning* of events, rather than their scientific *causes*. In fact, we generally classify objects in ways which would seem absurd to the scientist. Scruton explains:

… we group the stars into constellations according to fictions of our own, and in doing so we commit astronomical outrage. For the astronomer our concept of a 'constellation' displays nothing but the superstitious emotion of those who first devised it. For the astrologer it conveys the deepest insight into the mystery of things. For the rest of us this classification is a record of our familiarity with the world, a tribute to the human face which covers it. Thomas Hardy awakens us to much sadness when he writes, of young drummer Hodge, killed in the Boer war, that he 'never knew … / The meaning of the broad karoo': to die in surroundings that are opaque to our quest for meaning is to die unconsoled. And hence the bleakness of the 'strange-eyed constellations' that 'west/Each night above his mound'. [24]

The philosopher does not describe a distinct reality to that described by science. But he does describe it very differently. Whereas the concepts of science have an explanatory function, those of philosophy attempt to convey *meaning*. Their function, writes Scruton, 'is to divide the world in accordance with our interests, to mark out possibilities of action, emotion and experience which may very well be hampered by too great an attention to the underlying order of things'. It is true that such 'ordinary' descriptions of the world are vulnerable to the 'pressure of scientific explanation'. From the scientific perspective, 'it seems as though tables and chairs are not really as we describe them. They are not really coloured, not really solid, and so on'. However, even if we do experience such doubts about our everyday descriptions of the ordinary human world, those descriptions cannot be jettisoned. And that is because, for us, they classify 'the varieties of human "intentionality"'. [25]

The concept of intentionality, which Scruton borrows from the phenomenology of Franz Brentano and Edmund Husserl,[26] is of vital significance for an understanding of his thought. If science endeavours to describe and explain the world *as it is in itself*, intentional understanding seeks to describe, 'criticise and justify the world as it appears' to human consciousness. In so doing, 'it fills the world with the meanings implicit in our aims and emotions. It tries not so much to explain the world as to be "at home" in it, recognising the occasions for action, the objects of sympathy, and the places of rest.' Intentional understanding is the way the human subject finds meaning in an alien world of objects. It does not, for Scruton, possess the objectivity of natural science, but it does possess another kind of objectivity: 'a convergence upon a common fund of superficial truth' which entitles it to its own claims to knowledge.[27] Stated otherwise, intentional understanding does not seek to uncover the really real. Rather, it stays rooted *on the surface* where the human subject dwells and leaves its mark. As a form of knowledge, its aim is to reveal the personality of the world, and thus to bind us once more to what Scruton calls (again following the phenomenologists) the *Lebenswelt* or the 'lived world'.[28]

PHILOSOPHY AND THE *LEBENSWELT*

The *Lebenswelt*, argues Scruton, 'is not a world separate from the world of natural science'. It is, however, 'a world differently described – described with the concepts that designate the intentional objects of human experience'.[29] The objects of the *Lebenswelt* are, in other words, described in accordance with our human purposes. They are classified in such a way that they 'reflect our own practical and contemplative interest in them'. It is true that such descriptions are vulnerable to the withering gaze of the scientist in search of the 'underlying structure of reality'. But this does not mean that the descriptions of the world given by science are any substitute for those 'which order and direct our everyday experience'. And the reason for that is clear: 'We cannot replace our most basic everyday concepts with anything better than themselves, for they have evolved precisely under the pressure of human circumstance, and in answer to the needs of generations'. This suggests that the varieties of intentional experience which help us navigate our way around the *Lebenswelt* are not merely arbitrary or subjective constructs. They acquired their use and importance on the basis of our human needs and interests. And without such concepts, we run the 'risk of severing the vital connection which links our response to the world, and the world to our response, in a chain of spontaneous human competence'.[30]

We might put the point like this: natural science, or indeed the pseudo-sciences of Marxism, Freudianism and sexology, may attempt to peel away the personality of the world. They may seek to vanquish the appearances in favour of an underlying reality. For the charm of those sciences, according to Scruton, is one of 'demystification'. That notwithstanding, the charm of the *Lebenswelt* endures. It does so because it supplies us with concepts that make us feel at one with our world, thus enabling us to surmount the alienation and estrangement which is 'the poisoned gift of science'. Those concepts are neither 'consciously made nor deliberately chosen', but come gift-wrapped in culture. They are the bequest of what Edmund Burke called 'absent generations'. Scruton reflects:

> A rational being has need of such concepts, which bring his emotions together in the object, so enabling him – as the Hegelians would say – to find his identity in the world and not in opposition to it. A culture, moreover, is essentially shared; its concepts and images bear the mark of participation, and are intrinsically consoling, in the manner of a religious communion, or an act of worship. They close again the gap between subject and object which yawns so frighteningly in the world of science.[31]

Intentional understanding is not a gift of science, but of philosophy. That is so because only philosophy can reconnect us to the surface of the world where we naturally dwell. Only philosophy, that is, can salvage the sacred by restoring man to his rightful place at the acme of creation. Unlike science, philosophy's vocation is not to disenchant the world, and, unlike the pseudo-sciences, it does not set out to repudiate the *Lebenswelt*. For Scruton, this means that philosophy ought not to be considered 'the handmaiden of the sciences; it should be, rather, the seamstress of the *Lebenswelt*'.[32] For let us recall once more what Xanthippe teaches: when we look at things philosophically, she counsels, 'the world of nature is filled with meaning. Everywhere I encounter value, not as an abstract idea, but as a host of incarnate individuals, each of whom is unique and irreplaceable.'[33] In such circumstances, we do not consider other human beings as 'obedient to natural laws' only. Rather, we engage with them as free beings subject to moral laws, and we classify them 'in ways which could find no place in scientific theory'. With the use of one of his most dramatic and oft-cited examples, Scruton illustrates the point as follows:

When we see another's smile we see human flesh moving in obedience to impulses in the nerves. No law of nature is suspended in this process; we smile not in spite of, but because of, nature. Nevertheless, we understand a smile in quite another way: not as flesh, but as spirit, freely revealed. A smile is always more than flesh for us, even if it is only flesh.[34]

Put simply, a smile has *moral* significance for human beings. We can, of course, explain a smile with the use of scientific concepts. At that point, however, we would no longer be describing a smile, but the 'underlying mechanism that explains what we observe'.

Philosophically speaking, a smile reveals much more than 'human flesh moving in obedience to impulses in the nerves'. It is a way that free beings relate to one another and to their surrounding world. It is a gesture inspired by those features of human existence such as beauty, goodness and spirit, which spontaneously 'grow in the thin topsoil of human discourse'. And it is there, in that thin topsoil, 'that the seeds of human happiness are sown, and the reckless desire to scrape it away – a desire which has inspired all those "sciences of man", from Marx and Freud to socio-biology – deprives us of our consolation'.[35] Philosophy consoles because it re-moralises the ordinary human world, and saves it from the culture of repudiation. Hence, its true aim in the contemporary context is not to function as yet one more science of man. It should be understood, rather, as 'a last-ditch attempt to re-enchant the world ...'.[36]

For Scruton, philosophy consoles because it *re-personalises* the world of objects. It invites us to see the human subject as both sacred and free. Unlike other forms of life, the human self has the capacity to recall its past and project itself towards a future. Its freedom is characterised by its particular consciousness 'of time's passage'. Philosophically, says Scruton, '[t]he remembered order is an order of meaning, in which the uniform flow of physical time is "thickened" according to the subjective significance of events'. We have our being in time, but the temporal order is one of decay and anticipation. The 'now' of time, that 'infinitesimal fragment', is snatched away from us 'just as soon as we try to lay our hands on it'.[37]

But does this mean that we are slaves to time? Not so, for when we relate to one another as subjects or persons, we 'find ourselves enunciating "timeless" laws, which are not summaries of observation but prescriptions addressed to all rational beings'. These 'timeless laws' are universal moral principles that apply *solely to subjects*, or as Scruton puts it: 'It is as though subjects addressed one another from a point of view outside space and time – condemned to see one another "under the aspect of eternity".' In other words, the moral order possesses a 'timeless character: it is always with me, inscribed hereafter in my very self, regardless of subsequent events'. [38]

The consequence of looking at things in this way is clear: the 'world of nature is filled with meaning', because self-conscious subjects can defy time by looking upon the world of objects as though they were 'perforated by apertures'. And it is through those tiny gaps that 'we glimpse the "transcendental" province of another's will'. Lovers' glances, Scruton observes, cut a hole in the fabric of the world of objects, thereby revealing the light of eternity. A lover, he writes, 'shines his eyes into the depths of his beloved, calling the other subject to the surface: the world of objects falls away, and self presses to self at a common boundary'. [39] Now although this is something that happens *in time*, it has, nevertheless, *a timeless character*. The lovers' glances transcend the constraints of the empirical order and take us to a place 'which lies beyond the moment'. Perhaps, warns Scruton, 'there is an illusion at work here'; perhaps we are deluding ourselves regarding the timeless character of the other's gaze. That acknowledged, the belief that the world of objects simply cannot contain the subject, 'arises from our deepest thoughts about ourselves. In all our deliberations, we are acutely aware of this indescribable thing at the periphery of our mental vision: the subject who acts, who responds to reason, and who does not just show himself in the world of objects, but appropriates that world as his own.' Once again, Scruton is not suggesting that we are timeless beings. Rather, he is simply pointing out that to think of ourselves in that way is an inescapable feature of the human condition. For him, to repeat, we are both objects governed by nature's decrees, but also subjects 'who relate to one another as though bound only by reason and its immutable laws'. It is those laws which distinguish us as unique selves, and which make us the focus 'of those attitudes like erotic love, praise, accusation and remorse, which cannot be directed to something which is conceived merely as an object'.[40]

RELIGION AND THE *LEBENSWELT*

If all this appears to have a religious significance, that is because Scruton believes 'it is from religious ideas that the human world, and the human subject who inhabits it, were made'. The most destructive effect of the culture of repudiation has been the attempt to peel away the traditional idea of personhood which is the bedrock of the religious worldview. It has long been one of Scruton's principal aims to restore that notion of personhood, in an effort to make sense of man's sacred yearnings. As Scruton remarks in *Philosophy: Principles and Problems*: 'Our most pressing philosophical need, it seems to me, is to understand the nature and significance of the force which once held our world together, and which is now losing its grip – the force of religion'.[41] That is so because the notion of the transcendental subject, which is both in time and yet somehow beyond it, 'takes its sense from the new and "sacramental" bond that is established when people adopt common myths, common liturgies, and a common distinction between the sacred and the profane'.[42]

For Scruton, religion is nothing short of a social fact. While it may not supply objective truth, it does however furnish us with 'complex allegories of the human condition'.[43] And we have need of such allegories because, as self-conscious beings, we are somehow 'outside the natural order, looking into it from a "transcendental" perspective'. That is, the self is constantly aware that it is a free being constrained in its liberty by natural laws. It cannot, as it were, fully surmount the division between subject and object which characterises its temporal condition. Self-conscious beings are, thus, somewhat estranged from the natural order in which they have been placed. Or, to put it in Scruton's terminology: the rational being is *in* the world, but not *of* the world. But this in turn leads to 'a condition of metaphysical loneliness', whereby we are forced 'to meditate on our fallen state, and on the gap between human longing and human satisfaction: the gap which comes from being not *of* this world, but only *in* it'. Whereas animals are ignorant of this gap between the temporal and the timeless, 'it

24

is our awareness of it that leads both to religious ritual, and to the belief in a transcendental deity.[44]

Religious ritual provides for self-conscious beings a mode of membership based on a 'sacramental bond'. The religious rite enables people to overcome their estrangement by transporting them 'into the sphere beyond nature'. The function of the ritual, Scruton suggests, is to,

... mobilise words, gestures and dances – those forms of behaviour which are replete with the experience of self – and to turn them into a supernatural direction. The rituals are essentially shared, and each subject, repeating the magic words, or performing the magic gestures, is freed for a moment from the world of objects, flowing freely into a 'mystic communion' with the other subjects who worship at his side.[45]

By bringing us into direct communion with the Divine, the religious ritual redeems the self by cutting it free from the world of objects, thus setting it 'in the realm where subjects are fully at home with each other and transparently known'. Religion, in sum, provides the self with a form of salvation, in which the gap between the subject and the object is finally reconciled.

This means that Scruton follows Hegel and Søren Kierkegaard, in believing that there is much more to the philosophical question of God than the mere fact of his existence. Both of those philosophers were interested in how man could surmount alienation through his relationship to the 'God-man' of Christianity. For Hegel, Christ was 'the Mediator' through whom the self was dialectically reconciled with the objective world. For Kierkegaard, the God-man was a 'sign of contradiction' that shattered the speculative endeavour to become one with the Divine. That notwithstanding, it was only by emulating the life of Jesus, and by seeing him as the unconditional ethical prototype, that the self could, in faith, escape his fallen state. Neither philosopher had much use for the traditional philosophical proofs of the existence of God. What mattered for them was how man's relationship to God could purge him of guilt, thus expunging alienation and despair.[46]

Scruton places himself squarely in that same tradition.[47] He contends that 'the concepts of the holy and the sacred are, or ought to be, of considerable interest to the philosopher'. Such concepts endow the world of objects with a 'subjective' or 'personal' character. When the self recognises an object as sacred, the gap between the subject and the object miraculously diminishes. For in the experience of the sacred, the subject identifies the object as a portal to the timeless. Take, for example, a place of worship: the believer does not classify such a place as he would other objects. For him, the church, synagogue, shrine or mosque is a sacred location through which the eternal intersects with time. It is lifted from its 'mute contingency into the dialogue of reason', and it is then, while worshipping with others in that sacred place, that man's freedom is confirmed. In sum, the experience of the sacred supplies 'the mirror in which freedom can be seen. Nature then ceases to be a prison; its doors stand open, and no shadow falls between the intention and the act.'[48] In *A Political Philosophy*, Scruton explains this phenomenon as follows:

… the rational soul moves inevitably towards the belief in transcendental beings. This belief, which begins in wonder and ends in faith, conscripts the sacred to its purpose, as proof of a world beyond. It is not just because we are social beings, with emotions rooted in a past of solemn sacrifice and ritual cults, that we distinguish sacred from profane, and sanctity from desecration. We instinctively connect the sacred with the transcendental, seeing holy places, times and rituals as windows onto another realm – places in the empirical world where we look out in astonishment at something that we can understand through ritual and prayer, which we try to explain through theological doctrine, but which always in the end deludes our attempt to describe it.[49]

In a stunning commentary on the religious anthropology of René Girard's *La violence et le sacré*,[50] Scruton states that this experience of the sacred is neither 'an irrational residue of primitive fears, nor is it a form of superstition that will one day be chased away by science'. If anything, it is 'a solution to the accumulated aggression which lies in the heart of human communities'.[51] Whereas avowed atheists like Christopher Hitchens think that the religious urge results in violence and sexual obsession,[52] Scruton follows Girard in contending that 'religion is not the cause of violence but the solution to it'. By their very nature, all societies are formed in and through conflict due to the territorial ambitions of human beings in primitive contexts. Religion, Scruton asserts, emerges from a need to quell that primal violence. It is a response to the 'mimetic desire' of those who 'struggle to match each other's social and material acquisitions, so heightening antagonism and precipitating the cycle of revenge'.[53] In identifying a scapegoat with no deep attachment to the nascent community, and by uniting in opposition to him, 'people are released from their rivalries and reconciled'.[54] The hatred and division which previously existed between those in the primitive society is transferred onto the scapegoat, and through his destruction the community is finally purged of its 'accumulated violence'.

What fascinates Scruton in Girard's analysis of the 'sacrificial scapegoat', is the identification of 'Christ as a new kind of victim – one who offers himself for sacrifice, and who, in doing so, shows that he understands what is going on'. In asking His Father to forgive His tormentors from the Cross, Christ became not just another scapegoat, but one who inspired 'sacred awe' in all those who witnessed his agony. And he did so because, in willingly undertaking the role of sacrificial victim, he made 'the "love of neighbour" – which had featured in the oldest books of the Hebrew Bible as the standard to which humanity should aspire – into a reality in the hearts of those who mediate upon his gesture'. Consequently, Christ 'purified society and religion of the need for sacrificial murder'. The Christian sacrament of communion is precisely that – a ritual attempt to *commune* with the sacrificial victim in order to renew the 'awe, relief and visceral attachment to the community that was experienced at his death'.[55] It is an acknowledgement that, at the very core of the human condition, is a deep longing for 'a kind of self-forgiveness' which only religion (*qua* the experience of the sacred) can ultimately supply. Hence, the experience of the sacred will never be destroyed because 'it is in the nature of rational beings like us to live at the edge of things, experiencing our alienation and longing for the sudden reversal that will once again join us to the centre'.[56]

To sum up: by affording man a glimpse of eternity in the midst of time, the sacred provides an antidote to his temporal isolation. The sacred is, therefore, something that we humans connect with instinctively, supplying as it does our most fundamental form of membership. That is why, when undermined by science and secularism, we experience the loss of faith, not only at an intellectual level, but as 'a loss of comfort, membership and home: it involves exile from the community that formed you, and for which you may always secretly yearn'.[57] We might say, following Scruton, that when faith in the sacred subsides, the *Lebenswelt* is radically

27

transformed. The human subject is then plunged back into a world of objects from which there is no apparent escape. We become creatures locked in time without any windows through which we can peer onto that other transcendental realm.

The desecration of the holy signals, thus, the extirpation of the world's *personality*. And when that happens, 'the most ordinary things take on a new aspect, and concepts that inhabit the soul of believers and shape their most intimate experiences ... seem to make no contact with the world as it appears to the person ...'. We then find ourselves submerged in 'a culture of widespread desecration'. No longer are we surrounded by the consoling images of a *Lebenswelt* in which the idea of 'human distinction' permeates everything. We are instead stuck inside a world 'in which human relations are voided of the old religious virtues – innocence, sacrifice and eternal vows – and in which little or no public acknowledgement is afforded the ideas of the sacred, the holy and the forbidden'. With all apertures to the timeless sealed off, the sacred is then driven away, and with it the idea of the human being as subject, or 'as something removed from nature and destined for a higher sphere'. Where once it appeared as a reflection of divinity, the self is now squarely 'rooted in the natural world and obedient to its dark imperatives'. [58]

SCIENCE AND THE SACRED

As we shall see in Chapter 2, however, the old distinction between animal and human, which characterised the religious *Lebenswelt*, is difficult to abandon. In our postmodern existence, we may seek to repudiate the sacred and the sacramental. But despite the best efforts of those propelling the culture of repudiation and desecration, many still find it impossible to relinquish the religious urge. For such people, animals will never be 'seen as a centre of selfhood and freedom', being as they are 'a normal part of the empirical world, sharing some of our feelings with us, but never aspiring to the noble, the true or the good'. [59] Conversely, for those wishing to rid the world of the sacred, the priority is to undermine the metaphysical and moral differences separating humans and animals. The human, they declare, is no longer 'an object of awe' or of reverence. In so doing, they express 'a virulent desire to desecrate, to drag the human body down to its animal essentials and to show it as pure object, in which the light of selfhood and freedom has been extinguished'. What follows is nothing less than a pornographic paradise 'in which the human body is reduced to panting chunks on the screen, in which children are brought up on images that show the body not as the place where empirical and transcendental meet, the I-hole in the screen of nature, but as a target, a thing to be assaulted, ravaged and consumed, to be shown in all its contortions as a squirming, needing, agonising worm'. [60]

That is why, for Scruton, the pursuit of philosophy is a paramount task for those in search of consolation and temporal redemption. It promises a process of re-enchantment in which human action is lifted 'out of the web of causal reasoning in which it is ensnared by science'. [61] And it does so by 'reminding us that we did not create ourselves, nor did we create the world in which we live'. This is not to suggest, however, that we should think of religion and science as being mutually opposed. Humans are, to repeat, 'natural beings, part of the biological order', and, as natural beings, 'we exist in time and therefore change over time. That we should evolve is inevitable. If we ask the question how we humans came to be as we are, then any conceivable answer will refer to the unfolding of a process – and processes take time. The surprising fact is not that we should have evolved from the humble chemistry of the oceans but that it should have taken so long to discover this.' [62]

Put simply, science tells us '*how* the world is spread out in time', while 'the story of creation tells us *why*'. There are no answers to 'the why of the world' forthcoming from people like Charles Darwin or Richard Dawkins. [63] For when we ask the ultimate question regarding the origin of life, 'we are seeking a point of view outside all time and change, from which we can view the world as a whole'. Such is the point of view of God, and it is thus to Him 'that we must look for an answer'. Xanthippe explains:

Anaximander tells me that Xanthippe is descended from fish: all well and good. He tells me that Xanthippe's rational part is a product of the struggle for survival. Fine. He tells me that, just as the colours Xanthippe sees lie in her eyes, so do the meanings of her world lie in her intellect. Neither colour nor meaning is listed among the 'really real'. That too is fine. For the catalogue of the really real is no better a guide to our world than a book of anatomy is a guide to human beauty. I do not say that its list is false; merely that all the most important things are excluded from it. Even God is excluded.[64]

If science places all its trust in what it considers to be the 'really real', religion and philosophy focus on what science cynically denounces as mere 'appearance'. But, as Scruton repeatedly reminds us, it is on the surface of the world that we, as self-conscious beings, dwell and act. It is from the thin topsoil of culture that the moral person is formed. And it is to God that the moral person looks when searching for *meanings*, as distinct from *causal explanations* of his existence. It is towards the sacred, in other words, that we must turn when contemplating 'the mystery of the individual'. Xanthippe puts it like this: 'The meaning of an experience is not its cause. Those who communicate with the Creator through prayer are no more cut off from him by the knowledge that nature does not contain him, than the knowledge that words, smiles and gestures are nothing but movements of the flesh.'[65]

As self-conscious beings, we are, for the most part, impervious to scientific explanations of reality. What matters to the rational agent, are the 'meanings, connections, harmonies and symmetries' that are revealed only in the human *Lebenswelt*. That, to repeat, is not to say that Dawkins is mistaken about how we evolved as creatures in the natural world. It is simply to suggest that 'we want the world to make sense to us, and to answer our questions not merely in the way the laws of nature answer the enquiries of the scientist, but in the ways the laws of harmony answer the aspirations of the musician'.[66] There are many things that moral beings consider 'intrinsically worthwhile' that are not to be found on the scientific grid. Standing out amongst those are 'love, duty, virtue and kindness'. It is true, says Scruton, that 'we cannot mount a deductive or a scientific argument in favour of those values. But we condemn those who condemn them, and believe reason is on our side.'[67]

So, for Scruton, science and the sacred can, and indeed *should* coexist in harmony, for 'nothing in the scientific view of things forbids the experience of the sacred'. But if that is so, then we must also admit that nothing in the sacred view of things should forbid the experience of science. Only ignorance would make us deny that the existence of the earth 'is part of a great unfolding process, which may or may not have begun with the Big Bang, and which contains many mysteries that physicists explore with every increasing urgency'.[68] But that is not how the scientist views the matter. Unlike philosophy and religion, which urge that we look upon the human being as both subject and object, science 'invites us to regard the subject as a myth, and to see the world under one aspect alone, as a world of objects'.[69]

To do so, however, would mean no longer looking upon the human being as somewhat set apart. It would be to assume that the scientist has all the answers to the mysteries of the universe. It would be to see him perched 'upon the throne from which God was taken away for burial'. For we must remember, that in the naturalistic view of man, human freedom is 'nothing but an appearance on the face of nature'. And beneath that appearance, warns Scruton, 'rides the same implacable causality, the same sovereign indifference, which prepares death equally and unconcernedly for all of us, and which tells us that beyond death there is nothing'.[70] It was this image of man as mere object which inspired both the Communists and the Nazis, thus licensing 'forms of government in which the scientific view of our condition was for the first time in power'. The result was a supreme triumph for the 'desacralised view of the world'.[71]

The sacred acts as a barrier to that totalitarian temptation. It warns us that 'there are things which cannot be touched, since to meddle with them is to open a door in the world of objects, so as to stand in the I of God'. Man is then robbed of his personhood, subjectivity and liberty. He becomes a 'new kind of creature', one that has been 'de-personalised' and severed from the 'network of personal responsibility'. That is why we simply cannot afford to jettison the idea of man as both object *and* subject, for it is our rational and moral nature, or what Scruton occasionally refers to as 'the human soul', which bears witness to the *why* of creation. The soul, 'its freedom, translucency and moral presence are', he explains, 'never mentioned in the book of evolution'.[72] They are present, however, 'when we look at the world from "I" to "I"', or from subject to subject.[73] For it is then, when we view 'human life as a vehicle for freedom – to see a face where the scientist sees flesh and bone', that we catch a glimpse of how God truly intended us to be:

God intended that we live in such a way, that we see into the subjectivity of one another, and into the subjectivity of the world – which is God himself. That we can do this is self-evident. How we do it is an unfathomable mystery. And if, in order to bring this mystery about, a process of evolution was required, so that the soul became incarnate at last in a creature which rose only by degrees to such an eminence, then so be it. God moves in a mysterious way. When you look on people as objects, then you see that Darwin was right. When you look on them as subjects, you see that the most important thing about them has no place in Darwin's theory.[74]

PREFIGURING ETERNITY

God, for Scruton, *is* the subjectivity of the world. By seeing in another's eyes a vision of the sacred, the miraculous and the mysterious, we look upon that person as though he were not of this world. That is to say, we look upon him from the religious perspective, one that philosophy endeavours to rescue from the culture of desecration. In his beautifully composed memoir *Gentle Regrets*, Scruton recalls that his 'years as a voyeur of holiness brought me into contact with true believers, and taught me that faith transfigures everything it touches, and raises the world to God'.[75] Without faith in the sacred, we are, however, simply condemned to wander in a 'depersonalised world: a world where all is permitted, and where nothing has absolute value'.[76] Such, for Scruton, is the sad predicament of the present age. Having abandoned the idea that human life is set apart from the rest of nature, we have in turn lost 'the instinctive awe and respect towards our own being that the Romans called *pietas*'.[77]

The consequences of losing piety can be dramatically seen, for example, in the way Europe is currently being 'colonised by secular ways of thinking'. Although we may not be witnessing the return of the 'totalitarian system, and the death camp which is its most sublime expression',[78] we are nonetheless submerged in a culture where 'embryo research, cloning, abortion and euthanasia – subjects which go to the heart of the religious conception of our destiny – proceed in once-Catholic Europe as though nothing were at stake beyond the expansion of human choices'. The idea that the beginning and end of life are untouchable has been summarily cast into the dustbin of history. We no longer cultivate natural piety for the young and the old, for the unborn and the dead. Instead, the 'piety and humility that it was once natural to feel before the fact of creation have given way to a pleasure seeking disregard for absent generations. The people of Europe are living as though the dead and the unborn had no say in their decisions.'[79]

Still, we are not of necessity bound to this 'loveless culture'. We can, says Scruton, always choose to 'turn away from desecration and ask ourselves instead what inspires us and what we should revere'.[80] But in order to do so, we must rediscover the sacred beauty of the *Lebenswelt*. That means renouncing the idea of progress which the culture of repudiation has transfigured into an idol. By worshipping progress, Scruton warns, 'we bow before an altar on which our own sins are exhibited. We kill in ourselves both piety and gratitude, believing that we owe the world nothing, and that the world owes everything to us.'[81] Once again, the ever-present temptation for the self is to perch on the throne once occupied by God. The sacred view of life suggests, however, that human beings 'have *always* been wrong to look to the future for the test of legitimacy, rather than to the past. For the future, unlike the past, is unknown and untried.'[82] What the past offers, which the future never can, is the insight of hindsight. It tells us that if we are to embrace modernity, we should do so critically, 'in full consciousness that human achievements are rare and precarious, that we have no God-given right to destroy our inheritance, but must always patiently submit to the voice of order, and set an example of orderly living'.[83]

In submitting to that challenge, we shall not strive to turn the world of our forebears into a wasteland. Rather, we shall look upon it not merely as a world of objects, but a world in which subjectivity has etched its sacred mark across the surface. We shall, in turn, perceive the surface of the world as revealing 'the sense of God's presence'. It will be for us 'a direct encounter with the divine, which eludes all explanation in natural terms, and stands isolated and apart'.[84] If science sought to redefine humanity as 'part of the natural world', Roger Scruton's philosophy invites us to view the world as that which is 'made in the image of humanity'. In so doing, he endeavours to revive the old theological understanding of man as the locus of freedom in an otherwise determined world.

Science, Scruton says, is devoid of the theological understanding because it is impervious to 'the way of freedom, since this is not the way of the flesh'. But to know freedom, and to identify it as the source of the sacred, is to encounter 'a vision of eternity' and to know God. It is to cross 'the barrier of time', and to be placed in direct contact with the timeless. And in discovering this essential truth,

... We encounter what is permanent – or what is beyond time and change, the eternal peace that serves as the divine template, so to speak, for our brief homecomings here on earth. When we take those tentative backward steps ..., trying to restore this or that little precinct of our mutilated Eden, we are creating icons of another pasture, outside time and space, where God and the soul exist in dialogue. We are prefiguring our eternal home.[85]

NOTES

1. Roger Scruton, *Xanthippic Dialogues* (London: Sinclair-Stevenson, 1993), p.165.
2. *Ibid.*, p.166.
3. Roger Scruton, *Death-Devoted Heart: Sex and the Sacred in Wagner's Tristan and Isolde* (Oxford & New York: Oxford University Press), p.123.
4. *Ibid.*, p.124.
5. Roger Scruton, *Gentle Regrets: Thoughts From a Life* (London: Continuum, 2005), pp.33–34.
6. *Ibid.*, p.35.
7. *Ibid.*
8. Roger Scruton, *Thinkers of the New Left* (Harlow: Longman), p.32. Scruton's repudiation of the 'new Left' is something to which I shall return in Chapter 5.
9. *Ibid.*, p.2.
10. I shall expand upon this point in Chapters 4 and 5 below.
11. Scruton, *Thinkers of the New Left*, p.7.
12. *Ibid.*
13. Roger Scruton, *The West and the Rest* (London: Continuum), p.71.
14. *Ibid.*, p.72.
15. Roger Scruton, *Modern Culture* (London: Continuum), p.128.
16. *Ibid.*, p.130.
17. *Ibid.*, p.134.
18. Roger Scruton, *A Political Philosophy: Arguments for Conservatism* (London: Continuum), p.135.
19. Roger Scruton, *Philosophy: Principles and Problems* (London: Continuum), pp.11–12.
20. *Ibid.*, p.12.
21. *Ibid.*, p.14.
22. *Ibid.*, p.15.
23. *Ibid.*, p.19.
24. Roger Scruton, *Sexual Desire: A Philosophical Investigation* (London: Continuum, 2006), p.6 (hereafter *Sexual Desire*).
25. *Ibid.*, p.7.

26. See Franz Brentano, *Psychology from an Empirical Standpoint* (London: Routledge, 1995), and Edmund Husserl, *The Crisis of the European Sciences and Transcendental Phenomenology* (Evanston: Northwestern University Press, 1970). See also Scruton's detailed account of 'Intentionality' in the 'Appendix' to *Sexual Desire*, pp.377–391, and his analysis of 'Intentional Understanding' in *Modern Philosophy: An Introduction and Survey* (London: Pimlico, 1994), pp.243–244. He also includes a fine appraisal of 'Phenomenology and Existentialism' in *A Short History of Modern Philosophy* (London: Routledge, 2002), pp.263–280.

27. Roger Scruton, *The Philosopher on Dover Beach* (Manchester: Carcanet, 1990), p.108.

28. See Scruton, *A Short History of Modern Philosophy*, pp.268–269.

29. Scruton, *Sexual Desire*, p.8.

30. *Ibid.*, p.9.

31. Scruton, *The Philosopher on Dover Beach*, p.109.

32. *Ibid.*, p.112.

33. Scruton, *Xanthippic Dialogues*, p.166.

34. Scruton, *Philosophy: Principles and Problems*, pp.22–23.

35. *Ibid.*, pp.24–25.

36. *Ibid.*, p.25.

37. *Ibid.*, p.76.

38. *Ibid.*, p.82.

39. *Ibid.*

40. *Ibid.*, p.83.

41. *Ibid.*, p.85.

42. *Ibid.*, p.90.

43. Scruton, *A Political Philosophy*, p.121.

44. Scruton, *Philosophy: Principles and Problems*, p.89.

45. *Ibid.*, p.90.

46. See G.W. F. Hegel, *Lectures on the Philosophy of Religion*, Peter C. Hodgson (ed.) (Berkeley: University of California Press, 1988); Soren Kierkegaard, *Practice in Christianity* (Princeton: Princeton University Press, 1991). For a detailed analysis of the Hegel-Kierkegaard relationship, see Mark C. Taylor, *Journeys to Selfhood: Hegel and Kierkegaard* (Berkeley: University of California Press, 1980), and Mark Dooley, *The Politics of Exodus: Kierkegaard's Ethics of Responsibility* (New York: Fordham, 2001).

47. That notwithstanding, Scruton is highly critical of Kierkegaard's claim that 'subjectivity is truth'. See Scruton, *A Short History of Modern Philosophy*, pp.191–195. Elsewhere, however, Scruton praises Kierkegaard as a philosopher who 'saw the aesthetic as the one true path to man's redemption, the posture towards the world which preserved, as best it could, the ethical vision which makes sense of our time on earth. In dressing up the aesthetic gaze in the attributes of holiness, Kierkegaard showed us the meaning of high culture.' Scruton, *Modern Culture*, p.54.

48. *Ibid.*, p.96.

49. Scruton, *A Political Philosophy*, p.130.

50. René Girard, *La violence et le sacré* (Paris: Grasset, 1972).

51. Roger Scruton, 'The Sacred and the Human', *Prospect Magazine*, Issue 137, August 2007, p.6. See also Scruton's analysis of Girard in *A Political Philosophy*, pp.126–128.

52. See Christopher Hitchens, *God is not Great: The Case Against Religion* (London: Atlantic Books, 2007).

53. Scruton, 'The Sacred and the Human', p.4. See also, *Death-Devoted Heart*, p.166.
54. Scruton, *Death-Devoted Heart*, p.166.
55. Scruton, 'The Sacred and the Human', p.5.
56. *Ibid.*, p.6.
57. Scruton, *Gentle Regrets*, p.222.
58. Scruton, *A Political Philosophy*, p.135.
59. *Ibid.*, p.137.
60. *Ibid.*, p.136.
61. Scruton, *Philosophy: Principles and Problems*, p.106.
62. Scruton, *Gentle Regrets*, pp.235–236.
63. See Richard Dawkins, *The God Delusion* (Black Swan, 2007). Scruton debated Dawkins, Hitchens and Anthony Grayling in Central Hall, London, on 27 March 2007 on the theme: 'We'd be better off without religion', a podcast of which is available at: *www. youtube.com/watch?v=Q8NnGenJa8w*. More recently, he has dealt with Dawkins in 'The Return of Religion', *Axess Magazine*, No. 1, 2008. I am citing from the online edition which is available at: *www.axess.se/english/2008/01/theme_scruton.php.htm*. See also Scruton, 'Dawkins is Wrong about God' in *The Spectator Magazine*, 14 January 2006 (available at: *www.spectator.co.uk/the-magazine/features/14728/dawkins-is-wrong-about-god.thtml*) and my 'Saving the Sacred: Roger Scruton and Richard Rorty on Religion' in *Human Destinies*, Fran O'Rourke (ed.) (Southbend: Notre Dame University Press, 2009).
64. Scruton, *Xanthippic Dialogues*, p.162.
65. *Ibid.*, p.167.
66. Scruton in debate with Dawkins, Central Hall, London, 27 March 2007.
67. *Ibid.*
68. Scruton, 'The Return of Religion', *Axess Magazine*, No. 1, 2008.
69. Scruton, *Philosophy: Principles and Problems*, pp.107–108.
70. Scruton, *The Philosopher on Dover Beach*, p.8; *Philosophy: Principles and Problems*, p.108.
71. Scruton, *Philosophy: Principles and Problems*, p.108.
72. Roger Scruton, *On Hunting* (London: Yellow Jersey Press, 1998), p.78.
73. In 'The Return of Religion' Scruton puts the matter like this: 'The atheists beg the question in their own favour, by assuming that science has all the answers. But science can have all the answers only if it has all the questions; and that assumption is false. There are questions addressed to reason which are not addressed to science, since they are not asking for a causal explanation. One of these is the question of consciousness. This strange universe of black holes and time warps, of event horizons and non-localities, somehow becomes conscious of itself. And it becomes conscious of itself in us. This fact conditions the very structure of science. The rejection of Newton's absolute space, the adoption of the space-time continuum, the quantum equations – all these are premised on the truth that scientific laws are instruments for predicting one set of observations from another. The universe that science describes is constrained at every point by observation. According to quantum theory, some of its most basic features become determinate only at the moment of observation. The great tapestry of waves and particles, of fields and forces, of matter and energy, is pinned down only at the edges, where events are crystallised in the observing mind.' See *www.axess.se/english/2008/ 01/theme_scruton.php.htm*.

74. Scruton, *On Hunting*, p.79.
75. Scruton, *Gentle Regrets*, p.63.
76. Scruton, *The Philosopher on Dover Beach*, p.11.
77. Scruton, *Gentle Regrets*, p.232. Elsewhere, Scruton defines piety as 'respect for sacred things'. It demands, he writes, 'that we honour our parents and ancestors, the household deities, the laws and the civil order, that we keep the appointed festivals and public ceremonies – and all this out of a sense of the sacred given-ness of these things, which are not our invention, and to which we owe an unfathomable debt of gratitude'. *Philosophy: Principles and Problems*, p.117.
78. *Ibid.*, p.108.
79. Scruton, *Gentle Regrets*, pp.232–233.
80. Roger Scruton, 'The Flight from Beauty', *Axess Magazine*, No. 7, October 2008. I am citing from the online edition which is available at: *www.axess.se/web/main.nsf/0/FF3E886DA47856C9C12574F300411FAA*.
81. Scruton, *Gentle Regrets*, pp.237–238.
82. Scruton, *Philosophy: Principles and Problems*, p.163.
83. Scruton, *A Political Philosophy*, p.208.
84. Scruton, *Philosophy: Principles and Problems*, p.96.
85. Scruton, *Gentle Regrets*, p.239.

2
Personhood, Sex and the Sacred

Restoring those little precincts of our mutilated Eden is the task Roger Scruton has set himself in each of his major writings. We could say, therefore, that he is a philosopher who seeks to mend the world by restoring its meaningfulness. And he does so by showing how the culture of desecration is predicated upon a wholesale pillaging of the human person. We saw in Chapter 1 how the scientific aspiration to plumb the depths of our everyday human world threatens 'to destroy our response to the surface'. But it is there, on the surface of the world, that free subjects dwell. It is there, in the spheres of culture, religion and politics that identity and personhood are formed. While such things fail to show up on the grid of science, they nevertheless enable us to 'see into the subjectivity of one another, and into the subjectivity of the world'.[1] The unscientific surface of the world, that place where we live and love, is, in other words, where 'the seeds of human happiness are sown'. It is the point at which human subjectivity infuses the 'mute objectivity' of the world with its soul.

Roger Scruton believes, in sum, that if we are to save the sacred, man must look seriously again at human nature. He must do so in order to rediscover those artefacts 'which stem directly from social existence and which form the basis for the construction of personality'.[2] But what exactly does Scruton mean by the term '*construction* of personality'? He means that where once there was only 'mere nature', now there is a sacred place, 'one in which personality and freedom shine forth from what is contingent, dependent and commonplace – from a piece of stone, a tree, or a patch of water'. Where once we were confronted by nature 'in all its senseless impersonality', now we behold a world across which 'the mysterious lining of the human organism' has been gently strewn.[3] With the dawn of the culture of desecration, however, there has been a 'gradual erasure from nature of the human face which covers it'.[4] The personality of the world has been peeled away, thereby resulting in a loss of human meaning.

Meaning, writes Scruton, 'is a feature, not of the "objective" world of natural science, but of the *Lebenswelt* with which we engage through our spontaneous thought and action'. It has its source in man's sense of *moral obligation* which 'irradiates the world with a peculiar "luminosity"', that Scruton equates with the holy, the miraculous, the mysterious and the sacred. So, in order to salvage what is meaningful, the personality of the world must be reconstructed – unless, of course, we desire to supplant that 'vision of ourselves as free beings, in a world that is "open to our agency"', with one that sees us as just another 'part of nature, subservient to the laws of causality of which science alone provides knowledge'.[5]

For example, liberalism is quite happy to endorse Nietzsche's belief that man is nothing but a dying animal. That is so because, for most liberals, 'obligations do not surround us in the *Lebenswelt*, but are created by our individual choices'. According to Scruton, this means that liberalism is 'the natural philosophy of the "desacralised" world'.[6] For those satisfied to dwell on the surface of the world, however, we cannot simply jettison that vision of ourselves as subjects. And it is for such people that philosophy performs its most important task in the modern world: 'to resurrect the human person, to rescue it from trivialising science, and to replace the sarcasm which knows that we are merely animals, with the irony which sees that we are not.'[7] So what, for Scruton, constitutes the human person? The best way of answering that important question is to look at how he differentiates human beings from animals.

PERSONS AND ANIMALS

As we saw in Chapter 1, Scruton refuses to follow thinkers like Richard Rorty who contend that 'Darwinian evolutionary theory made it possible to see all of human behaviour – including the "higher" sort of behaviour previously interpreted as fulfilment of the desire to know the unconditionally true and do the unconditionally right – as continuous with animal behaviour'.[8] Neither does he subscribe to Peter Singer's view that animals can and must be 'liberated', nor to the notion that animals are victims of what Richard Ryder calls 'speciesism' – a term which implies that 'like racism and sexism, our attitude to other animals is a form of unjust discrimination, lacking both rational and moral title'. These writers, Scruton rightly complains, 'have so changed the climate of opinion that no thinking person could now treat animals as our ancestors did, ignoring their feelings and desires and thinking only of their human uses. In a world dominated by humans and their appetites, animals are now widely perceived as a victim class.'[9]

In sum, the traditional distinction between human and animal has collapsed beneath the weight of liberalism's assault on the old idea that the person is somehow different *in kind* from other species. Scruton insists, however, that we cannot dissolve that distinction. Yes, he holds that we are indeed animals, 'but animals of a very special kind – animals who are conscious of themselves as individuals, with rights, responsibilities and duties, and who are capable of extending their sympathies to other species'.[10] We are, to invoke Aristotle's terminology, 'rational animals'. That is, human beings 'have a need and an ability to justify our beliefs and actions and to enter into reasoned dialogue with others'.[11] Scruton does not deny that animals are conscious and have desires, but he does dispute that they can make choices, engage in long-term planning, imagine future possibilities and ponder the world 'as an object of disinterested contemplation'. In all sorts of ways, he tells us, 'the passions of animals are circumscribed. They feel no indignation but only rage; they feel no remorse but only fear of the whip; they feel neither erotic love nor true sexual desire, only a mute attachment and a need for coupling.' They are, moreover, 'humourless and unmusical'. The birds of the air, he laments, do not sing. Neither does the hyena laugh. Rather, 'it is we who hear laughter in the hyena's cackle and music in the song of the thrush'.[12] What this implies is that 'the reasoning being exists and acts on another plane, forming intentions, making plans, perhaps with some long-term and unlikely prospect. He may set himself to oppose his own desires, and, in all that he does, he is motivated – or believes himself to be motivated, which is itself to have a kind of motive – not merely of self-interest but by a conception of the good'.[13]

Humans are, in short, *self*-conscious beings. While it is true that animals possess consciousness, they nevertheless lack the capacity to stand back from their immediate needs and desires so as to contemplate who and what they are. We might say, following Heidegger, that they are incapable of asking the question of being. Whereas humans can 'distinguish self from other and identify themselves in the first person,'[14] animals can do no such thing, in as much as no animal can say 'I':

The rational being is also a self-conscious being, and this self-consciousness lies at the root of his existence as a person. It is this feature which enables us to adopt towards him (and he towards himself) the peculiar posture which underlies our use of the concept of the person. Of course, there is a use for the concept of the self in describing the behaviour of animals. A dog distinguishes himself from other dogs, and his own interests from those of his fellows. But he does not distinguish himself as a self, since he lacks what I shall call the 'first-person perspective' – a feature of consciousness that is distinctive of language-using beings.[15]

PERSONHOOD AND LANGUAGE

In order to shed some light on what Scruton means here, it is useful to compare his philosophy of language, and its role in the formation of personhood, with that of postmodern philosopher Richard Rorty. Like Rorty, Scruton owes an immense debt to Ludwig Wittgenstein's insight that there is no way, as Rorty puts it, 'to come between language and its object'.[16] As such, both thinkers reject what Scruton calls 'the Cartesian view of consciousness',[17] or what Rorty labels 'the Cartesian mind'.[18] The 'Cartesian picture', explains Scruton, 'envisages the mind and mental processes as private to the person who possesses them: only he can really know of their existence and nature; others have to guess from his words and behaviour, which are at best the effects of mental processes, and not the things themselves.'[19] In other words, Descartes incarcerates the thinking self in a mental prison, and he does so by insisting that 'the mind is a non-physical entity whose states are essentially "inner" – that is connected only contingently (by no necessary connection) with "outer" circumstances'.[20]

Scruton and Rorty believe that Wittgenstein supplied the definitive philosophical response to Descartes. Most especially, they focus on Wittgenstein's famous 'private language argument' to rebut the notion that mental states are private, 'and therefore knowable, only to the person who has them'.[21] Wittgenstein rejected that contention, in as much as he held that everyone is subject to the rules of a common public language. There is, he argues, no such thing as a private language which enables me to refer to objects and sensations that only *I* can know. Scruton explains:

It is part of the 'grammar' of sensation words that we do not make mistakes when using them of ourselves, provided that we understand them. That is what our first-person certainty amounts to. The inventor of a private language is supposing just the same guarantee is available to *him*. But it was a guarantee provided by the grammar of our public language; so he is not entitled to assume that he has. For him the question can arise: how do I know that this, that I have now, is a private object …? Once the question has arisen, we find that there is no answer to it. There is no criterion to be found, which would guarantee to the user of the private language, that he really has identified a *private* object, and really has succeeded in endowing his words with a private reference, or indeed with any reference at all. He could be wrong about this, and yet never know that he is wrong. And if he is right, he could not know that either. Since nobody knows anything about the matter, he cannot appeal to other speakers. So there simply is no criterion of correctness, no rule that attaches his terms to intrinsically private entities. The private language is impossible.[22]

Stated otherwise, sensation words, or indeed any words for that matter, cannot be detached from the *public language* that guarantees their proper use and meaning. Consequently, the inventor of a private language deprives himself of the public criteria that would make his words intelligible. It follows that private objects cannot be referred to in a public language, for to do so would force the inventor to use the grammar of a public 'language game', thereby exploding his contention that he has identified a *private* object. In short, 'no language can refer to a sphere of merely private things. Every language, even one that I invent for myself, must be such that others too can learn it. If you think about your thinking, then you must do so in a publicly intelligible discourse.'[23] You must, in other words, 'be part of some "public realm", in which other people could wander'.[24]

For Wittgenstein and Scruton, thus, the public world *is* the 'fundamental reality'. Richard Rorty concurs. He tells us that human beings 'shall never be able to step outside language, never be able to grasp reality unmediated by a linguistic description'.[25] Moreover, Rorty would wholeheartedly subscribe to Scruton's observation that no philosopher 'who has studied the argument of Hegel's *Phenomenology of Spirit*, or that of Wittgenstein's *Philosophical Investigations*, would dissent from the view that self-consciousness and language emerge together, that both are social phenomena and that the Cartesian project – of discovering the essence of the mental in that which is private, inner and hidden from external view – is doomed to failure'.[26] But in sharp contrast to Scruton, Rorty thinks the failure of the Cartesian project should encourage us in the direction of Darwin. Indeed, he urges that we should think of human beings as nothing more than 'animals doing their best to cope with the environment – doing their best to develop tools which will enable them to enjoy more pleasure and less pain. Words are among the tools which these clever animals have developed.'[27]

From the perspective of the postmodern pragmatist, therefore, language does not correspond to the way the world is *in itself*. As tools for coping with the surrounding environment, linguistic descriptions cannot accurately represent language-independent reality. That is because, for people like Rorty, there is 'no way of formulating an independent test of accuracy of representation – of reference or correspondence to an "antecedent determinate" reality – no test distinct from the success which is supposedly explained by this accuracy'. We cannot, in other words, leap outside 'our language and our beliefs' in order test them against 'something known without their aid'.[28] On this reading, language is not a *medium* that stands between language-users and the world (*qua* language-independent reality), neither is it something that mirrors 'nonhuman reality'. Its principal function is simply to help us accomplish our everyday tasks and purposes. And, as with any tool, once our linguistic descriptions have served their particular purpose, they can always be replaced with more useful alternatives. As Rorty argues:

All the descriptions we give of things are descriptions suited to our purposes ... Just as it seems pointless to ask whether a giraffe is really a collection of atoms or really a collection of actual and possible sensations in human sense organs, or really something else, so the question 'Are we describing it as it really is?' is one we never need to ask. All we need to know is whether some competing description might be more useful for some of our purposes.[29]

But can we really dispense with our linguistic descriptions of the surrounding world so casually? Scruton does not believe that we can. Neither does he follow Rorty when the latter declares that 'we cannot regard truth as the goal of inquiry'. [30] Yes, Scruton does hold that the 'human world is a social world, and socially constructed'. He also believes that 'language is the principal criterion of rationality'. But he rejects Rorty's claim that linguistic constructs can be randomly jettisoned, or that the social world can 'be constructed as we please'. For there are, Scruton insists, 'constants in human nature – moral, aesthetic and political – which we defy at our peril, and which we must strive to obey'. [31] These 'constants in human nature' are not to be found in some private or pre-linguistic realm. For Scruton, they are revealed *in and through language*, and are, as such, gifts of community and culture.

Still, the question persists: if such gifts are disclosed in and through language, are they not susceptible to the type of insouciant reformulation that Rorty recommends? Once again, Scruton responds in the negative. He is happy to follow Rorty in believing that 'we can know the world only from the point of view that is ours', and that it is impossible to 'step outside our concepts so as to know the world "as it is in itself", from no point of view'. However, he refuses to concede that just because we have no God's-eye standpoint from which to assess the accuracy of our beliefs and representations, we ought to simply abandon the quest for objective truth and meaning. Following Kant, Scruton asserts that without the concept of objectivity, and the belief that our 'judgements are representations of reality', we could not even 'begin to think'. [32] In other words, while it may be true that 'we cannot attain God's perspectiveless view of things … the thought of it inhabits our procedures as a 'regulative idea', exhorting us always along the path of discovery'. [33]

Let me explain it like this: for Scruton, the world as revealed to us through language and culture is the only world that we have. Science may strive to rob the human world of its personality by burrowing below its surface so as to reveal the hidden reality behind the appearances. Try as it might, however, 'science can provide no substitute for the concepts which order and direct our everyday experience'. [34] Such concepts are, to repeat, gifted to us by language and culture, but that does nothing to deprive them of their truth-content. They are part and parcel of what we described in Chapter 1 as our 'intentional understanding' – or that mode of understanding which seeks to 'describe, criticise and justify the human world'. In short, even though the concepts of intentional understanding may be difficult to 'bring into focus', embedded as they are in 'feeling and activity', they nevertheless disclose 'genuine, objective truths about the human world', or what we have come to know as the *Lebenswelt*.

The concept of personhood is, for Scruton, one such truth, as are the related concepts of 'freedom, responsibility, reason for action, right, duty, and justice'.[35] And it is through those concepts of intentional understanding that the human being is described and defined as a subject, as distinct from an animal or object. The description of a human being, *qua* person, is not, therefore, a description that can be discarded once its usefulness has been exhausted. For to do so would be to look upon human beings as objects, which, according to Scruton, 'is not to see them as they are, but to change what they are, by erasing the appearance through which they relate to one another as persons'.[36] Rorty's belief that we should follow Darwin and Nietzsche in redescribing the human subject as a 'clever animal', consequently threatens to strike at the heart of social harmony. And that is so because, in denying that language can reveal 'constants of human nature' such as that of personhood, it follows science in destroying our spontaneous response to the surface of the world.

In the end, therefore, Rorty's pragmatism is yet one more exercise in Darwinian disenchantment.[37] By discounting the possibility that language might be something more than just a set of useful tools for particular purposes, he fails to appreciate the power *inherent in language* to force upon us those intentional concepts that guarantee long-term human happiness. Had he taken intentional understanding seriously, however, Rorty would surely have recognised that the human being 'is not merely part of the natural order: he has a world of his own, created in part by the concepts through which he perceives it'. But animals, as Scruton explains, 'suffer from no such disadvantage. Their world is entirely ordered according to their interests: it is a world of the edible, the drinkable, the dangerous, the comfortable, and the unreliable. There is no place in this world for "if" or "perhaps", no place for "Why?", "When?" or "How?", no place for the unobserved, or the unobservable'.[38] Neither is there any evidence that animals, when 'left to their own devices, can achieve the particular form of social interaction required by language'.[39]

THE MORALITY OF HUNTING

Animals, in sum, 'have neither rights nor duties nor personality', for only those creatures who are 'duty-bound to respect the rights of others' can be said to have rights. To argue, therefore, that a fox has rights is equivalent to saying that it is 'duty-bound to respect the right to life of the chicken'. But because the fox does not respect the right of the chicken, he should, on that logic at least, 'be condemned out of hand as criminal by nature'. [40] Such is what motivates Scruton to insist that we stop treating animals as our equals:

By ascribing rights to animals, and so promoting them to full membership of the moral community, we tie them in obligations that they can neither fulfil nor comprehend. Not only is this senseless cruelty in itself; it effectively destroys all possibility of cordial and beneficial relations between us and them. Only by refraining from personalising animals do we behave towards them in ways that they can understand. [41]

So what then is the proper way for humans to behave towards the lower animals? Controversially, Scruton believes it is by restoring the old equilibrium that has enabled humans and animals to live together on realistic terms, one that is 'maintained by the old arts of hunting'. Through those arts, he tells us,

... you glimpse another, more ancient and more healthy relation between man and beast – the relation between Homer's Odysseus and the old hound Argus, first to recognise his master on his return to Ithaca, or the relation between Alexander and Bucephalus, which caused the conqueror to found a city in memory of his heroic horse. The unsentimental love between man and beast that comes about when they are engaged together in some act of war or predation is, indeed, the nearest that animals attain to equality with the human species – and it is a love that is deeply horrible to the defenders of animal rights for that very reason. For it is a love founded in the aspect of animals that they put out of mind – the relentless life-and-death struggle that is the normal condition of life in the wild. [42]

One of the many things for which Roger Scruton has been vilified, is his robust and passionate defence of fox hunting. As the above citation makes abundantly clear, however, Scruton has a deep and abiding love for the 'lower animals'. That love emanates from every page of *On Hunting* – Scruton's scintillating memoir of how he first discovered horses, the countryside and the 'community of hunters'. It is evident too in *News from Somewhere*, a fascinating account of daily life among the animals on his farm in Wiltshire. But it is not, as he insists, a sentimental love. Rather, it is based on an awareness of the fact that animals are not persons, in as much as they do not form moral communities. Their world is, thus, devoid of judgement, 'embarrassment, remorse, guilt, and penitence'.[43] But does this mean that we can treat animals as we wish? Does it suggest that because we are 'the guardians of the natural order', we can use the lower creatures in any fashion we see fit? Not so, according to Scruton. To repeat, as moral beings we have a duty to care for those that destiny has placed under our care. Consequently, we 'should behave towards the natural world with piety, for we are its present trustees'.[44] But we must also exercise the 'ethic of virtue', which condemns 'those ways of dealing with animals which stem from a vicious motive', or that relishes in the gratuitous suffering of the beasts.[45]

Of course, the animal liberation lobby condemns hunting as the cause of such gratuitous suffering. Scruton profoundly disagrees. There is, he argues, a distinction that must be drawn between the obligations we have towards animals 'whom we have caused to depend on us', and those in the wild. In the first case, our pets become 'honorary subjects, who borrow a soul from those who love them'.[46] Wild animals do not, however, participate in the human world. It is true that 'we have a duty to protect their habitats, to secure, as best we can, the balance of nature, and to inflict no pain or fear that is not a necessary part of our legitimate dealings with them'.[47] It is, thus, 'morally dubious' to seize an animal from its natural environment simply for the purpose of exhibiting it in a zoo. But there is nothing morally suspect about the hunting of wild animals *in the right circumstances*. Indeed, from Scruton's perspective, it may even be 'a positive good', and anyone who has seriously studied the substance of his arguments in defence of the hunt would, I contend, find it difficult to disagree.

Fox hunting cannot be condemned as cruel, simply because it does not involve 'unnecessary suffering'. Its principal aim is not to destroy the fox population, 'but to establish a *modus vivendi*, one that will make the fox and his predations tolerable to those whose livelihood he threatens or whose domestic life he inconveniences'.[48] Scruton invites us to compare that 'economically sound system of species control' with the legal alternative of trapping, a practice which 'subjects a wild animal to unaccustomed, unnatural stress and fear, since it renders superfluous and impotent the animal's natural "fight or flight" response. This stress often lasts for many hours, culminating in a moment of terror when the executioner approaches.'[49] In contrast, the 'average hunt lasts for 17 minutes, and more often than not ends in escape. There is no attempt either to eke out the suffering of the fox or to deprive it of it natural defence, which is to fly from the danger'. True, the huntsman does experience a certain degree of pleasure from the chase. But the pleasure does not derive from seeing the fox suffer or being dispatched. Rather, it has its source in 'the intricate relationship of hounds with one another and with the huntsman, as they work together in pursuit of a scent'. For the true hunt-follower, Scruton adds, 'even the pleasures of horsemanship are subordinate to this one, of observing the mysterious relation between species in the moment of the chase …'.[50]

And what precisely is the nature of this 'mysterious relation'? Within each of us, Scruton observes, 'are psychic residues inherited from our hunter-gatherer ancestors, which speak to us of another and simpler world'. That was a world in which man was fully at one with the natural order, having been 'adapted to it by evolution'. No more. Today, we have all but lost touch with those primal feelings. But if we are not to completely succumb to the strains of modern life, we must, on occasion, 'rehearse the spontaneous psychic movements that were implanted in us by the species, and which are as important for our proper functioning as it is important to a dog that he should bark from time to time, or to a chicken that she should lay an egg'. We must, that is, revive the 'instincts of the hunter-gatherer', by relating to our own and other species 'in a herd-like way'. And this, he argues, is accomplished by approaching one's prey with 'a quasi-religious attitude'. While the hunted animal is hunted as an individual, the hunted species 'is elevated to divine status as the totem, and a kind of mystical union of the tribe with its totem seals the pact between them forever'.[51] Stated simply, the huntsman worships the species as spiritually embodied in the individual creature. In so doing, he 'guarantees the eternal recurrence of his prey' by identifying the species as a 'sacred object'.[52] The hunt awakens in him, in other words, those 'old instincts and desires, the old pieties and the old relations with our own and other species'.[53]

Scruton is quite aware, however, that these arguments will 'carry little weight in modern times'. Today, people are happy to live in a state of estrangement from their tribal moorings. They view the world 'as a vast suburban garden, an artificial and third-rate paradise, which we must maintain as kindly and responsibly as we can. This means taking the interests of all creatures into account and refraining from pursuits which cause needless suffering, lest the spectacle of suffering should cease to trouble us'.[54] In the end, modern people would prefer that we left nature to itself. But for Scruton, that is not a serious option. If we opted to 'turn our backs' on the natural world, the consequences would be catastrophic both for us and for the animals who abide there. For, whether we like it or not, we are 'guardians and keepers of the natural order', and are thus responsible for it. If, however, we decided to renege on that duty, if, let us say, 'deer were never culled, Exmoor would contain nothing else besides suburban houses, and the highlands of Scotland would be treeless crags. If foxes were never killed, lambs, ducks and chickens would be reared indoors, in conditions that no decent person should tolerate. If angling ceased, our waterways would never be maintained and mink, coote and moorhen would drive all their rivals to extinction.'[55] If, in other words, it is biodiversity that we are seeking, then 'culling and pest control will remain incumbent on us'.

The decision, therefore, is ours: either we opt to poison the pests, which Roger Scruton perceives as 'the truly callous way of doing these things'. Or we can choose to control them in accordance with the ancient rituals of the hunter-gatherer. If we take the second path, it is then that we shall come to appreciate the 'true graciousness of hunting'. For unlike those who have recourse to bait, the trap or the gun, the hunter understands that the fox 'can be cleanly killed only in the open', and is 'never more quickly dispatched than by a pack of hounds'. This, moreover, 'requires great labour and the cooperation of three species if he is to be hunted in this way'.[56] In a remarkable passage from the final pages of *On Hunting*, Scruton substantiates these arguments by outlining the moral foundations of the chase:

Grieving is an offshoot of love – love for the individual, under a duty of care. It has no place in the wild, and those who grieve for hunted animals see things wrongly. The screams of a rabbit caught by a weasel move us to pity, even horror. But, unless the rabbit is our loved companion, we must not grieve for him. The moral law does not tell us to save this suffering creature, but rather to consider his death in the context of his life. Is it, on the whole, better for rabbits that they should live in an environment where they are preyed upon by weasels? Only if such questions come first in our thinking will we fulfil our duty towards other species, all of which now depend upon us for their survival. If it is true, as I and many others believe, that the fox is better served by hunting than by any other form of cull, and that all rival practices expose him to far more suffering, then it is not just permissible to hunt, but morally right.[57]

SEX AND THE SACRED

Rescuing the world from the culture of desecration requires us, therefore, to re-establish the old metaphysical distinction between persons and animals. It demands, moreover, that we revive 'the *Lebenswelt* as religion shapes it'. For in that sphere of the sacred, an animal 'is not seen as a centre of selfhood and freedom'. Neither is it perceived as 'a source of shame or judgement, but a normal part of the empirical world …'. When we look at things in this way, it is possible 'to show that there are no grounds for attributing rights to animals, or for believing that they either desire or are capable of "liberation"'.[58] It also follows that there is something morally suspect in treating people as animals and animals as people. In *A Political Philosophy*, Scruton explains the matter as follows:

Dogs have no conception of what it is to be naked, and their calm unembarrassability before the sight of human flesh reminds us of how very different the human form is, in their eyes and in ours.[59]

Dogs do not become embarrassed when confronted by nudity, simply because they are essentially driven by lust. Unlike persons, theirs is not a world of interpersonal negotiation. It is true that, like us, animals 'feel a need to unite' and 'experience a compelling physical pleasure' in the process. However, even though sex is 'the sphere in which the animal and the personal meet', it is also the domain in which the ineluctable distinctions separating human and animal are most obvious. For, in contrast to human subjects, animals 'are never sexually aroused; they do not feel sexual desire, nor do they have sexual fulfilment. Almost all that matters in sexual experience lies outside their capacities, not because they reach for it and fail to obtain it, but because they cannot reach for it.'[60] Animals, in short, do not have sexual *intentionality*.[61]

In the desacralised world, however, people are indifferent to those fundamental distinctions. They believe themselves to be part of 'the natural order, bound by laws tying them to the material forces that govern everything'. Convinced that 'the gods are their invention, and that death is exactly what it seems',[62] they summarily discard those concepts 'which are indispensable to our lives as rational beings, yet which have no place at all in the scientific view of the world: concepts like person, responsibility, freedom and the subject, which shape the world in readiness for action, and which describe the way in which we appear to one another, regardless of what, from the point of view of science, we are'.[63] The result, according to Scruton, is a demoralised world in which interpersonal relations are voided of their sacred aspect. It is a world where the 'pseudo-science of sexology' has 'redescribed the human world as a world of things …, and presented sex as a relation between aliens'. No longer is the other approached as a person, but simply as 'an instrument of pleasure'.[64]

The 'pseudo-science of sexology' was inaugurated by Sigmund Freud, when he wrote that the objective of sexual desire is 'union of the genitals in the act known as copulation, which leads to a release of sexual tension and a temporary extinction of the sexual instinct – a satisfaction analogous to the sating of hunger'.[65] But Freud's account is not, as Scruton argues, 'a theory of human sexual desire in the social conditions which emerge spontaneously between human beings'. Rather, it is 'a description of sexual feelings transformed by a kind of scientistic prurience, and by an obsession with the human object that clouds awareness of the subject'.[66] By reducing human sexuality to genital satisfaction, Freud (and successive sexologists such as Alfred Kinsey and Richard Posner[67]) pillages the phenomenon of personhood as it emerges in and through the *Lebenswelt*. In doing so, he contaminates the realm of the sacred by 'dragging the subject into the world of things'.[68] That is why, if the sacred is to be saved from the 'charm of disenchantment', Freud's purely biological account of human desire must be repudiated. For it is, according to Scruton, a dangerous caricature that leads only to perversion:

Freud's description of desire is the description of something that we know and shun – or ought to shun. An excitement which concentrates on the sexual organs, whether of man or of woman, which seeks, as it were, to bypass the complex negotiation of the face, hands, voice and posture, is perverted. It voids desire of its intentionality, and replaces it with a pursuit of the sexual commodity, which can always be had for a price.[69]

Scruton's objective in his magisterial *Sexual Desire*, and subsequently in his equally compelling *Death-Devoted Heart*, is, as he remarks, to shore up 'the human world against the corrosive seas of pseudo-science'. It is to demonstrate that, when conceived from a philosophical perspective, sexual desire trades in 'the currency of the sacred'.[70] This means that the experience of desire, far from announcing the 'eclipse of the subject', fundamentally enriches our experience of the sacred. For in the moment of desire, I confront a subject incarnate within the object, or a free self situated in a body which 'is not you but *yours*'. In true desire, we actually encounter the 'mystery of our incarnation', and while we might 'not necessarily *see* it as a mystery', it is one that 'affects us nonetheless, through the caresses, glances, and blushes that work upon us like spells'. This leads, in turn, to a 'process of idealisation' that is 'shaped by culture and feeds automatically into our sense of the sacred'. And it does so by 'prompting lovers to single each other out as incarnations of a unique and possible selfhood'.[71]

Today, however, we are witnessing the ascendancy of a pornographic culture, whose supreme purpose, for Scruton, 'is to eliminate the encounter between subjects and to put the contact of objects in its place'.[72] It achieves that goal by ignoring the human face, while making a shameless spectacle of the body. The face must be ignored by the pornographer, simply because the eyes and mouth bear witness to the transcendence of the subject. Unlike that of an animal, the human face is endowed with feeling and emotion; it is a revelation of freedom in the midst of a mute world of material objects. But in pornography, the face is no longer a portal to personality. 'The burden of contact' is carried instead by the sexual organs, which, in contrast to the face, 'can be treated as instruments' or as 'rival means to the common end of friction …'.[73] No longer is desire focused on another *person*, but merely on the gratification of the flesh. Scruton contends that the consequences of this for society could not be more serious:

The intentionality of the sexual act, conceived in this disenchanted way, is radically changed. It ceases to be an expression of interpersonal longing, still less of the desire to hold, to possess, to be filled with love. It becomes a kind of sacrilege – a wiping away of freedom, personality, and transcendence, to reveal the obscene contortions of what is merely flesh ... A kind of Baudelairean Satanism moves people to look for new ways of desecrating the sexual object, of hunting down what is unpolluted, innocent, or forbidden, so as to expose it to some violating abuse. More important even than pornography is the tendency to sexualise children and to render them enticing – not enticing as premature adults but enticing precisely as *children*, as people unequipped for responsible emotion, whose bodies are still out of bounds and who can therefore be profaned and polluted by the sexual act. The lust for desecration is the other side of the belief in sanctity and can be seen as the inevitable outcome of the attempt to sever desire from commitment and to put sex on sale.[74]

The lust for desecration, that characterises so much of modern life, is an attempt to abolish the personhood of the other and of oneself. It views both your body and mine as just that: bodies devoid of soul and meaning. No longer is desire directed at the moral subject who says 'I', but merely at his flesh. Consequently, the desacralised world is one in which personal commitment is no longer valued. For when a person is desired for his body alone, it is then possible to circumvent the emotionally challenging rituals that lead to commitment. What you seek in that moment, is not the long-term happiness that lasting union guarantees. It is, rather, the type of quick-fix pleasure that either fantasy or prostitution can easily satisfy. In both of these cases, sex is 'seen as a commodity: something that we pursue and obtain in quantifiable form, and which comes in a variety of packages: in the form of a woman or a man; in the form of a film or a dream; in the form of a fetish or an animal'.[75] This is not so much casual sex, as im*personal* sex. In disregarding the other as a source of sacredness, his freedom, subjectivity and personhood are expunged. All that remains is the *object* of desire, one that can very easily be substituted by another object. Hence, in the sexual world of the fantasist, 'others appear as objects only. And when a person is targeted by a desire nurtured on fantasy – when a real subject is treated as a fantasy object – the result is a sin against love'.[76]

In order to counter this lust for desecration, it is not sufficient to renounce our 'animal nature' in favour of pure reason. Such was the course that Plato recommended when he drew his notorious distinction between 'erotic love and sexual desire', a distinction that has, in Scruton's mind, 'caused considerable confusion in subsequent debate'. According to Plato, 'our animal nature is the principal vehicle of sexual desire', whereas in erotic love 'it is our nature as rational beings that is primarily engaged'.[77] To cultivate the soul requires us, therefore, to decontaminate love of sexual desire, thereby rendering it 'intrinsically rational and morally pure'. Scruton opposes Platonic love, not because it is founded on the distinction between the rational and the animal – a distinction which is for him, as we have seen, 'crucial to the understanding of our condition'. Rather, he sets himself the task of combating the Platonic theory, because he can see no value in the 'moral and philosophical impulse that leads us to assign sexual desire to the animal part of human nature'.[78] The result is that when Plato talks of love, he is simply describing 'a bloodless philosophical passion that has nothing of the erotic about it at all, and which is not even directed toward a human being'.[79]

We will recall that Scruton follows Kant in holding that human beings are both object *and* subject, animal *and* person. To love, therefore, is to love another who is ineluctably situated *in her body*. We are, in other words, 'incarnate persons in whom animal and self exist in an intricate unity, each both exalted and compromised by the other'.[80] Hence, as properly conceived, sexual desire is desire for another *person*, the very thought of whom causes me to become aroused. And it is through the phenomenon of arousal that the true intentionality underlying sexual desire is revealed:

Sexual arousal has, then, an intentionality that is not merely epistemic, but also interpersonal. In its normal form it is a response to another individual, based in revelation and discovery, and involving a reciprocal and cooperative heightening of the common experience of embodiment. It is not directed beyond the other to the world at large; nor is it straightforwardly transferable to a rival object who might 'do just as well'. Of course, arousal may have its origin in highly generalised thoughts, which flit libidinously from object to object. But when these thoughts have concentrated into the experience of arousal their generality tends to be put aside; it is then the other who counts, and his or her particular embodiment, as well as I myself and the sense of my bodily reality in the other's perspective.[81]

Through the body, a particular subject is made visible, becoming thus an object of desire – 'of the desire to be united with this person, which is also a desire to possess'. In blushes, smiles and glances, I respond to you as a 'responsible agent … in the realm of embarrassment and self-knowledge'. The reason why an animal cannot blush is because it does not possess the 'intentionality of sexual emotion'.[82] It is incapable, in other words, of being consumed with desire for a particular individual, seeking as it does only instinctual gratification, and for that purpose any other will suffice.

In contrast, human sexual emotions are 'founded on individualising thoughts: it is *you* whom I want and not the type or the pattern'. Properly speaking, therefore, desire proposes 'a relation between subjects'. It demands and requires negotiation and consent, and is founded on compromise and trust; it is 'an expression of my freedom, which seeks out the freedom in you'.[83] When observed thus, it is easy to understand why we condemn rape, for it is, quite literally, a desecration of another's freedom – 'a dragging of the subject into the world of things'. But when the human being is perceived as a soulless entity, as it is by Freud and Kinsey, the moral and legal prohibitions against rape begin to seem inexplicable. For rape, as properly conceived, is a crime against *the person*. But because the person, as a locus of freedom, fails to feature in the pseudo-science of sexology, 'the outrage and pollution of rape become impossible to explain'.[84]

For Scruton, sexual desire leads to an epiphany of the sacred. No longer is the body of the other perceived as mere flesh that may be despoiled without moral consequence. In authentic desire culminating in erotic love, it is seen as a 'free self-conscious being' that must be approached through what he calls 'the rite of mutual acquiescence'.[85] That rite demands that we recognise in both self and other, the transcendental freedom that invites us to sacrifice. The basis of all true love is sacrifice, whereby the self sets aside the claims of the empirical world and dies to itself for the sake of the other. That, claims Scruton, is 'a goal that only free beings can embrace or conceive', and it 'sanctifies the one who performs it.

It brings the sacred into being.'[86] In sexual love, the individual is redeemed from selfishness and brought to the realisation that devotion to another is inordinately preferable 'to life without the other'. Erotic love is, therefore, the key to redemption *in time*. It reveals to us that salvation is not to be found by following Plato in a wholesale purging of our physical passions. Rather, it consists in recognising that 'freedom really does exist in this world and that we too possess it. And this freedom is discovered in the most earthbound of our passions ...'[87]

PRIORITISING THE 'THIRD-PERSON'

If Scruton is correct, which I believe he is, then it clearly follows that society has a vested interest in maintaining a morality of erotic love. For this, we need to look in the direction of Aristotle, and his theory of virtue ethics as outlined in the *Nicomachean Ethics*.[88] Unlike Plato, who prioritised the rational at the expense of the animal, Aristotle seeks to establish *equilibrium* between the rational and the animal, resulting in happiness (*eudaimonia*). But human happiness is not to be confused with pleasure, for as Scruton remarks, 'pleasure comes with the fulfilment of desire – getting what you want and wanting what you get'. True happiness, on the other hand, 'comes with the fulfilment of the person'.[89] And what counts as fulfilment of the person? According to Aristotle, it is *the cultivation of virtue as habit*. Aristotle believed that happiness is 'an activity of the soul in accordance with virtue', meaning that only virtuous people can be happy. And because happiness is the end (*telos*) towards which all human life aims, only virtuous people are truly fulfilled.

Following Aristotle, Scruton contends that the good life 'is the life that reproduces itself'. This means that if we are to be true to ourselves as rational animals, we must aim to reproduce moral personality in our young. But for that purpose 'you need parents who take charge of their children, who defend them and nurture them and instil in them the habits which will lead them, in turn, to do the same. You need, in short, the life of self-sacrifice which is part of virtue and dependent on virtue for its long-term success.'[90] Put simply, the successful reproduction of personhood depends on a strong moral education, one that inculcates those dispositions 'which lead of their own accord to fulfilment'.[91] Only then will the child flourish in accordance with his essence as a rational being:

It is clear that virtue is a part of rational fulfilment. For without the disposition to want what is reasonable, there is no such thing as an *exercise* of reason. And while this may seem a rather trivial assertion, it is, in the context, far from trivial. For if I have reason to aim at anything, I have reason to acquire the dispositions that enable me to fulfil my aims. I therefore have reason to acquire courage – and perhaps other virtues too. I will also try to inculcate these dispositions in my child, since whatever his desires his long-term fulfilment will depend upon his acquisition of the habits which prevent their frustration. And these habits will constrain his desires, so that he will learn to want what is reasonable.[92]

The Aristotelian believes that rational fulfilment never results from the transitory pleasures of the present. For him, the key to a happy life is the cultivation of a moral disposition that shuns immediacy in favour of the long-term perspective. This suggests that there are virtues which, if judged from the immediate point of view, appear wholly irrational and arbitrary. However, if judged from 'the third-person view of moral agency', a point of view that sees my action 'in the context of my life as a whole',[93] then the value of such virtues becomes abundantly clear.

To understand what is at issue here, we must recall that for Scruton the 'first-person perspective' is predicated on an abstraction. It invites me to withdraw from the *Lebenswelt*, shed my empirical trappings, and remove 'from my thought every consideration which ties me to the "here and now"'.[94] This applies, as we have already seen, in the case of Descartes' *ego cogito*, but also in the case of Kant's 'transcendental self'. In his formulation of the categorical imperative, Kant seeks to establish reason as the sole basis for moral judgement. As he argues, the principles of moral agency 'must have an origin entirely and completely *a priori*, and must at the same time derive from this their sovereign authority – that they expect nothing from the inclinations of man, but everything from the supremacy of the law and from the reverence due to it, or in default of this condemn man to self-contempt and inward abhorrence'.[95] This, however, results in a paradox regarding moral motivation: in responding to reason to the point where it loses touch with the empirical world, the Kantian self is deprived of *concrete* moral motives. It becomes, as it were, a 'minimal self' divorced 'from the conditions which distinguish *me*'. Consequently, Scruton argues, 'either I am a transcendental self, obedient to reason, in which case I cannot act; or else I am able to act, in which case my motives are part of my circumstance and history, and remain unresponsive to the voice of reason, which calls away from beyond the horizon of the empirical world'.[96]

This suggests that the first-person perspective, which abstracts from 'the historical givenness of my aims and projects', is a misrepresentation of the human condition.[97] As a person, I am ineluctably subject to the constraints of a public world which supplies me with real motives for action. Recall how Scruton follows Wittgenstein in arguing that the idea of transcendental freedom is not a feature of some private and self-vindicating entity outside the natural order. Rather, 'I can see myself as free only because I have intentions, which I acquire through the practice of public criticism and argument, whereby I am situated in a moral community and made answerable for what I do'.[98] It follows that the rational agent is a 'gift of community', one in which 'people are seen to be immersed in the contingencies of social life, acting from passions which respond to the changing circumstances of existence'.[99] Hence, I cannot *be* a transcendental self, for the simple reason that 'I speak a public language which confers that privilege upon me, by enabling me to formulate and reflect upon my thoughts, feelings and desires'. From the moment of my birth, I am 'nurtured and protected by forces the operation of which they could neither consent to nor understand'. The family is, of course, the most important of those forces, and is that through which the person begins to recognise and respond to 'the power of "ought"'. This, however, is not the abstract 'ought' of Kantian liberalism, but the concrete, 'immediate "ought" of family attachments'.[100]

Scruton is here reinforcing the familiar Hegelian intuition that 'communities are not formed through the fusion or agreement of rational individuals: it is rational individuals who are formed through communities'.[101] From the outset of his existence, the individual is surrounded by obligations, and it is 'an essential part of rationality to recognise these obligations which are not self-imposed'. And so, the abstract rationality of the Kantian ego is rejected in favour of that which is *socially* formed. It is, says Scruton, 'only in the condition of mutuality, when he recognises himself as a social being bound by a moral law which constrains him to recognise the selfhood of others, that the individual acquires (or "realises") his autonomy'.[102] The rational agent evolves, therefore, from those institutional structures which burden him with 'a debt of love and gratitude'. And to recognise this fact is to acquire real autonomy, as distinct from the empty autonomy of the Kantian ego. It is the freedom that only socially-situated selves enjoy.[103]

What we may conclude from this is that Roger Scruton's conservative convictions put him squarely on the side of Aristotle and Hegel, thinkers who prioritise the 'third-person perspective'. This does not mean, however, that we can simply jettison the Kantian theory of freedom upon which so much of Scruton's philosophy relies. While the transcendental self may very well be an illusion, it is, he stipulates, a 'well founded' illusion. Why so? Because 'if I am to be fulfilled at all, I must belong to a world in which this illusion can be sustained, so that my projects are also values for me, and my desires are integrated into a vision of the good'.[104] It seems then, that *there are good third-person reasons for sustaining the 'necessary' illusion of the first-person perspective.* While 'there is no "real transcendental self" behind appearances', there is nevertheless 'a way of treating people *as if* there were such a thing: addressing them as free beings governed by reason, with a point of view that uniquely identifies them and which is not revealed to them in empirical observation'.[105] Without the first-person perspective, in other words, the idea of the rational person as source of the sacred would be compromised.

To see the world from the first-person perspective is to 'perceive it in sacral terms'.[106] It is to observe the world, and all those in it, as subjects who possess the capacity to transcend their empirical condition through wilful acts of freedom. And, by redeeming man from the 'causal order', the transcendental illusion provides for his long-term happiness. The restoration of the sacred depends, therefore, on nurturing 'the sense that our transcendental identity and freedom are not illusory but real', and that the world's 'steely objectivity has been breached'.[107] But that, as we have seen, requires an institutional or social setting, in which moral education 'is directed towards the special kind of temperance which shows itself, sometimes as chastity, sometimes as fidelity, sometimes as passionate desire'. For without an ethics of sexual virtue, in which we are enjoined 'to respect the other person, and to respect, also, the sanctity of his body, as the tangible expression of another self', a person can easily be 'driven from its incarnation, and its habitation ransacked'. [108]

SAVING SHAME

When looked at from this perspective, it becomes easier to appreciate the reasoning that guides Scruton's defence of *shame*. For the latter, ours is a culture dominated by lavatory humour and Reality TV, in which all 'fig leaves, whether of language, thought or behaviour, have now been removed ...'. [109] This is true, not only of adult society, but also within the classroom, where 'sex education' teaches more about technique than about tenderness. Hence for those brought up in the current climate, shame is regarded as a 'lingering disability'.

For Scruton, however, shame is not only essential for the proper development of sexual desire, but is 'an integral part of the human condition'. Take it away and sexual feeling ceases to be moralised. In traditional society, sexual feelings were imbued with 'psychological sanctions'. And, by becoming part of a person's moral character, such feelings were then regulated from inside 'by the will'. This 'inward control', as Scruton calls it,

... set people at a distance from one another; it also made them safe to one another by ensuring that sexual advances were not just smash-and-grab raids aimed at the goods in the window, but the first steps towards love and commitment. Take this inner control away, and what was previously a source of social cohesion becomes the cause of social decay. [110]

Indeed, according to Scruton, the abolition of shame has contributed to the morally corrupting virus of screen addiction. Cyber pornography is an obvious case in point. But, as a recent case of an American boy who chose to webcast his suicide live shows, there can be deadly consequences in a world where shame has been banished. In responding to that tragedy, Scruton declared that when he views the world from behind the screen, the internet addict 'can relish every kind of narcissistic, sadistic and hateful feeling without cost'. He can do so because he is invisible to those who might judge him. There he sits in isolation, savouring the spectacle un-perturbed by the public gaze.[111] Those who watched the boy commit sui-cide live on screen 'could enjoy a cost-free sadistic spree, and – when the dreadful event was over – turn their vicarious lives in another direction, as though nothing had happened'. Such is the 'enormous moral cost' of screen addiction, one which will not only result in a 'widespread hardening of the human heart', but – worse still – a 'replacement of true relationships with their cyber substitutes'.[112]

And that is why there is now such a pressing need to nurture real rela-tionships founded upon commitment, obligation and genuine devotion. Otherwise, we shall succumb to 'the culture of masturbation', in which there are no lasting attachments, but only fleeting encounters for the sake of immediate gratification. In such a culture, love is never the goal of sexual union, and children are considered an unwanted burden. Indeed with cybersex, proclaims Scruton, 'the risk of children is finally elimi-nated'. There is, in other words, no place for the family in the shameless paradise of 'Onanistan'.[113]

THE MEANING OF MARRIAGE

In love, we see each other, not as 'cost-free' substitutes, but as transcenden-tal beings. But we do so only because the idea of the transcendental self has been nurtured by particular institutions. Hence, if man is to success-fully sustain his sense of the sacred, 'unthreatened by the senselessness of a merely objective world', he must care for those institutions whose cer-emonies and rituals foster 'the idea of the sacred'. For Scruton, the most important of those ceremonies is that of *marriage*:

The marriage ceremony is therefore one of the most important of human cere-monies, and one which marks the transition from one state to another. At such moments, man is confronted with his fragility and dependence. As at the moments of death and birth, he is beset by awe. The feeling is a recognition of the sacred, of the intrusion into the human world of obligations that cannot be created by an act of choice, and which therefore demand a transcendental meaning. The sacred is 'the subjectivity of objects' – the presentation in the contours of day-to-day things, of a meaning that sees 'from I to I'. Out of the mute objectivity of the surrounding world, a voice suddenly calls to me, with a clear and intelligible command. It tells me who I am, and enjoins me to enter the place that has been kept for me. In marriage I 'undertake' an obligation that precedes my choice, and which resides in the scheme of things. Not surprisingly, therefore, marriage is a religious 'sacrament', comparable to the sacraments of baptism and extreme unction. The universal participation of religions in the marriages of believers is testimony to the shared perception of this sacred quality.[114]

Marriage embodies the 'experience of a sacred obligation'. It invites the participants to publicly sacrifice their former selves in favour of a transcendent union. It bears witness to the coming together of two people whose commitment is based not simply on a *contract*, but on an eternal vow. Hence, a wedding 'is a rite of passage, in which the couple pass from one social condition to another'. And it is one that society has a vested interest in sustaining, because latent within the marriage vow there is the promise of 'social reproduction'. When the couple promise to remain faithful 'in sickness and in health', they are concomitantly pledging to assume 'responsibility for the socialising and educating of the children'.[115] Marriage has, thus, both a subjective meaning and a social function. Its subjective meaning, Scruton writes, 'lies in the exaltation and ennobling of our sexual urges, which are lifted from the realm of appetite and reconstituted as rational commitments'. But as the institutional expression of desire, marriage also facilitates 'the sacrifices on which the next generation depends'.[116] It is through marriage, in other words, that the social and moral capital of a community is transmitted from one generation to the next.

We might say, therefore, that it is through the vow of love, as witnessed in the marriage ceremony, that personhood, as the basis of the moral order, is reproduced. However, when marriage is no longer perceived as a religious sacrament, when it becomes devoid of sacred obligations, and when it ceases to be endowed with lifelong responsibility and obligation, it is then that it succumbs to the 'ideology of contract'. The ideology of contract, which results in the 'de-sacralisation of the marriage tie', leads to 'a transitory agreement between people living now'. Consequently, marriage loses its 'transcendental meaning', becoming instead 'a partnership in things subservient only to the gross animal existence of a temporary and perishable nature'.[117] And when that happens, the other ceases to be idealised as a sacred being.

Put simply, when vows are reduced to contracts, the sacral character of human experience is destroyed. The ideology of contract may indeed result in the individual's liberation from conventional constraints, but it does nothing to promote the long-term prospect of human happiness. And that is because human joy does not result solely from the short-term sating of bodily appetite. Rather, as Scruton tirelessly endeavours to explain, it demands that the other be loved as a *person* – a being characterised by subjective freedom and transcendence. Without love, in other words, the re-sacralisation of the depersonalised world is nothing but a vain hope.[118]

NOTES

1. Scruton, *On Hunting*, p.79.
2. Scruton, *Sexual Desire*, p.348.
3. Scruton, *The Philosopher on Dover Beach*, p.9.
4. Scruton, *Sexual Desire*, p.349.
5. *Ibid.*
6. *Ibid.*, p.355.
7. Scruton, *Philosophy: Principles and Problems*, p.59.
8. Richard Rorty, *Philosophy and Social Hope* (London: Penguin, 1999), p.68.
9. Roger Scruton, *Animal Rights and Wrongs* (London: Continuum, 2000), pp.1–2.
10. *Ibid.*, p.4.
11. *Ibid.*, p.16.
12. *Ibid.*, p.19.
13. Scruton, *Sexual Desire*, p.32.
14. Scruton, *Animal Rights and Wrongs*, p.21.
15. Scruton, *Sexual Desire*, p.44.
16. Richard Rorty, 'The Challenge of Relativism' in *Debating the State of Philosophy*, Jozef Niznik and John T. Sanders (eds.) (Westport: Praeger, 1996), p.42.
17. Scruton, *Sexual Desire*, p.46.
18. Rorty, 'The Challenge of Relativism', p.38.
19. Scruton, *Philosophy: Principles and Problems*, p.48.
20. Scruton, *Modern Philosophy*, p.48.
21. *Ibid.*, p.50. For more on the 'First Person' and the 'Private Language Argument', see Scruton, *Sexual Desire*, pp.364–376; *Modern Philosophy*, pp.46–57 & pp.481–495; *A Short History of Modern Philosophy*, pp.289–294.
22. Scruton, *Modern Philosophy*, p.53.
23. Scruton, *Philosophy: Principles and Problems*, p.49.
24. Scruton, *Modern Philosophy*, p.54.
25. Rorty, *Philosophy and Social Hope*, p.48.
26. Scruton, *Animal Rights and Wrongs*, pp.24–25; *Philosophy: Principles and Problems*, p.65.

27. Rorty, 'The Challenge of Relativism', p.38.
28. Richard Rorty, *Objectivity, Relativism and Truth* (Cambridge: Cambridge University Press, 1991), p.6.
29. Rorty, 'The Challenge of Relativism', p.41.
30. *Ibid.*, p.40.
31. Scruton, *Modern Philosophy*, p.495.
32. *Ibid.*, p.107.
33. *Ibid.*, p.108.
34. *Ibid.*, p.242.
35. *Ibid.*, p.244.
36. Scruton, *Philosophy: Principles and Problems*, p.109.
37. For Scruton's final verdict on Rorty, see his 'Richard Rorty's Legacy' on *www.open-democracy.net*. See also, Scruton, *A Political Philosophy*, pp.103–117.
38. *Ibid.*, p.54.
39. *Ibid.*, p.65.
40. Scruton, *Animal Rights and Wrongs*, p.80.
41. *Ibid.*, pp.80–81.
42. Roger Scruton, 'Animal Rights', *City Journal*, Vol. 10, No. 3, Summer 2000. I am citing from the online edition of this article: *www.city-journal.org*.
43. *Ibid.*
44. Scruton, *On Hunting*, p.132.
45. Scruton, *Animal Rights and Wrongs*, p.124.
46. Scruton, *On Hunting*, p.79.
47. Scruton, *Animal Rights and Wrongs*, p.125.
48. Roger Scruton, 'Fox-Hunting: The Modern Case', A Written Submission to the Committee of Inquiry into Hunting Chaired by Lord Burns. Available at: *www.defra.gov.uk/rural/hunting/inquiry/evidence/scruton.htm*.
49. *Ibid.*
50. *Ibid.*
51. Scruton, *On Hunting*, p.73.
52. *Ibid.*, p.75.
53. Scruton, *On Hunting*, p.77; *Animal Rights and Wrongs*, p.154.
54. Scruton, *Animal Rights and Wrongs*, p.162.
55. *Ibid.*, pp.162–163.
56. *Ibid.*, p.163.
57. Scruton, *On Hunting*, p.154.
58. Scruton, *A Political Philosophy*, p.137.
59. *Ibid.*, p.138.
60. Scruton, *Sexual Desire*, p.36.
61. There is a superb interview (and podcast) with Scruton on the theme of 'Sex and Perversion' on *Ethics Bites*, *Open2.net*, in which he says: 'I would say the first thing to be clear about is that sexual desire in the human case has an individualizing intentionality. That is to say, I desire another person as the person he or she is. That is not the case with animals; they have sexual instincts and sexual pleasures and they pursue them. But they do not have desire for the other individual in that way, partly because they don't have the concept of the individual. Now once you are set on this path of desiring another individual there are all kinds of obstacles along the way and

also un-clarity, often, as to what it is you want to do with that other person. You can desire somebody without having the first desire to perform the sexual act. And indeed Plato thought that, in the normal case, we are under an obligation to somehow transcend that carnal appetite and unite with the other person in a completely different way. Now I don't think that is normal. But I do think the normal course of sexual desire does involve courtship, the soliciting of consent from the other as an individual to you as an individual so that when you do finally achieve the result it is in the way of a mutual possession where each gives himself to the other. And that of course is something that doesn't always occur. But if you define normality in that way, that gives you a grip on the moral essence of the thing'. And that, in a nutshell, is a perfect summary of Scruton's theory of sexual desire. Both the interview and podcast can be downloaded by going to: *http://www.open2.net/ ethicsbites/sex-perversion.html.*

62. Scruton, *Death-Devoted Heart*, p.12.
63. Scruton, *Philosophy: Principles and Problems*, p.106.
64. *Ibid.*, p.135.
65. Sigmund Freud, 'Three Essays on Sexuality' in *On Sexuality*, J. Strachey and A. Richards (trans. & eds) (London: Harmondsworth, 1977), p.61. Cited in Scruton, *Death-Devoted Heart*, p.137.
66. Scruton, *Death-Devoted Heart*, p.137.
67. Scruton critically confronts Kinsey and Posner in his chapter on 'Sex' in *Philosophy: Principles and Problems*, pp.127–139. However, the real target of all his discussions of sexual desire is Michel Foucault's *History of Sexuality* (3 Vols.) (London: Penguin, 1997–1998).
68. Scruton, *Philosophy: Principles and Problems*, p.133.
69. *Ibid.*, p.132.
70. Scruton, *Death-Devoted Heart*, p.7.
71. *Ibid.*, p.178.
72. *Ibid.*, p.181.
73. *Ibid.*
74. *Ibid.*, pp.181–182.
75. Scruton, *Sexual Desire*, p.345.
76. Scruton, *Death-Devoted Heart*, p.146.
77. Scruton, *Sexual Desire*, p.1. See also Plato, *The Symposium* (trans. Walter Hamilton) (London: Penguin, 1951), a satirical send-up of which Scruton provides in 'Phryne's Symposium', *Xanthippic Dialogues*, pp.175–265.
78. Scruton, *Sexual Desire*, p.2.
79. Scruton, *Death-Devoted Heart*, p.136.
80. *Ibid.*, p.137.
81. *Ibid.*, pp.139–141; *Philosophy: Principles and Problems*, p.130.
82. Scruton, *Death-Devoted Heart*, p.141.
83. *Ibid.*, p.142.
84. *Ibid.*, p.143.
85. *Ibid.*, p.179.
86. *Ibid.*, p.183.
87. *Ibid.*
88. Aristotle, *The Nicomachean Ethics* (trans. J. A. K. Thomson) (London: Penguin Books, 1955). See also 'Sexual Morality' in Scruton, *Sexual Desire*, pp.322–347.

89. Roger Scruton, 'Do the Right Thing' in *The Good Life*, Ian Christie and Lindsay Nash (eds), Demos Pamphlet, 1998, p.64.

90. *Ibid.*, p.67.

91. *Ibid.*, p.68.

92. Scruton, *Sexual Desire*, p.329.

93. Scruton, *The Philosopher on Dover Beach*, p.265.

94. Roger Scruton, 'Philosophical Appendix: Liberalism versus Conservatism' in *The Meaning of Conservatism* (South Bend: St. Augustine's Press, 2002), p.188.

95. Immanuel Kant, *Groundwork of the Metaphysic of Morals*, H. J. Paton (trans.) (New York: Harper Torchbooks, 1964), p.93.

96. Scruton, *The Meaning of Conservatism*, p.189.

97. *Ibid.*, p.190.

98. Scruton, *Modern Philosophy*, p.494.

99. Scruton, *The Meaning of Conservatism*, p.190.

100. *Ibid.*, p.192.

101. Scruton, *Modern Philosophy*, p.494.

102. Scruton, *The Philosopher on Dover Beach*, p.49.

103. I return to this aspect of Scruton's thought in Chapter 4, below.

104. Scruton, *The Meaning of Conservatism*, p.192.

105. Scruton, *Death-Devoted Heart*, p.123.

106. Scruton, *Sexual Desire*, p.352.

107. *Ibid.*, p.353.

108. *Ibid.*, p.340.

109. Roger Scruton, 'Shameless and Loveless' in *The Spectator Magazine*, 16 April 2005. I am citing from the online edition which is available at: *www.spectator.co.uk/the-magazine/ features/13530/investigation-shameless-and-loveless.thtml*.

110. Roger Scruton, 'Bring Back Stigma' in *City Journal*, Autumn 200. I am citing from the online edition which is available at: *www.city-journal.org*.

111. 'The same force led to the perfecting of the photograph, the video camera, and the movie screen. What is new is the withdrawal of pornography from the arena of shame. People could see you entering the "adult" video shop; they could discover the photographs in your drawer or the books on your shelf. Your secrets were not just guilty, but shameful. Technology now enables you to escape from the public eye. You can enjoy your sexual encounters in cyberspace, without the shaming contact with your fellow human beings. Sex on the internet recalls Wilde's quip about masturbation: "cleaner, more efficient, and you meet a better class of person." Sex has been confiscated by the machine, and virtual sex has come in place of it. Virtual sex is shame-free, since no one knows you are having it, not even the person with whom you are having it. And that which is shame-free soon becomes shameless.' Roger Scruton, 'Very Safe Sex' in *National Review*, 28 July 1997. Available at: *http://findarticles.com/p/articles/mi_m1282/ is_14_49/ai_59451084/print*.

112. I am citing here from a press release issued by Scruton in response to the internet suicide, and posted on the website of The Institute for the Psychological Sciences. It is available at: http://ipsciences.edu/pages/what-is-new/prof.-scruton-comments-on-virtual-suicide.php. Scruton wrote a lot on the morally corrosive effects of internet addiction. See especially Roger Scruton, 'Virtual Reality: Its Distortion of Self and Others', delivered as part of The Institute for the Psycholog-

ical Sciences' 'John Henry Cardinal Newman Lecture Series 2008–2009', 31 October 2008. A podcast of the event is available at: *www.frc.org/content/ips-lecture-roger-scruton-hiding-behind-the-screen-the-philosophy-of-virtual-reality*. See also his sensational column 'Can Virtual Life Take Over from Real Life?' in *The Sunday Times*, 16 November 2008, in which he says: 'In real life, friendship involves risk. The reward is great: help in times of need, joy in times of celebration. But the cost is also great: self-sacrifice, accountability, the risk of embarrassment and anger, and the effort of winning another's trust. Hence I can become friends with you only by seeking your company. I must attend to your words, gestures and body language, and win the trust of the person revealed in them, and this is risky business. I can avoid the risk and still obtain pleasure; but I will never obtain friendship or love.

When I relate to you through the screen there is a marked shift in emphasis. Now I have my finger on the button. At any moment I can turn you off. You are free in your own space, but you are not really free in mine, since you are dependent on my decision to keep you there. I retain ultimate control, and am not risking myself in the friendship as I risk myself when I meet you face to face. Of course I may stay glued to the screen. Nevertheless, it is a screen that I am glued to, not the person behind it.' Available at: *http://technology.timesonline.co.uk/tol/news/tech_and_web/the_web/article 5139532.ece*.

113. See Scruton, 'Very Safe Sex': 'The encounter in cyberspace is merely the imaginative seed, brought to fruition by an act of masturbation. Ever since Americans accepted the view of sex propagated by such pseudo-scientific documents as the Kinsey report, they have been deprived of the concepts that would enable them to understand why masturbation is wrong. If all sex is a matter of pleasurable sensation, then what does it matter how it is produced, provided those involved consent to it? Masturbation has ceased to be self-abuse and become the most innocent form of sexual exploit – the only one in which no one but the agent is at risk. And other forms of sex are described and understood as a kind of masturbation *a deux* (or more). The sex of the partner is no longer morally relevant, and the single permitted moral question is the question of consent. The result is not Sodom or Babylon but a universal Onanistan.'

114. Scruton, *Sexual Desire*, p.357.

115. Scruton, *A Political Philosophy*, p.83.

116. Roger Scruton, 'The Moral Birds and Bees: Sex and Marriage Properly Understood', *National Review Online*, 15 September 2003. Available at: *http://findarticles.com/p/articles/mi_m1282/is_17_55/ai_107223562/print*.

117. Edmund Burke, *Reflections on the Revolution in France*. Cited in *Conservative Texts: An Anthology*, Roger Scruton (ed.) (London: Macmillan, 1991), p.39.

118. For more on this, see Roger Scruton, 'Sex in a Commodity Culture', in *Rewriting the Sexual Contract*, Geoff Dench (ed.) (New Jersey: Transaction Publishers, 1999).

3

Gazing Aesthetically

In one of his most arresting phrases, Roger Scruton says that 'art has grown from the sacred view of life'.[1] It is the portal through which the personality of the world is proclaimed. That is why, for him, it is 'of the greatest import to beings like us, who move on the surface of things'.[2] Like religion, art exposes us 'to an experience saturated by meaning, whose value overwhelms us with the force of law'.[3] Indeed, Scruton shares with Hegel the conviction that art and religion are dialectically inter-twined at a most intimate level. Both sacralise 'the core experiences of society', thus elevating 'the human person to the summit of creation'. Properly construed, art 'ennobles the human spirit, and presents us with a justifying vision of ourselves, as something higher than nature and apart from it'. It is an aperture through which the timeless enters time, or through which freedom contravenes contingent constraints.

But whereas religion demands ritual, faith and worship, art 'engages our sympathies without compelling any doctrine'. It invites us to view the world not as something to be merely used or manipulated. Rather, we are asked to 'set aside the relentless curiosity of science, and the habit of instrumental thinking', so as to incorporate what art expresses into 'a life of lasting commitment and serious feeling'. Put simply, art shares with religion the belief that while the human subject is situated in this world, it is not totally of the world. And by enabling us to 'close again the gap between subject and object which yawns so frighteningly in the world of science', the aesthetic experience reveals 'the human spirit as a thing redeemed'.[4]

This suggests that there is a deep connection between the sacred, the aesthetic and the experience of sexual desire. We will recall that in erotic love, the person is lifted from the world of objects and idealised as a source of the sacred. In that moment, his face and form are 'endowed with a moral and spiritual significance'. Scruton writes:

We see the beloved face as in some way lifted out of the ordinary commerce of human features, shining with a radiance of its own, in which virtues (specifically male or female virtues) achieve a kind of sensory embodiment. This experience is often invoked by Dante and other mediaeval poets influenced by the Platonic theories of erotic love. But it is there, in one form or another, in all the literature of love, right down to Proust and James, and it has suggested to many writers a close proximity between erotic feelings and the sense of the sacred: this face and form are for me somehow *outside* the polluted world of ordinary transactions, in something like the way sacred things exist apart from the world – in it, but not of it.[5]

So too with the objects of aesthetic interest: being irreplaceable and without substitutes, they are 'part of the continuing human attempt not just to observe the world but to idealise and sanctify it, to make it into an object of reverence, and to present images and narratives of our humanity as a thing to live up to, and not merely a thing to live'.[6] Both art and love are, in sum, expressions of the sacred. They reveal to us who we are and what we ought to value. But they do so only because of the latent religious impulse that lies at the heart of all cultural awareness.

COMMON CULTURE VERSUS HIGH CULTURE

In order to illustrate his point, Scruton draws an important distinction between 'common culture' and 'high culture'. From the outset, people participate in a set of cultural practices which precede them. These include those ceremonies and rituals which serve as a rite of initiation into one's tribe or community. A common culture is, therefore, a means to communal membership. It is certainly true that we can study and learn about a particular common culture, but 'no amount of study can suffice to take us from outside to inside the privileged relation'. That is because the common culture is the *background* context through which a human being first encounters the world. Through it, 'a person is joined to something greater than himself, and the world as he perceives it (his

Lebenswelt) is transformed accordingly'. He thinks as his tribe thinks, and finds meaning through a common fund of signs, symbols, ceremonies and customs. This is what Scruton means when he argues that each common culture 'defines a distinct intentionality – a "way things seem" – which is offered to the participant, but not to those who stand outside'.[7] It is a *lived* experience rather than one that is consciously learned, and one that we tamper with only with supreme caution and sensitivity:

The attitude of a common culture to innovation is necessarily one of suspicion and hostility. Much more is at stake than the scoffing rationalist can conceivably imagine (if he *could* imagine it, he would cease to scoff). Innovation can take place, if at all, only in the spirit advocated by Burke: the spirit of a reform which aims to conserve. Innovation must therefore be construed as a renewal of something more fundamental than the detail changed: a casting away of accidents and perversions. The innovation must *prove* itself, by showing that it already *belongs* to the tradition which it seems to challenge. It must adapt itself to the tradition, and in doing so it will adapt the tradition to itself.[8]

But in making this assertion, Scruton is not solely relying on the insights of Edmund Burke. He is also making subtle reference to another of his intellectual heroes: T. S. Eliot. In his essay 'Tradition and the Individual Talent', Eliot speaks of tradition as involving an appreciation of 'the timeless as well as of the temporal and of the timeless and the temporal together'.[9] Belonging to a tradition means having a sense of oneself as being situated in a dialectic between past, present and future. We always already belong, as it were, to an 'existing order', one which cannot be radically altered or changed without doing a disservice to both the living and the dead. That is why Eliot cautions that, 'for order to persist after the supervention of novelty, the *whole* existing order must be, if ever so slightly, altered'.[10] If novelty is to chime harmoniously with the spirit of the past, in other words, it must adapt to the 'existing monuments' of the tradition. That is so because tradition, conceived as common culture, 'gives meaning to the world, by offering occasions for action, a right and wrong procedure, and those ready concepts which close the gap between thought and action – concepts of virtue and vice, of sacred and sacrilege, of seemly and unseemly'.[11] Hence, because the common culture 'impresses the matter of experience with moral form', it cannot admit of too much *individual* innovation. For it is through the sacred rituals of the common culture, which convey the 'core experience of membership, that 'I see the world no longer as an object of my own paltry needs and appetites, but as it really and eternally is'. Or, as Scruton majestically expresses it: 'Through the ceremony of membership, therefore, God enters the world, and makes himself known'.[12]

In less exalted language, we might say that most – though not all – common cultures originate from a tribe's primal desire for communion with the eternal. Through their 'meticulous' rituals and sacrifices, in which the dead and the unborn are sanctified, the members of the tribe congregate in honour of sacred times and sacred places. At the core of common culture is, thus, a deeply implanted religious urge, one that 'unites the present members by dedicating them to the past and future of community'.[13] And because all religions nurture and sustain 'the ethical vision of man', it is through the common culture that 'the vision of human beings as objects of judgement' first takes root.[14] The reproduction of personhood requires, therefore, a strong common culture in which the idea of a free or transcendental subject stands supreme. Scruton explains:

The ethical vision endows human matter with a personal form, and therefore lifts us above nature, to set us side by side with our judge. If we are judged then we must be free, and answerable for our actions. The free being is not just an organism: he has a life of his own, which is uniquely his and which he creates through his choices. Hence he stands above nature in the very activities which reveal him to be part of it. He is not a creature of the moment, but on the contrary a creature extended through time, and compromised forever by his actions. ... This long-term answerability means that the free being is set apart from the natural order. His acts and omissions flow from the inner well-spring of intention. His motives are ranged on the scale of virtue and vice, and he is seen as supernatural beings are seen: subject, not object; cause, not effect; the invisible centre of his world, but in some way not truly a part of it. Kant referred in this connection to the 'transcendental self' which is the locus of our freedom. But older idioms strive for the same idea. Soul, spirit, self; the 'I am' of God's word to Moses, the *nafs* (soul, self individual) of the Koran, and St Paul's metaphor of the face (*prosopon*).[15]

To recall what I said in Chapter 2: the 'revelation of the individual in his freedom' is not a natural, or even a functional kind. It is a gift of community and culture, one which permits those 'deeper feelings, and at the same time educates them'.

But what happens to the ethical (*qua* sacred) vision of man when, as we are witnessing in our own time, the religious source of the common culture dries up? In *Modern Culture*, Scruton observes that a 'community that has survived its gods has three options. It can find some secular path to the ethical life. Or it can fake the higher emotions, while living without them. Or it can give up pretending, and so collapse, as Burke put it, into the "dust and powder of individuality".' [16] Scruton opts for the first of those options, which amounts to following the path of *high culture*, which in turn teaches us 'to live *as if* our lives mattered eternally'. This, however, does not mean that high culture is a purely secular phenomenon – far from it. Having its roots in common culture, high culture also springs from religious soil, and has, in its most sublime manifestations, 'religious experience as its object'. It is true that what distinguishes high from common culture is that it is not accessible to every member of the tribe, and can indeed be severed from its origins 'as the art of our civilisation has grown away from the Christian Church which first inspired it'. That said, high culture, even when detached from its sacred source, will still retain within itself 'the memory of a religious sentiment: a core experience of membership in which God was once revealed'. It is nothing less than a glorious 'meditation on its own "angel infancy".' [17]

Following Scruton, I might put the point like this: high culture captures in abstract and symbolic form, the sacred yearnings of the common culture. It is, as such, a form of participation which engages the living and the dead. But unlike the common culture, which is immediately available to all merely by virtue of their belonging to a community, high culture must be *consciously* taught and learned. It therefore requires both induction and initiation. As a form of *knowledge* that conveys in 'heightened and imaginative form the ethical vision that religion made so easily available', high culture depends for its transmission on education. Or, to be more precise, high culture requires and involves an education of the emotions.

There are, according to Scruton, three distinct kinds of knowledge: 'knowledge *that*, knowledge *how*, and knowledge *what*'. [18] If knowledge *that* amounts to the accumulation of information, then knowledge *how* is the acquisition of a technique or skill. Knowledge *what*, on the other hand, is much more than the accumulation of facts or the mastery of techniques. It is the acquisition of *virtue* and *wisdom*, or knowledge not of means, but of ends:

Knowing what to do, Aristotle suggested, is a matter of right judgement (*orthos logos*); but it also involves *feeling* rightly. The virtuous person 'knows what to feel', and this means feeling what the situation requires: the right emotion, towards the right object, on the right occasion and in the right degree. Moral education has just such knowledge as its goal: it is an education of the emotions. The virtue of the Greek hero is of a piece with his emotional certainty, and this certainty is the gift of culture, and of the higher vision which culture makes available. By setting the individual within the context of the group, by providing him with ritual expressions and the path to collective release, by uniting him in thought with the unborn and the dead, and by imbuing his thoughts with ideas of sanctity and sacrilege, the culture enables the hero to give safe and sincere expression to the feelings that social life requires.[19]

High culture emulates the redemptive function of religion by cultivating and expanding the individual's emotional range. Through art and literature, the self is made whole in being reunited to 'its rightful congregation'. Knowledge *what* is, thus, a precondition of human happiness.

HIGH CULTURE AND HUMANE EDUCATION

But how, we might ask, is such knowledge of the human heart taught, or through what means can such 'practical wisdom' (*phronesis*) be transmitted? Scruton believes the answer lies in the cultivation of imagination. In studying the great works of art and culture, we 'rehearse in ritual form the joys and sufferings of revered and exemplary people'. On those occasions, when the imagination momentarily frees us from our finitude, we encounter the 'emotions and motives' of individuals who exemplify the virtuous disposition. That, in turn, arouses our sympathy for the lives they lead, lives which we now recreate in imaginative space. It is not, as Scruton instructs, 'that we imitate the characters depicted, but that we "move with" them, acquiring an inner premonition of their motives, and

coming to see those motives in the context that the writer or artist provides.'

Through imagination, in other words, our emotions are ethically elevated.[20] In being exposed to the plight of people in challenging situations,
and in coming to understand their motives for responding in the way
they do, we are 'preparing ourselves for the joys and calamities that we
will someday encounter'.[21] And here, once again, we see the deep affinity
between high culture and the religious disposition: by sacralising the core
experiences of society, Scruton writes, 'religion eternalises our commitments …, and gives sense and direction to our lives'.[22] Likewise, "[w]hen
a work of art conveys a view of things, our interest is not in the truth of
that view, but in the extent to which it can be incorporated into a life
of lasting commitment and serious feeling'.[23] Both are forms of moral
education in which the person is taught *what to do* and *what to feel*.

If knowledge of such 'ideal visions' of humanity is to be conserved,
enhanced and passed down, it will, however, require teachers who are prepared to row against the tide in order 'to keep those skills alive'.[24] Such
teachers will be those who recognise the value and worth of expanding the
student's emotional horizon – something they will do by perpetuating
'knowledge of the human heart', and also by nurturing 'a sense of what is
intrinsically worthwhile in the human condition, a recognition that our
lives are not consumed in the fire of means only, but devoted also to the
pursuit of intrinsic values'.[25] That is to say: *high culture serves to sacralise
the world of the student.* Through works of art and literature, he learns
that life is not something simply to be squandered, but something to be
idealised, sanctified and made 'into an object of reverence'. He learns,
moreover, that humanity is not 'merely a thing to live', but a thing 'to live
up to'.[26] The student comes to realise, in short, what it means to be an
emotionally balanced and morally discerning *person*. On this reading,
therefore, high culture serves as a *rite of passage* from the adolescent to the
adult state.

According to Scruton, the humanities are not simply 'what is left over
when science and technology have been counted out', but are 'forms of
true education …'.[27] For what they study is the surface of the world, or the
thin topsoil that issues from humanity's creative interaction with its
surrounds. Or, as Scruton puts it in *Philosophy: Principles and Problems*:

'The "human sciences" are really attempts to reorder the appearance of the human world, not so as to explore its underlying causes, but so as to enter into dialogue with it, and discover its meaning as an object of human interest'.[28] Unlike natural science, 'humane education' does not strive to 'divide nature at the joints'. Rather, it endeavours 'to articulate our moral interests, drawing lines of sympathy across the lived surface of the world'. It seeks, therefore, to stimulate our understanding of the world of *appearances*, or of 'the world as intentional object, conceived prior to any "method" or "discovery"'. It is a form of education that has as its subject-matter the world of culture – a world that reflects our 'human' aspirations. Hence, humane education contains a wealth of truth, but not of the kind that science aims at. It fills the world with meaning, thus enabling us to 'classify objects according to their felt significance'. And this, in turn, directly impacts on how we describe the world and its objects, for our descriptions of things will always bear the mark of human feeling and human response.

Following Wilhelm Dilthey, Scruton asserts that 'I see the world under the aspect of my own freedom, and describe and respond to it accordingly. This before me is not a member of the species *Homo sapiens* but a person, who looks at me and smiles; that beside her is not a piece of bent organic tissue but a *chair* on which I may sit; this on the wall is not a collection of tinted chemicals but a *picture*, in which the face of a *saint* appears; and so on'.[29] The aesthetic description that we give of things is, therefore, inseparable from the way they are *for us*, and there is no way of knowing them that involves bracketing out those descriptions in the manner of a 'pure' phenomenology. We are, as such, 'in constant dialogue with the world of objects, molding it through our descriptions so as to align it with our rational purposes'.[30]

Is Scruton suggesting here that 'convergence' between our aesthetic descriptions of the world, and the way the world actually is, should simply be dropped as the ultimate goal of enquiry? The answer is 'no', because he firmly rejects the assumption, as advanced by postmodern philosophers like Rorty, that we should aim for 'a culture in which questions about the "objectivity of value" or the "rationality of science" would seem equally unintelligible'.[31] As suggested in Chapter 2, Scruton does not believe that human beings can access mind or language-independent reality in any unmediated manner. He believes that objects, no less than our fellow-subjects, always appear for us 'in the light of our human interests'. But that, he maintains, does nothing to undermine his commitment to truth as the *goal* of enquiry. Yes, it may very well be that 'we cannot take for granted the ideals of convergence of opinion and of progress, which stem from the scientific view of the world'. And it may also be the case that the 'end of our enquiry may not be a single body of recognised truths that state how things are independent of our capacities to observe and discover them'. For, in this 'more human world, our natural capacities to observe and discover, to feel and respond, enter into the natural descriptions of how things are, and convergence, if it is to be secured at all, must be secured in some other way'. But that is not the same as saying that convergence, even if it is in fact never realised, does not persist 'as an ideal'. Indeed, for Scruton, the ideals of convergence and truth must become what he calls a 'common pursuit', and there are, he insists, 'distinctive educational processes through which this common pursuit can be advanced and retarded'. [32]

Convergence is advanced by humane education as I have defined it in this chapter. It is, however, retarded by the twin cultures of repudiation and desecration, both of which seek to 'turn aesthetic judgement against itself, so that it no longer seems like a judgement of *us*'. [33] The result is an adolescent culture in which 'the transition from raw human material to a responsible adult member of the community' is never made. [34] Modern adolescents, Scruton declares,

… have neither the tribal nor the modern urban experience of membership. They exist in a world protected from external and internal threat, and are therefore rescued from the elementary experiences – in particular the experience of war – which renew the bond of social membership. They have little or no religious belief, and what religion they have is detached from the customs and rituals that form a congregation. Television has confined each young person from childhood onwards before a box of intriguing platitudes. Without speaking, acting or making himself interesting to others, he nevertheless receives a full quota of distractions. The TV provides a common and facile subject of communication, while extinguishing the ability to communicate. The result is a new kind of isolation, which is as strongly felt in company as when alone. [35]

Without the emotional knowledge that is contained in high culture, and which is transmitted through humane education, the modern adolescent is divorced from both his common culture and religion. He is, consequently, incapable of responding to the demands of freedom, subjectivity and truth. For him, the other person is neither a source of the sacred nor an end-in-himself, but simply a means to easy pleasure. In such circumstances, erotic feelings are no longer a prelude to the idealisation of another human being in marriage, for marriage has also ceased to be 'the principal means to pass on moral knowledge and the habits of social constraint'. Indeed, the marital bond is now perceived as 'a condition of partial servitude, to be avoided as an unacceptable cost'. The security of real membership, in which life and love are sanctified, is therefore rejected in favour of an alienated culture which deifies 'youth as the goal and fulfilment of human life ...'.[36]

DECONSTRUCTING HUMANE EDUCATION

This situation has been exacerbated by a sustained attack from within the academic establishment on both the common culture of the West, and on the old educational curriculum that sought to transmit its humane values. In Chapter 1, we saw how Michel Foucault's assault on 'bourgeois' society resulted in an 'anti-culture' that took direct aim at holy and sacred things, condemning and repudiating them as oppressive and power-ridden. But the same applies to more recent trends such as multiculturalism, feminism and postmodernism, each of which dismisses Western culture as having no objective or universal status. For proponents of these movements, the values of the West, as enshrined in its high culture, are simply the product of a parochial mindset that endeavours to silence the equally legitimate voices of competing cultures. Hence the academic Left's obsession with what it terms 'the Other' – meaning that which stands opposed to everything Western. It does not matter that many of these 'other' cultures are significantly more parochial, exclusivist, patriarchal and ethnocentric than their Western counterpart. The only thing that matters in the mind of postmodern intellectuals is that such cultures *are not Western*. And that is because it is an article of faith for postmodernists to side 'with "them" against "us"', irrespective of the nature of 'them'. It is, moreover, a badge of honour for such people 'to denigrate the customs, culture

and institutions that are identifiably "ours". Scruton labels that disposition 'oikophobia' (as distinct from 'xenophobia'), by which he means 'the
repudiation of inheritance and home'.[37]

One such intellectual is Jacques Derrida, founder of the movement
popularly known as 'deconstruction'. Over the years, Scruton has deployed
some of his most trenchant polemics in the direction of Derrida and his
disciples. In one searing critique worth quoting at length, Scruton attacks
Derrida's style as indicative of someone dedicated to the pursuit of mean-
inglessness:

If I were to describe what is really going on in Derrida's style, I would say that its
principal movement is one of 'taking back': each passage cancels in its second
half what is promised in the first. That which enters the text enters by association
rather than statement, so that no commitment is truly voiced. And once an idea
has entered it drifts at once into its negation, so that the brief promise of a statement remains unfulfilled. There are those who dismiss the result as pretentious
gobbledegook, which refrains from meaning anything largely because the author has nothing to mean. And there are those who are mesmerised by it, awe-
struck by its majestic vacuity, and convinced that it contains (or at least conceals)
the mystery of the written word. Strangely enough readers of this second class
often agree with those of the first, that the author refrains from meaning anything, and indeed that he has nothing to mean. But they regard this as a great
achievement – a liberation of language from the shackles of a dictated meaning,
by showing that meaning, in its traditional construction, is in a deep sense impossible. In my view neither of those attitudes is exactly right. It is not right to
dismiss this jargon-infested delirium as meaningless; nor is it right to welcome
it as the proof that nothing can be meant. For it does mean something – namely
Nothing. It is an exercise in meaning Nothing, in presenting Nothing as something that can and should be meant, and as the true meaning of every text. And
that is its meaning.[38]

A philosopher who certainly was awe-struck by Derrida's 'majestic vacuity'
was Scruton's friend Iris Murdoch.[39] In the course of a discussion on
Wittgenstein in her last great philosophical work, *Metaphysics as a Guide
to Morals*, Murdoch assesses Derrida's contribution as follows:

Derrida is an 'authority' who sets up laws of contingency and rules of grammar.
He cannot but appear as a sort of moralist, his work carries a strong emotional
charge, a whiff of some new style liberation. He is far more like Nietzsche and

Freud than like Wittgenstein. He is a remarkable thinker, a great scholar, a brilliant maverick polymath, a *pharmakeus*. But if thought of as philosophy, the aesthetic requirement of the doctrine itself tends to exclude sober plodding reflection, slow lucid explanation, simple clear thinking. ... What is disturbing and dangerous is the presentation of his thought as philosophy or as some sort of final metaphysic, and its elevation into a comprehensive literary creed and model of prose style and criticism, constituting an entirely (as it were compulsory) new way of thinking and writing.[40]

That, it seems to me, is as good an assessment of Derrida as you are likely to come across. But it misses something which troubles Scruton deeply, something that he perceives at the core of Derrida's work and that causes him to associate the latter with the more outlandishly extreme wing of French postmodernism – the view 'that the human world is also a human construct'.[41] Scruton concedes this form of 'antirealism' is of a kind with the philosophical position adopted by the 'medieval nominalists, Hegelian idealists and American pragmatists against the common-sense conception of reality'. The latter share with Derrida the belief that it is simply impossible, as Scruton puts it, 'to step outside language and confront the thing in itself'. Rather, 'to know reality is to know it through signs, and these are our invention. If at times we have the impression that we compare our thought with the world, that we measure our utterances against the standard of some absolute reality, then this is no more than a comforting illusion, engendered by our complacent posture within language, and our inability to transcend language to the point where its initiations can be grasped'.[42]

What differentiates those philosophers from Derrida, however, is that they have, at least, 'tried to distinguish objective and subjective, truth and falsehood, reality and perspective, in some other way. For most of them the belief that we cannot (in Wittgenstein's words) use language to get between language and the world, has gone hand in hand with a scrupulous attempt to distinguish right and wrong ways of thinking, and to show that thinking is constrained by conceptions of validity and truth'.[43] Like Scruton, they also do not consider it possible to get a perfect convergence between our descriptions of the world and *the way the world is in itself*. But that does not prevent them from holding fast to convergence 'as an ideal'.

That said, I don't believe Derrida ever actually denied the existence of the external world. But in failing to adequately clarify such nebulous statements as 'The thing itself is a sign', or 'There is nothing outside of the text',[44] he failed to dampen the widely held suspicion that he believed the outside world was something of our own making. If, for example, he had followed Rorty and said something luminous on the issue like: 'Both the words we use and our willingness to affirm certain sentences using those words and not others are the product of fantastically complex causal connections between human organisms and the rest of the universe. There is no way to divide up this web of causal connections so as to compare the relative amounts of subjectivity and objectivity in a given belief',[45] then perhaps Derrida's brand of anti-essentialism might not have been dismissed so casually. He did not, however, set things up quite so clearly, thus compounding the belief that he was indeed a maverick who purposely hid his shallow convictions in a thick haze of gratuitous 'gobbledegook'.

But what worries Scruton even more than his semantic incoherence, is Derrida's *oikophobia* and the impact it has had on a generation of university graduates. As he writes:

Deconstruction has been adopted as a weapon against the 'hegemonic' and 'authoritarian' structures of our culture; and it has been associated with the unchanging agenda that unites Marx, Sartre and Foucault under the banner of 1968. Whether feminist, neo-Marxist or radical anarchist, the one thing that the deconstructionist cannot do is endorse the powers that be, uphold Western civilisation, affirm the values of bourgeois society, or betray the ordinary conservative instincts that make the world go round – as opposed to those 'destabilising' and 'unsettling' postures which cause it to fly off at a tangent.[46]

Now, Derrida was no Foucault. He was never a dangerous iconoclast who sought the demolition of existing institutions and settled things. Indeed, notwithstanding the popular caricatures, he was a man of great personal charm and grace, who very often said things which would have made Foucault squirm. On one occasion, for example, Derrida forthrightly declared: 'So, you see, I am a very conservative person. I love institutions and I spend a lot of time participating in new institutions, which sometimes do not work. At the same time, I try to dismantle not institutions but some structures in given institutions which are too rigid or are dogmatic or which work as an obstacle to greater research.'[47] That is something you would never hear from Foucault or his anarchic followers, people for whom all bourgeois institutions were nothing but citadels of oppression. It should also be remembered that, like Scruton, Derrida was intensely opposed to the autocratic regimes of the Soviet Bloc. In 1981, he founded the Jan Hus Association to help persecuted Czech intellectuals. Later that year he was arrested in Prague after running an underground seminar, and was released only after the intervention of the Mitterrand government.[48] Derrida's deconstruction cannot be characterised, therefore, as *wanton* anarchy. However, if by 'anarchy' one means a repudiation of origins and home, then yes, Derrida was an anarchist of sorts.

In the notorious distinction that he draws between the 'voice and 'writing', Derrida explicitly deploys theological categories, as when he says: 'Natural writing is immediately united to the voice and to breath. Its nature is not grammatological but pneumatological. It is hieratic, very close to the interior holy voice of the Profession of Faith, to the voice one hears upon retreating into oneself: full and truthful presence of the divine voice to our inner sense.'[49] It is in opposition to the belief that human beings can construct an identity based around a theological and literary canon, that Derrida promotes the idea of *arche-writing*. Pure self-presence, he tells us, is impossible because once speech is set down in writing it automatically succumbs to multiple interpretations. Indeed, speaking itself is a form of writing in that, once articulated, the original intention of the speaker is forever lost. This suggests that any attempt to recover an original meaning is in vain, for there is only writing, and all writing is devoid of pure intention.

The consequences of this could not be more devastating: the theological foundations of the Western literary canon are rendered illusory. Now that Derrida has denied the presence of a signified behind the written signifier, the idea of 'the Book', as that which contains meaning and memory, is fatally deconstructed. It can no longer be thought of as 'the encyclopaedic protection of theology', but must give way to the 'disruption of writing' and its 'aphoristic energy'.[50] Meaning is, as Derrida puts it, 'disseminated', and any hope of retracing our steps back home is endlessly deferred. To use the theological vernacular, we might say that our route back to the Father (*qua arche*) is perpetually blocked. Everything has been placed 'under erasure'.

Scruton identifies this as a symptom of what he calls the 'religion of alienation' which 'has been a motivating force behind much of modern art and politics, and is the spiritual bond that unites the romantic and the modernist against the bourgeois normality'. It is a religion which preaches to 'a congregation of rebels', all of whom seek to reject the 'existing order'. However, 'the God of deconstruction is not a "real presence", in the Christian sense, but an absence: a negativity'. And this religion of alienation has a singular objective, which is to 'invert the central idea of our religious tradition: the idea of a sacred utterance, the word of God, enshrined in a text. The text remains sacred, but is no longer the word (the *logos*). It is the absence of the word, the "taking back" of God's primeval utterance'.[51] Gone are all claims to objectivity – even as an ideal. Having been severed from our origins, we are left to wander aimlessly without hope of reconciliation. Mankind is perpetually lost, the texts and institutions through which salvation was once possible having been deemed arbitrary and merely contingent.

Derrida is a classic *oikophobe* in so far as he repudiates the longing for home that the Western theological, legal and literary traditions satisfy. If, as Scruton maintains, high culture conveys 'the original experience of community', then Derrida's deconstruction seeks to block the path to this 'core experience' of membership, preferring instead a rootless existence founded 'upon nothing', a life akin to that of Abraham, as described by Hegel in his essay 'The Spirit of Christianity':

He was a stranger on earth, a stranger to the soil and to men alike. Among men he always was and remained a foreigner, yet not so far removed from them and independent of them that he needed to know nothing of them whatever, to have nothing whatever to do with them. The country was so populated beforehand that in his travels he continually stumbled on men already previously united in small tribes. He entered into no such ties. … He steadily persisted in cutting himself off from others, and he made this conspicuous by a physical peculiarity imposed on himself and his posterity.[52]

Now, although it is true that, for Scruton, our culture has from time to time 'been suspicious of the written word', Western civilisation is nevertheless 'founded upon the written record, and the core religions of our culture – Judaism and Christianity – are, like their close cousin, Islam, religions of the book, in which Latin, Greek and Ancient Hebrew have achieved the sacred status of the voice of God, through being written down: a fact that enabled them to retain their importance long after they ceased to be spoken'. You cannot say, in other words, that just because things have been written down or inscribed, they somehow lose their essential meaning. According to Scruton, 'writing is a permanent sign of human intentions'. It is a 'momentary self-presence' that guarantees 'the *spoken* performance', thus enabling it to be 'recuperated at a later time'.[53] Indeed, the same applies to all spheres of culture that rely on representation for their transmission. The big problem for the deconstructor is, thus, that the 'sacred text, the sublime harmony, the forms of art, poetry and liturgy' persist in 'whispering over again the same troubling message', which is that,

The old order is sacred ... and its meanings secure. When all institutions have been exposed as fraudulent; when all laws have been re-cast as human interests; when the human person himself has been depersonalised, and set down unprotected in the sterile void of science, those ancestral voices still murmur in the void, and prevent us from becoming content with our liberation.[54]

THE 'IRRELEVANCE' OF HUMANE EDUCATION

Humane education, defined by Dr Johnson as 'the common pursuit of true judgement', is the natural enemy of the religion of alienation, or that disposition which seeks to 'rupture the chain of sympathy that binds us to our culture'.[55] Hence, contrary to what is claimed by the high priests of postmodernism, the humane curriculum was never driven by a political agenda. Neither did it serve to consolidate arbitrary social divisions. On the contrary, those lucky enough to have been schooled in the traditional humanities emerged with 'a shared frame of reference, a body of weighty utterance and refined expression, an understanding of the past and its uses, which could be deployed in a thousand ways, so enabling the student to find his feet among his contemporaries and to communicate with them on equal terms'.[56]

The new multicultural curriculum differs fundamentally from its traditional counterpart. There is no longer a common frame of reference that supplies the student with the moral and emotional knowledge of which he is in need. Instead, his only exposure to classical literature, music and architecture is by way of deconstructing it. Consequently, 'by destroying the durable frame of reference and the web of human sympathy which make serious communication across generations possible', the student is wrenched from his inheritance and deprived of his 'only hope of competing on equal terms'.[57] Such, for Scruton, is the inevitable consequence of treating education as 'an instrument of social engineering', rather than as an end in itself.

True education does not seek to undermine the foundations of Western civilisation, but to nurture them. It eschews 'relevance' in favour of a 'knowledge-centred' approach, the focus of which is on the intellectual discipline 'rather than the things that might make the subject for the time being "relevant" to matters of no intellectual concern'.[58] This suggests that there is immense virtue in *irrelevance*. Indeed, most subjects on the traditional curriculum were 'wilfully irrelevant – like Latin, Greek, ancient history, higher mathematics, philosophy and literary criticism'. Indeed, Scruton believes the more irrelevant a subject 'the more lasting is the benefit that it confers'. That is so because such subjects do not equip the student with transitory knowledge. Rather, they transmit an 'understanding of the human condition, by forcing the student to stand back from it', thereby 'enhancing the appetite for life, by providing material for thought and conversation'.[59] When trained in the Classics, for example, the world of the student is no longer one of fact, but of *meaning*. It enables him to interpret his world, thus becoming 'master of his condition'.

The 'relevant curriculum' is, on the other hand, 'child-centred'. By aiming to fulfil the immediate needs of the student, it destroys the 'majestic irrelevance' which may seem futile now, but which is likely to be exactly what is needed at some unforeseen point in the future. Scruton gives substance to this point through a delightful reflection on his Cambridge tutor, Laurence Picken. It was, in fact, Picken who turned Scruton in the direction of philosophy. More importantly, he taught Scruton the virtue of irrelevance in education, and in so doing proved to him why the egalitarian agenda of the new educationalists is profoundly at variance with human nature. For Picken, knowledge was not there to help the student, but rather the student was there to help knowledge. Young people such as Scruton mattered to him, because 'they had brains into which the reservoir of learning could be poured'. And so, the purpose of education is not to pretend that all children are equally talented. For that will only result in stymieing the progress of the best, while giving a false sense of genius to the rest. Rather, it means 'making a radical distinction – the distinction the egalitarians refuse to make – between those who can be taught and those who can't'. It means sustaining the old division between 'knowledge and opinion, culture and philistinism, wit and stupidity, art and kitsch'. It means nurturing the idea that a culture without distinctions, criticism and judgement is no culture at all. It is simply the apotheosis of ignorance and mediocrity:

That, I think, is what I principally took away from my school and college: the thought of culture as the heart of education, and of both as founded in the pursuit of distinction. My school taught me that a discipline is available, which permits us to absorb the works of our culture, to discriminate between them, and to venture safely into hitherto uncharted areas. This discipline is criticism, and criticism is necessary if culture is to be protected from decay.[60]

All of this serves to highlight Scruton's particular antipathy to what he calls 'those second-order subjects or metadisciplines', such as Women's Studies, Queer Studies and Equality Studies. The object of those 'subjects' is, once again, strictly ideological. They do not serve to inculcate what Matthew Arnold called 'the best that has been thought and said'. Rather, having no genuine field of study which is constrained by a tried and tested body of knowledge, they are best characterised as 'a collection of intellectual fragments: applications of this or that humane discipline by students who have neither the time nor the interest to master any of them ...'.[61] Hence, they do not aim at convergence of truth and opinion, but strive merely to undermine truth, reason and objectivity. And they do so by cultivating 'a culture without judgement, which is therefore incapable of imparting the knowledge on which the ethical life depends'.[62] But without the cultivation of judgement and criticism, the student of the radical curriculum becomes detached from his 'true community'. Having been schooled in the theology of alienation, he remains 'incapable of receiving or passing on the inherited capital of moral knowledge'.[63] He has no way of identifying the cultural 'touchstones' upon which genuine moral education relies for its survival. He has, in short, no way of identifying the *objectivity* of aesthetic values.

THE OBJECTIVITY OF ART

Let us recall once again what Scruton says regarding the nature of truth: in the human world of appearance, as distinct from the scientific realm of the 'really real', the end or goal of inquiry 'may not be a single body of recognized truths that state how things are, independent of our capacities to observe and discover them'. This means that the scientific realist is mistaken when he dismisses *human* classifications of the world as 'merely arbitrary, interest-relative, or intellectually confused'.[64] For no matter how hard we try, we simply cannot filter out our intentional understanding in order to apprehend unvarnished reality. Rather, the ways we observe and discover, feel and respond inevitably 'enter the description of how things are'.[65] This means, that in its 'negative' or 'critical' employment, philosophy can only 'tell us whether our concepts are in order, but not whether our beliefs are true'. If so, the question then is this: how can we, as Scruton puts it, 'vindicate a concept'? Without reference to the 'really real', how can we determine whether a particular concept is warranted or justified? Or, if complete convergence persists only as an ideal, how are we to decide between a true and false application of a concept?

In his response, Scruton reaches for what he calls 'an old dispute, made central to philosophy by Locke, concerning the nature of "secondary qualities" – qualities like colours, which seem intimately tied to the way things appear to us, but connected only obscurely with the underlying reality'. That is to say, if you inquire as to what a particular colour (say red) *really is*, you won't get very far. The best you will come up with is that 'redness is a way of appearing'. There is, of course, no way of *testing* to see if such 'everyday' beliefs about secondary qualities or the human world (*Lebenswelt*) are true. Nevertheless, we can *justify* 'the distinction between true and false colour-judgements', thereby vindicating 'the concept of colour'.[66] Likewise, it may very well be, as Marxist pseudo-science asserts, that beliefs about justice 'are adopted merely because they legitimize "bourgeois" power'. But, once again, this does not mean that such concepts 'have no claim to truth of their own', or that the concept of justice is discredited.[67] By drawing a distinction between justice and injustice, we show 'that there is a difference between a true and a false claim of justice'. Hence, the concept of justice is also thereby vindicated. Science has, in other words, no more authority than the study of appearances. Indeed, the only authority it has derives from the fact that 'it explains how things appear', meaning that it can 'never have more authority than the appearances that it strives to replace'.[68] If, in other words, the human world (*qua* the sphere of appearances) is 'riddled with error', then so too is science.

Our everyday human concepts represent the surface of the world, or the *Lebenswelt*. For Scruton, this means they cannot be replaced 'with anything more useful than themselves – even if we find concepts with greater explanatory power', such as those supplied by science. They therefore contain their own justification, in so far as any attempt to replace them with those that answer to 'the requirements of scientific objectivity', will 'render the surface unintelligible'.[69] Critically, it is 'by the use of such concepts that the moral reality of our world is described: concepts of good and evil, sacred and profane, tragic and comic, just and unjust ...'.[70] Strip them away in favour of an 'unobtainable objectivity', and you risk undermining the 'vital link' that we humans have with the lived world of everyday experience.

This explains why Scruton believes that philosophy, 'to the extent that it takes the study of the *Lebenswelt* as its primary concern, must return aesthetics to the place that Kant and Hegel made for it: a place at the centre of the subject, the paradigm of philosophy, and the true test of all its claims'.[71] For it is through aesthetic concepts that we learn how to engage with the world *as it appears*. It is through them that we mediate with others, thereby finding our home in an otherwise alien world. It is through aesthetic concepts, in sum, that the human urge for belonging and membership is satisfied. And that is why, following F. R. Leavis, Scruton believes that the pursuit of culture is nothing less than a sacred task:

For Leavis the task of culture was a sacred task. Culture had in some way both to express and to justify our participation in the human world. And the greatest products of culture – those works of art that [Matthew] Arnold called 'touch-stones' – were to be studied as the supreme distillations of this justifying force. In them we find neither theoretical knowledge, nor practical advice, but life – life restored to its meaning, vindicated and made whole. Through our encounter with these works our moral sense is liberated, and the fine division between good and evil, positive and negative, affirmative and destructive, made once more apparent, written everywhere across the surface of the world.[72]

The upshot of this is that aesthetic understanding is not tangential or peripheral to the subject of philosophy. In so far as it conveys those concepts that enable the human person to navigate his way across the surface of the world, aesthetics should be of pivotal concern to philosophers. What is more, the values and truths that it supplies, which are at the core of humane education, are neither arbitrary nor subjective. They are objective, not by virtue of corresponding to the really real, but in the sense that they can be supported 'with reasons "valid for all men", reasons which one must accept on pain of being irrational'.[73]

In *The Aesthetics of Music*, Scruton substantiates this contention by means of a meditation on the complex notion of *aesthetic value*. Following Kant, he suggests that most of our interests, whether in food or information, are satiable. There are, however, certain human interests that are 'by their nature insatiable, since they have no goal'.[74] They are, in other words, not a means to some further end, but an end in themselves. Such is the nature of aesthetic objects: they repeatedly call on us to discover their latent meaning. And each time we engage with such objects they reveal something new, some deeper significance that resisted the critic's previous attempts to understand them. But the important point is that aesthetic objects invite us to set aside our immediate interests with a view to experiencing their intrinsic value. They do not satisfy any spontaneous desire or need, but call to us from a place where the demands of the empirical world have no purchase.

Is that enough to satisfy those sceptics who believe that aesthetic judgements are arbitrary and subject to cultural contingencies? Why, asks Scruton, 'is it not enough to describe our various aesthetic *preferences*, and to leave it at that?' The response he provides is replete with philosophical ingenuity: it is true, he argues, that 'values are preferences', but it is also the case that 'not all preferences are values'. And when precisely does a preference become a value? In that moment, he says, 'when it matters to us in a certain way whether others share and accept it'. We consider an aesthetic object valuable when we identify with it, and when it enables others to identify with us as members of a shared moral order. In arguing thus, Scruton is relying on Hegel's insight that self-identity is not something immediately given, but is a process whereby the individual discovers meaning and value by dialectically engaging with the artefacts of the community. In so doing, the sacred longings of the community become the self's own, thus satisfying his need to surmount alienation and find an enduring home. Scruton explains in the context of a discussion on architecture and morality:

Self-realisation requires then that the agent have some real sense, in the present, of his continuity into the future. His future satisfactions must in some way enter into his present calculations, even though they are not the objects of present desire. Until he has achieved that rational balance between himself at one time and himself at another, he lives as it were expended in the present moment. But what makes this achievement possible? On the idealist view art, and the aesthetic impulse, play an important part in the process of 'spreading oneself' on the objective world. The view gains support from our reflections on the art of building. The process of 'self-realisation', of breaking from the prison of immediate desire, is a kind of passage from subject to object, a making public and objective what is otherwise private and confused. But a man can set his feet on the ladder of self-realisation only when he has some perception of its reliability, and this cannot be achieved by subjective fiat. He must first find himself at home in the world, with values and ambitions that are shared. We must first be able to perceive the ends of his activity not in himself but outside himself, as proper aims in a public world, endowed with a validity greater than the validity of mere 'authentic' choice.[75]

Aesthetic values permit the self to look upon the world of objects and recognise therein the spirit of the living and the dead. In so doing, the world appears not simply as a functional or instrumental entity, but as one surrounded with a sacred aura. That is why appearances matter: the manner in which we shape and mould the surface of the world is not merely a random or gratuitous endeavour without consequence. It is nothing less than 'the all-pervasive background to our lives as social beings', and one through which 'we make sense of our being with the strangers upon whom our lives depend'. As rational beings, we cannot therefore dispense with an interest in appearances, or in aesthetic value, without ceasing to be human. For to do so would be to view the world as animals do – namely, in terms of one's immediate appetites. It would be to lapse 'into a kind of solipsism, an estrangement from the world of objects, in which all relations to things take on a purely instrumental character'.[76] In such circumstances, nothing would be desired for its own sake. Nothing would have intrinsic value, all things being simply a means to instinctual satisfaction. That is why Scruton believes that our need for beauty is not 'something that we could lack and still be fulfilled as people'. It is, he asserts, 'a need arising from our metaphysical condition, as free individuals seeking our place in a shared and objective world'.[77]

This point can be further explained by looking at what Scruton terms 'everyday beauty'. When we plant a garden, lay a table or dress for an occasion, we do so in order to 'fit in'. We want the garden, the table and the costume to *look right*. But what does 'look right' mean in this context? It means that we wish our aesthetic preferences to gel seamlessly with those of our neighbours. Through the process of making and decorating, we are striving to build a home, while endeavouring to make others *feel at home*. My garden must chime harmoniously with that across the fence, and if it fails that test then I risk being condemned by the community for my bad taste. Likewise when I set a table for an important occasion, or when I dress for a public engagement: both are attempts to project order and harmony so as to satisfy the aesthetic preferences of my guests and hosts. In other words, I justify my aesthetic preferences on the basis of what *looks* right and wrong. There is nothing 'merely' subjective or arbitrary in those judgements. For in violating aesthetic norms I violate the order, harmony and symmetry that rational beings naturally seek in the surrounding world. That is what possessing bad taste means: it is *bad* because, in defying order, it offends those who are forced to share my space.[78] Expressions of bad taste serve, thus, to alienate me, not only from my surrounds, but also from my community. They mark me as an 'outsider', or someone who rejects the values upon which the identity of my tribe rests:

Implicit in our sense of beauty is the thought of community – of the agreement in judgements that makes social life possible and worthwhile. That is one of the

91

reasons why we have planning laws – which, in the great days of Western civilisation, have been extremely strict, controlling the heights of buildings (nineteenth
century Helsinki), the materials to be used in construction (eighteenth century
Paris), the tiles to be used in roofing (twentieth century Provence), even the
crenellations on buildings that face the thoroughfares (Venice, from the fifteenth
century onwards) ... Think of clothes, interior decor, and bodily ornaments: here
too we can be put on edge, excluded or included, made to feel inside or outside
the implied community, and we strive by comparison and discussion to achieve
a consensus within which we can feel at home. Many of the clothes we wear
have the character of uniforms, designed to express and confirm our inoffensive
membership of the community (the office suit, the tuxedo, the baseball cap, the
school uniform), or perhaps our solidarity with a community of offenders (the
'convict' style of black American 'gangstas'). Others, like women's party clothes,
are designed to draw attention to our individuality, though without offending the
proprieties.... [F]ashion is integral to our nature as social beings: it arises from,
and also amplifies, the aesthetic signals with which we make our social identity
apparent to the world. We begin to see why concepts like decorum and propriety
are integral to the sense of beauty: but they are concepts that range equally across
the aesthetic and the moral spheres.[79]

It is true that aesthetic judgements are to some extent *subjective*, in as
much as they 'attempt to articulate an individual experience'. However, stat-
ing that you like something is not the same as *justifying* why you like it,
or indeed why it should be appreciated and approved by others. To account
for one's particular taste in music, architecture or painting, one must give
reasons that will serve to justify your preferences 'to all beings with aesthetic understanding'. That is what Scruton means by the 'objective validity' of aesthetic judgement. But how is objective validity obtained? This is
a complex issue that goes to the heart of analytic aesthetics, but one across
which Scruton sheds much light. He begins by asserting that there is a big
difference between those with taste and those without it. Analogously, there
is a big difference between good people and bad people. Human beings
are capable of identifying this difference, not by referring to 'a set of rules of
conduct' or to a compendium of moral truths. Rather, they possess the
capacity to 'recognise moral virtue *in* action'.[80] Through experience, they
become acquainted with instances of vice and virtue, thereby enabling
them to empathise with the feelings of morally motivated individuals.
While this is an indirect process, in so far as it is undertaken 'without ref-

erence to a universal rule', the resulting precept may still be considered objective. Scruton defends his position in the following Aristotelian terms:

… taste is not simply a set of arbitrary preferences. It is a complex exercise of sympathy, in which we respond to human life, enhanced and idealised in artistic form. Good taste is not reducible to rules; but we can define it instead through a concept of virtue: it is the sum of those preferences that would emerge in a well ordered soul, in which human passions are accorded their true significance, and sympathy is the act of a healthy conscience.[81]

The person with good taste will, therefore, have an instinctive aversion towards those objects, such as depictions of violence and pornography, which 'contaminate his conscience, and tempt him towards sympathies he should not have'.[82] Taste is, in other words, bound up with character. If a person's moral character is correctly ordered, he will naturally respond to the demands of virtue. So too with aesthetic interest: beauty, Scruton believes, is 'as firmly rooted in the scheme of things as goodness. It speaks to us, as virtue speaks to us, of human fulfilment, not of things that we want, but of things that we ought to want, because human nature requires them.'[83] How, for example, could a human being find lasting fulfilment without cultivating manners, politeness or decency?

Consider again what Scruton means by 'everyday beauty': beauty is central to the life of a human being because everything we do is ordered aesthetically. That is obvious in the case of clothes and gardens, where appearances matter. But Scruton asserts that the aesthetic is an intrinsic feature of the human condition itself, in so far as it is that which 'lifts the human form above the level of animal life, so as to become fully human, fully sociable, and fully self-aware'. As social beings, we naturally yearn to be liked and loved. We want to appear attractive to those around us. But that requires much more than beautifying one's body. It demands that the person himself be polished, that he radiates an 'inner' beauty as it were. And, as Scruton points out, 'polished' is connected etymologically to 'polite'. Hence to be a polished person means to be an 'agreeable' person, someone who makes himself attractive through physical gestures ('manners') which bear witness to his essence as a conscious subject.

We can see this at work in the context of the meal. In contrast to animals, eating is for us a ceremonial activity. We gather around a decorated table, not merely to feed, but to 'combine conversation and consumption'. Without table manners, however, the ritual would collapse into a feeding frenzy. And that is simply because table manners ensure 'that the mouth retains its social and spiritual character at the very moment when it is supplying the body's needs'. Like all other creatures, we are sustained through the mouth. But the human mouth is also that through which we smile, kiss and speak. It is, therefore, 'second only to the eye as the visible sign of self and character'. How we present the mouth has thus enormous social and spiritual significance:

We shield it when we yawn in public; we dab at it with a napkin rather than wiping it with the back of the hand. The mouth is a threshold, and the passage of food across it is a social drama – a movement from outer to inner and from object to subject. Hence we do not put our face in the plate as a dog does; we do not bite off more than we can chew while conversing; we do not spit out what we cannot swallow; and when the food passes our lips, we strive to make it vanish, to become unobservably a part of us.[84]

The rude person, on the other hand, is one who views 'manners, forms, courtesies, and graces' as 'mere ornaments'. For him, style is far too heavy a burden to shoulder, and so he rejects it in favour of obscenity. But acts of obscenity, rudeness and brashness are not without consequence. For if, as Scruton suggests, the 'moral being is the creature of dialogue, and politeness is his way of making a place for himself in the conversation of his kind', then the impolite or unpolished person will never be at home in this world. He will not be invited to contribute to the conversation, because the way he *appears* is threatening to those around him. That is why, for Scruton, it is imperative that we teach manners to the young. As he writes:

The fact that we can survive without manners ... does not show that human nature doesn't need them in some deeper way. After all, we can survive without love, without children, without peace or comfort or friendship. But all those things are human needs, since we need them for our happiness. Without them, we are unfulfilled. And the same is true of manners.[85]

The purpose of manners is to polish personality. Hence, to deprive a child of civility and courtesy is tantamount to making him unattractive and unwanted. Yes, his 'mother may love him, but others will fear or dislike him'. And by not fitting in, he is condemned to a life of alienation and isolation. If Scruton is right (which he undoubtedly is) that morals and manners 'are continuous parts of a single enterprise, which is to forge a society of cooperative and mutually respectful individuals out of the raw material of self-seeking animals',[86] then we cannot flourish as human beings without them. They are, like good taste itself, *intrinsic* features of the human condition.

Not so for the proponents of cultural relativism. For them, taste, manners and morals differ from culture to culture and epoch to epoch. Indeed, to claim that certain aesthetic preferences are objectively or universally valid is, they argue, simply to pay an empty compliment to one's own subjective prejudices. The Marxist goes even further: for those like Terry Eagleton and Pierre Bourdieu, taste is not a human universal, but just a 'piece of bourgeois ideology'. To argue, as does Scruton, that the true objects of aesthetic interest are intrinsically valuable, is for such writers simply an attempt to portray a 'transient social order' as permanent, fixed and natural. Ideas such as those of good taste and intrinsic value are, they say, elaborate fictions, 'designed to inscribe the class interest of the bourgeoisie on the face of nature'.[87] If the Marxists are correct, then the notion of the objective validity of aesthetic judgements is rendered groundless. For what they will have shown is that 'there is no such thing as holiness, justice or beauty, but only the belief in it – a belief that arises under certain social and economic relations and plays a part in cementing them, but which will vanish as conditions change'.[88]

In response, Scruton concedes that the word 'aesthetic' has its historical provenance in the 18th century. But that fact, he argues, does nothing to disprove his belief that aesthetic interest is a *human universal*. For example, when Kant described aesthetic interest as being 'disinterested' in the *Critique of Judgement*, he was carrying on a tradition begun by Plato in the *Republic* and Aristotle in the *Poetics*. The phenomenon cannot, in other words, be confined to any particular historical epoch or culture. It is certainly the case that the aesthetic impulse will only flourish in certain cultural conditions, especially 'those which the bourgeois order most readily promotes'. It is also true that this impulse will take many forms. However, 'cultural variation does not imply the absence of cross-cultural universals'.[89] Symmetry, order and harmony are, Scruton instructs, as natural to man 'as law or mathematics, and just as free from the "ideology of domination"'.[90]

Put simply, the urge to be part of something larger than oneself, to find a home in an otherwise alien world, 'seems to have a permanent hold on the human psyche'. This process of self-discovery, of finding value and meaning in the appearances – the attempt 'to make sense of the world as home' and of striving to 'fit in' through expressions of good taste, may indeed differ from place to place, community to community and from tribe to tribe. But, suggests Scruton, 'the root distinction between safety and danger, between love and hostility, is a human universal, and requires of every society that emancipates itself from need that it spread its image before itself in poetry, architecture, image-making, and music'.[91]

All human beings, that is, possess the aesthetic impulse. For when we contemplate the world, we do so with a view to seeing ourselves projected in and through it. We do so, in other words, in order to idealise it as a sphere of value, or what Kant called a 'kingdom of ends'. We long for the things of this world to answer not only to our 'present purposes', but more importantly to that sacred sense of self that transcends 'the sum of present purpose and desire'. But that can only happen when those things acquire a subjectivity of their own, or when they are perceived not merely as a means to utilitarian satisfaction, but as *persons* in their own right.

Take, for example, the home itself. The home is a place where I can truly be myself – a place that reveals to the world who I am and the values that I cherish. That is why when my home is burgled it is equivalent to an act of defilement. When the thief ransacks my belongings, it is as though he were debasing my very existence. It is deemed an act of desecration because the burglar has reduced my home to a mere house – a subject to an object. A house becomes a home when it is decorated in accordance with the taste and style of its occupants. It then acquires character, charm and colour. Hence, to defile the order and harmony of a home is, quite literally, to plunder its personality, or the sense it comes to possess when it is transformed from mere object to a concrete expression of someone's subjectivity. The same, of course, applies to places of worship, in as much as a church or mosque embodies the sacred yearnings of an entire community.

Aesthetic judgement, thus, 'fills the world with intimations of value – and this is perhaps part of what Kant had in mind in arguing that in aesthetic attention the object is always seen as in some sense "purposeful", though without specific purpose. In the choice of clothes, as in all other areas where appearance counts, a man will naturally try to herald his adopted character in his present choice – otherwise reason engages only with transient satisfactions.'[92] And when everything is perceived in purely functional terms, meaning and value disappear from a person's life. No longer can he find purpose or permanence in the world, because nothing stands as an enduring monument to his existence. No longer can he identify with a particular community through common expressions of taste and style. Alienation and disenchantment are, thus, the lot of those who engage only with 'transient satisfactions'. But, as Scruton rightly points out, 'there can be no self-knowledge in a private world, and no self-knowledge in a world that does not bear the mark of human action'. Happiness, defined as 'the complete satisfaction of a rational being', can only become a reality 'if it coexists with sufficient self-consciousness, with a consciousness able to look on itself and on the world and say: it is well with me'.[93]

The long-term happiness of the self is predicated, therefore, on the correct cultivation of the aesthetic sense. Without it, a person would lack the practical wisdom necessary for knowing what to do and what to feel in the course of his daily affairs. He would, to repeat, lack a sense of the *value* of things. And that is so because, in asking which of his multifarious desires he should satisfy, the individual must be capable of standing back from his immediate situation so as to rationally reflect upon 'which aim it is right to pursue'. But that, in turn, demands a sense of self that transcends the 'totality of existing desires' and appetites. It demands the capacity to judge what is appropriate with an eye to long-term contentment. Someone who can make such a judgement must be, according to Scruton, 'in a position to see himself from outside ...'. His stance towards the world is 'essentially anti-individualistic', in so far as it 'involves seeing oneself as of a kind, with fulfilments and satisfactions which can be described only in terms of values that transcend the sphere of individual impulse'.[94] I cannot, in short, hope to find lasting value if I cannot justify my choices to those with whom I live. Having a genuine sense of self requires, therefore, the affirmation of all those affected by the manner in which I choose to fulfil my desires:

The process of self-realisation is possible only when the world responds to my activity, when it reflects back to me an image of my true fulfilment. The aesthetic sense ... is precisely devoted to the task of endowing the world with an order and meaning of that kind. Not only the man who builds but the man who lives with the product must see the building in relation to himself, as an objective part of a process of *interaction* with the world; in that process his humanity may be either rebutted or confirmed. Every man has a need to see the world around him in terms of the wider demands of his rational nature; if he cannot do so he must stand towards it in an alienated relation, a relation based on the sense that the public order resists the meanings with which his own activity seeks to fill it.[95]

BUILDING AND BELONGING

The efficacy of Scruton's argument can be appreciated by analysing how he applies these observations to the spheres of architecture and music. In his first major statement on the role of architecture in human affairs, Scruton argued that a 'merely functional building' is both a declaration of alienation, and a significant cause of it in others. In its relation to its immediate surrounds, such a building resembles an 'individualistic ego, pursuing its own aim in defiance of, or indifference to, the aims of others'. That is so because it is constructed with the intention of fulfilling a singular purpose. Like a self that views the world from a utilitarian perspective, the functional building has no aim other than the satisfaction of an immediate impulse. It is neither built in consideration of aesthetic demands, nor of the needs of the community, and thus it 'contains no intimation of an objective world of values beyond the pursuit of limited desires'.[96] Hence, the functional structure, being devoid of character and failing to signify the values of society, alienates those who must live in its shadow. By satisfying transient needs only, it pays homage neither to the past nor the future. And by failing to fit in, it contravenes reason, order and social identity. Scruton explains, with reference to the desecration of the traditional street by what he calls the 'maddest of all Utopian schemes, the open-planned housing complex':

> … streets are replaced by empty spaces from which towers arise, towers bearing neither the mark of a communal order, nor any visible record of the individual house, and demonstrating in their every aspect the triumph of that collective individualism from which both community and individual are abolished. No less disturbing is the attitude which sees streets as mere conduits through a '*cité radieuse*', upon which buildings turn their backs, or (since they usually are conceived without any 'backs' to turn), against which buildings stand like indomitable cliffs of shining glass, spectacular, luminous and cold. It is surely absurd to think of the popular outrage at these things as no more than a 'matter of taste', rather than a re-affirmation of injured moral feeling.[97]

Scruton believes that the real enemy of architectural order is modernism. In housing, it has resulted in disaffection and dislocation, while modernist factories 'are universally received as blots on the landscape, whose raw functionality is profoundly at odds with the natural environment'. And the reason for that is simple: the modernist building is egocentric, paying 'scant respect to the surrounding fabric'. It is, as witnessed in London's South Bank and New York's Lincoln Center, a sad survival 'from the age of ill-considered and temporary things'.[98] The great sin of modernism is that it discarded 'the aesthetic discipline embodied in the classical tradition', something that was taken to even more perverse extremes by postmodernism. The result was that architects 'were deliberately *diseducated*', thereby rendering them 'ignorant of the Orders of classical architecture, with no conception of light and shade, or of the function of mouldings in articulating them, and without any idea of a building as something other than an engineering solution to a problem stated in a plan'.[99] That has been a disaster in so far as it has served to undermine the 'rule of obedience' to which all architects should submit if they are to rise to the moral task demanded by the 'aesthetics of everyday life'.[100] Once again, the objective of the architect should be to establish something permanent, something that fits seamlessly into its surrounds and that conveys a sense of home to all who dwell there. What he should not do (but which modernists such as Le Corbusier, Walter Gropius and Ludwig Mies van der Rohe took great pride in doing) is privilege function above 'the moral coordination of the community'.[101]

In his fictional account of the aesthetic way of life entitled *Perictione in Colophon*, Scruton explains that we need to understand the human urge to build in religious rather than secular terms. Our architecture, he tells us, 'derives from the temple, for the reason that the city derives from its protecting God'. He continues:

The stone of the temple is the earthly translation of the god's immortality, which is in turn the symbol of a community and its will to live. The temple, like the liturgy, is forever, and the community contains not the living only, but also the dead and the unborn. And the dead are protected by the temple, which immortalises them in stone. This is what you understand instinctively, when you see religious architecture. And it is the sentiment from which cities grow – the tribe's will to permanence.[102]

Functionalism, however, 'hurts both the eye and the soul, for it speaks not of us and our right of dwelling, but of *them*' – the architects, people 'who built these things, for inscrutable purposes that lie beyond our sympathies. That is why these buildings are perceived as a desecration: nothing of the sacred remains in them.'[103] Modernist architects, along with their postmodernist descendents, are devoted, in other words, to the twin cultures of repudiation and desacralisation. Their aim is to void the public world of the human form, thereby depersonalising the social space and depriving the community of its identity.

But for Scruton, architecture is a 'vernacular art', meaning that it is founded on a tradition of patterns, or of types, which may be deployed in 'awkward or novel situations so as spontaneously to harmonise with the existing urban decor, and so as to retain the essential nature of the street as a common home and dwelling-place'.[104] To repeat: the basic objective for those trained in the classical vernacular is to ensure that a building *fits in*, and that it responds to the long-term needs of the community. Unlike the modernist vernacular, which prioritised 'horizontal layers' over vertical order, the classical vernacular insists that one build with sensitivity for the street as conceived over time. Its guiding precept has been that of 'civility', defined by Scruton as 'the creation of a public world of mutual respect, the boundaries of which are permeable to the private interests that are sheltered by it'.[105] Manners, therefore, are pivotal for those trained in the classical orders. Such architects must adhere to the principles of civility and decency that prevailed when the temple stood as 'the perfect expression of the "settlement": of the collective decision to dwell'.[106]

The traditional architectural Orders attempt to preserve and affirm the timeless in the midst of time.[107] They do so by endorsing the community's right to exist. As such, they 'enshrine the gift of membership', for without the civility that they seek to uphold there is only anarchy. Modernism failed, according to Scruton, because its buildings repudiated permanence in favour of transience. In seeking the extinction of the sacred, the modernists endeavoured to 'recreate the town'. Their aim was to peel away its personality so as to render it literally lifeless: a soulless monument to a new world order, where all vestiges of the old bourgeois settlement had been sacrificed in the name of the 'new socialist man'. What emerged was an affront to tradition and taste, a 'frozen junkyard' where absolutely 'nothing of the sacred remains' – no temples, no streets, no shops, 'only access roads across the mud'.

In contrast, the classical tradition takes the temple as its template. Scruton calls it 'sacred architecture', for it answers not only to the needs of the living, but also to those of the dead and the unborn. Its aim is to harmonise with what has gone before, thereby synchronising with the soul of the street. And its ideals are those of permanence, identity and home. Hence, it has as its guiding motif the column:

The column stands before me as does a human being. It has a posture, inseparable from its visible role as a support. It also has proportion: like a man, it can appear too fat or too thin, too tall or too short, too delicate or too firm. It is visibly elastic, taking the weight that rests on it and passing it to the ground … Thus the column approximates to the statue of the god himself: it is the minimal representation of life in sculpture, and, by virtue of its very minimalism, conveys an idea of permanence, of life removed from the world of decay and transformation – in short, of life become divine.[108]

The column symbolises a building's will to exist in spite of change. It invites us to look upon the building as we would a human person: a self-conscious being 'with an enduring identity in a public world'. Isolation then gives way to belonging, the end triumphs over the means and value exceeds desire.[109]

What classicism in architecture provides, therefore, is constants that are not compromised by individualism and utilitarianism. In so doing, it prioritises scale, for to 'stand in a personal relation to a building, I must comprehend it visually, without strain, and without feeling dwarfed or terrorised by its presence'. There are, of course, classical buildings which defy scale, such as 'the spires of a Gothic cathedral' or the Pyramids of Egypt. But these wonders do not unsettle those who behold them. Rather, they convey a sense of awe, wonder and astonishment. That said, such buildings cannot serve as archetypes for the average builder. He must build, not to inspire or to overawe, but to fulfil the everyday needs of the ordinary man. Hence, his structures 'must face the passerby, who should not be forced to look up in awe, or to cringe in humility, beset by a sense of his own littleness'.[110]

Second, a building must possess a facade. It must, says Scruton, be capable of assuming the position of another human being, one who stands before us as we stand before it. It must, in other words, possess a face that looks with civility upon all those who encounter it. If modernist buildings are expressionless, classical buildings convey character, warmth and cheer. Their aim is not to alienate, but to confirm and affirm the values of the community in the midst of which they stand. Whereas modernist structures 'appear in our ancient towns like expressionless psychopaths', classical constructs are warm, inviting and welcoming. Theirs is a beauty that has been 'transfigured into a daily discipline', one that not only exploits light, shade and climate, but also one that relies heavily on the use of mouldings. Without mouldings, a building loses its character, its expression, its face and voice:

Without mouldings, no space is articulate. Edges become blades; buildings lose their crowns; and walls their direction (since movement sideways has the same visual emphasis as movement up and down). Windows and doors cease to be aedicules and become mere holes in the wall. Nothing 'fits', no part is framed, marked off, emphasised or softened. Everything is sheer, stark, uncompromising, cold. In a nutshell, mouldings are the *sine qua non* of decency, and the source of our mastery over light and shade.[111]

Such are the principles which have been adopted by Scruton's architectural hero, Léon Krier. Krier, who designed the new town of Poundbury in England in response to an invitation from the Prince of Wales, reacted to modernist vandalism with the idea of a civil city. In a recent article celebrating Krier's achievements, Scruton argues that planners are currently attracted 'only to exceptional buildings, usually designed, like the monstrosities of Daniel Libeskind and Frank Gehry, to stand out rather than to blend in – to focus attention on themselves, not on the ordinary solaces of the human community'.[112] What we need, however, is to follow Krier in removing the emphasis from exceptional buildings, and place it instead on 'inevitable buildings – such as the house, the workshop, the garage, and the corner store – that dictate the ambience in which ordinary people work and live'.[113] To do so, would mean returning to the wisdom contained in the classical pattern books, wisdom which Scruton has relentlessly defended in his multifarious declarations on the art of architecture. Poundbury is a living monument to the truth of that wisdom:

> By designing the street as the primary public space, by encouraging vertical syntax rather than horizontal spread, by suggesting materials, details and the number of storeys, and by embellishing here and there to ease the eye, [Krier] created a townscape into which any vernacular builder can insert the product of his craft, and which will grow organically without ever offending the eye, the soul or even the pocket. All who visit Poundbury, other than members of the architectural profession, are delighted and moved by it.[114]

They are moved by it because Poundbury's buildings speak to them as would a neighbour. They smile at them as would a friend. And, in so doing, they offer the prospect of permanence in a world ravaged by change and decay.

To sum up: in architecture, the 'aesthetic sense is not an optional addition to our mental equipment'. It is, argues Scruton, central to the way we perceive things as endowed with meaning. Hence, if we are to feel at one with the structures in which we labour and dwell, if they are to endorse our existence here on earth, the aesthetic sense 'must take precedence over all other factors – over function, structure, durability, even over economics'. Such factors are, of course, important, but they will not in themselves 'lead to a rational design, nor to a building that is truly suited to human purposes'. Only aesthetic value answers to our real human purposes which is why it 'contains the meaning of a building'. And by attending to it, 'we engage with the true task of architecture, which is to create our home'.[115]

MUSIC AND MORALITY

For Roger Scruton, music is no less essential to man's perennial quest for communal and spiritual membership. But the particular sense of home that it conveys is not of the here and now. Rather, it opens up to us another more transcendental realm, one 'whose order is only dimly reflected' in this world. This 'strange transformation', as he calls it, reaches into a sphere of pure abstraction, 'reconstituting there the movements of the human soul'. Through the process of listening, we surrender ourselves to an 'other-worldly voice which speaks to us in tones'. And because this ethereal voice is 'free from the obligation to represent the empirical world', it opens up a vision of an 'implied community' which is 'finer, nobler, and more generous in its feelings than anything that we could know'.[116]

In *Philosophy: Principles and Problems*, Scruton offers a highly condensed summary of the meaning of music explored in greater detail throughout *The Aesthetic Understanding* and *The Aesthetics of Music*. He explains that the process of listening is unique to rational beings or persons, in as much as animals are incapable of understanding what sounds *mean*. Finding meaning in sounds is what *we* do when we pause and reflect on 'the palpitating stones of melody and harmony'. In that experience, I *enter into the music* as it were, 'imbuing it with a life that originates in me'. The subject is then unshackled from its 'human prison' and brought to a place 'where bodily objects can no longer encumber it'. As such, 'it offers an image of the subject, released from the world of objects, and moving in response to its own caprice'. Music serves, therefore, to sanctify the subject by opening up a space which is 'incommensurate with physical space'. Likewise with musical time, as Scruton explains with heartfelt emotion for an art form he loves without measure:

It is only the greatest labour of style and architecture that can place the freely moving subject in this useless space and build there its 'godly home'. The masterpieces of music may, however, lift us from our time and space into an ideal time and space, ordered by an ideal causality, which is the causality of freedom. From the

it were, with the mystery of another's incarnation. In the dance, we set aside our immediate purposes, something that can be done 'only in company and only through the encounter with another soul'.[125] There is, accordingly, no functional or utilitarian purpose to real dancing. In fact, through the dance I am fully liberated from 'the tyranny of purpose'.

So what happens when the musical culture upon which the dance depends collapses? What happens when the likes of U2 replace Beethoven as the object of a child's cultural sympathies? Scruton invites his reader to ponder the issue in the following terms:

Listen to a gavotte from the late Renaissance, and imagine the mores of the people who danced to it. Then listen to a track by Nirvana, and imagine the mores of the people who can dance to *that*. Surely, you will not be tempted to think that these two sets of people could live in the same way, with the same habits of mind and character, and the same ways of responding to each other in the circumstances of social life.[126]

In listening, singing and dancing to classical music, young people enter a spiritual community with a strong moral code at its core. It is a community based on order, harmony, virtue and respect for the freedom of others. For example, something like the formation dance requires of the dancer that he 'fit his gestures to the movement of his partner and to the pattern of the whole'.[127] The analogy with architecture is once again apposite: those who build in order to belong do so with the aim of fitting in with the existing streetscape. To build contrary to those considerations is not only an affront to aesthetic decency and harmony, but, as we saw above, a self-indulgent snub to the rest of the community. Such is the problem with pop music: it does not have a life and force of its own. Genuine rhythm, harmony and melody are sacrificed in favour of an artificially manufactured beat. No longer does the music call from the transcendental sphere. Neither does it demand that we fit our gestures to the pattern of the whole. Instead, the lead singer 'projects *himself* and not the melody, emphasising his particular tone, sentiment and gesture'.[128] In contrast to a classical performance, 'in which the singer is the servant of the music', the pop performance has only one aim: to emphasise the persona of the performer. The deleterious consequence of this is, according to the Scruton, a 'fusion between the singer and the song', which leads, in turn, to a 'more mysterious fusion – that between the singer and the fan'. He explains:

You can sing the song only by becoming the singer. You are for a moment incarnate in him as he is in you. But the song is musically inept. Anybody (given the right machinery) can sing it, since nobody can. The fan knows this, and through his idolisation of the singer runs the thought: 'what has he got that I haven't?' The answer is: Nothing. To the fan in the audience, the greying figure on the stage is himself, enjoying his fifteen minutes of fame. As he fuses with the totem the fan is transfigured, relieved at last of his isolation.[129]

Compare an orchestra to a community. Each musician has a particular task that must be meticulously performed if the harmony of the whole is to be sustained. There is no room for egotism in such a context. Indeed, the individual musician serves only the music and his fellow-performers. The aim of this is, of course, to let the music be heard. That is what distinguishes the concert hall from the rock venue: in the first, the performer fits in, and, in so doing, does not stand out. In the second, the performer stands out, thereby failing to fit in. Thus we witness 'a reversal of the old order of performance':

Instead of the performer being the means to present the music, which exists independently in the tradition of song, the music has become the means to present the performer. The music is part of the process whereby a human individual or group is totemised. In consequence it has a tendency to lose all musical character. For music, properly constructed, has a life of its own, and is always more interesting than the person who performs it. Much as we may love Louis Armstrong or Ella Fitzgerald, we love them for their music – not their music for them. And this is music we can perform for ourselves.[130]

Dancing in these circumstances becomes, according to Scruton, 'a lapse into disorder, a kind of surrender of the body which anticipates the sexual act itself'.[131] The totemic superstars of pop speak only to the body as distinct from the soul. Their aim is to promote hedonism, anarchy and narcissism, thereby undermining the old civic virtues of loyalty and sacrifice. And because they feed off the insatiable desire of their fans, the idea of answering to anything as an end in itself is vanquished. People like Bono and Bowie are princes of the postmodern world, a world that 'denatures music only because it denatures everything, in order that each individual might have his chance to buy and sell'. In such a world, nothing is permanent because the very idea of permanence itself is repudiated. The fan believes he belongs to a community of fellow-travellers, but it is no such thing. For what is being championed is not homecoming and identity, but alienation and discord. The result is that those who become intoxicated by pop remain in a perpetual state of adolescence and personal discord. They are, to paraphrase the lyrics of Bob Dylan, complete unknowns with no direction home:

> Pop music, which presents the idealised adolescent as the centre of a collective ceremony, is an attempt to bend music to this new condition – the condition of a stagnant crowd, standing always on the brink of adulthood, but never passing across to it. It shows youth as the goal and fulfilment of human life, rather than a transitional phase which must be cast off once the business of social reproduction calls. For many young people, therefore, it constitutes an obstacle to the acquisition of a musical culture. It is the thing that insulates them from the adult world, and all other uses of music – singing, formation dancing, playing an instrument, listening – arouse their suspicion.[132]

That said, Scruton still believes that pop music, for all its power over the modern psyche, will not endure. Just as he recognises signs of an architectural revival in the work of Léon Krier and the New Urbanists, he sees 'rays of hope' emanating from the pens of composers such as Henryk Górecki and John Tavener. In conveying a sense of the higher life, their music provides a 'promise of release from the alienated world of popular culture'. And it does so by adapting itself to the ear of those 'raised on beat', which responds to relentless ostinato far more readily than to melody or to counterpoint'.[133] Indeed, when he listens to composers of his own, 'somewhat younger, generation – Colin and David Matthews, Oliver Knussen, David del Tredici, Robin Holloway', Scruton believes that the revival of melody and counterpoint is already well underway, thereby announcing the imminent demise of 'the bleak noise-factories of the postmodern orchestra'.[134]

* * * * * *

In the end, therefore, Roger Scruton believes that only when we reject the 'wilful desecration' of the culture of repudiation will we halt the flight from beauty. Only then will we 'find our home here, coming to rest in harmony with others and with ourselves'. Only then will we succeed in cultivating good taste in our children and in convincing them that 'if you want to know the meaning of life – of your own life as well as of the lives around you – you should explore your cultural inheritance with a critical eye, so as to repossess the meaning that has been distilled in it'.[135] But that will require, in turn, a rejection of the 'ubiquitous diseases of sentimentality and kitsch', in favour of the aesthetic ideals as outlined in this chapter.[136] And should you doubt that, Scruton invites you to consider what would happen if we were ever tempted to fully embrace 'a culture that wishes not to educate our perception, but to capture it, not to ennoble human life but to trivialise it'. Imagine, he writes,

… a world in which people showed an interest only in Brillo boxes, in signed urinals, in crucifixes pickled in urine, or in objects similarly lifted from the debris of ordinary life and put on display with some kind of satirical intention – in other words, the increasingly standard fare of official modern art shows in Europe and America. What would such a world have in common with that of Duccio, Giotto, Velazquez, or even Cézanne? Of course, there would be the fact of putting objects on display, and the fact of our looking at them through aesthetic spectacles. But it would be a degenerate world, a world in which human aspirations no longer find their artistic expression, in which we no longer make for ourselves images of the ideal and the transcendent, but in which we study human debris in place of the human soul. It would be a world in which one whole aspect of the human spirit – the aesthetic – would have become stunted and grotesque. For we aspire through art, and when aspiration ceases, so too does art.[137]

So yes, art does indeed grow from the sacred form of life, for it is through the aesthetic that human beings can fulfil their deepest longings – the longing to love and to belong. We can, says Scruton, 'wander through this world, alienated, resentful, full of suspicion and distrust'. That, however, need not be our fate, for if we have the courage to enter 'the cathedral of culture', we shall suddenly find that the experience of beauty guides us elsewhere. It will bring us into a culture of love, one that 'tells us that we are at home in the world'.[138] But that is not all: we shall be reminded that we also belong to the 'sphere of consecrated things', and that beauty is the mark of that transcendental sphere in time. And that is why, when we despoil art, we commit nothing less than an act of sacrilege.

This is all a way of saying that Roger Scruton's aesthetics is an attempt to save the sacred from the profanities of the present age. He urges us to rediscover beauty in those things that we once loved – 'the woods and streams of our native country, friends and family, the "starry heavens above" '.[139] In so doing, he reveals the true meaning of our lives here on earth.

NOTES

 1. Roger Scruton, *Modern Culture* (London: Continuum, 2005), p.40.
 2. Scruton, *The Philosopher on Dover Beach*, p.111.
 3. *Ibid.*, p.110.
 4. Scruton, *Modern Culture*, p.42.
 5. Roger Scruton, 'The Judgment of Beauty', Lecture 1 of *Beauty and Its Modes*, a course delivered to The Wynnewood Institute, Spring 2007. Available at: *www.wynnewood.org*.
 6. *Ibid.*
 7. Scruton, *The Philosopher on Dover Beach*, p.118.
 8. *Ibid.*, p.119.
 9. T. S. Eliot, 'Tradition and the Individual Talent', cited in Scruton, *Conservative Texts*, p.87.
10. *Ibid.*
11. Scruton, *The Philosopher on Dover Beach*, p.118.
12. *Ibid.*, p.119.
13. Scruton, *Modern Culture*, p.9.
14. *Ibid.*, p.11.
15. *Ibid.*, pp.11–12.
16. *Ibid.*, 14.
17. Scruton, *The Philosopher on Dover Beach*, p.120.
18. Scruton, *Modern Culture*, p.15.
19. *Ibid.*, p.16.
20. It should be pointed out at this juncture that, from the very beginning of his career, Scruton has sought to show how ethics and aesthetics are fundamentally related. In his first book, *Art and Imagination*, he writes for example that 'Rules, conventions and artistic forms have an immense importance in art, and this importance cannot be accounted for in any simple way. Nonetheless, we seem to have discovered one reason for their importance. In daily life our sense of what is appropriate must be held in abeyance, and only in the enjoyment of art is it allowed total freedom. In art everything that occurs is deliberate and reasoned; art presents us with a world entirely circumscribed by human intention. Every work of art is created in a medium, under the guidance of pre-established rules which may be broken but never ignored, for they embody the tradition of thought without which no work of art would be meaningful. Each word or gesture on the stage strikes us as in place or out of place, and no feature

of the work of art can escape making some contribution to the effect. In the absence of rules and traditions our sense of what is appropriate could hardly be aroused, and appreciation of art would remain inchoate and primitive. But our sense of the appropriate, once aroused, entirely penetrates our response to art, dominating not only our awareness of form, diction, structure and harmony, but also our interest in action, character and feeling. It is inevitable, therefore, that we should make the connection between artistic and moral experience.' Scruton, *Art and Imagination: A Study in the Philosophy of Mind* (London: Methuen, 1974), pp.247–248.

21. Roger Scruton, *Culture Counts: Faith and Feeling in a World Besieged* (New York: Encounter Books, 2007), p.38.

22. Scruton, *Modern Culture*, p.41.

23. *Ibid.*, p.42.

24. Scruton, *Culture Counts*, p.40.

25. *Ibid.*, pp.40–41.

26. Scruton, 'The Judgment of Beauty'; see n.5.

27. Roger Scruton, *The Aesthetic Understanding: Essays in the Philosophy of Art and Culture* (South Bend: St Augustine's Press, 1998), p.252.

28. Scruton, *Philosophy: Principles and Problems*, p.157.

29. *Ibid.*, pp.156–157.

30. *Ibid.*, p.157.

31. Rorty, *Objectivity, Relativism and Truth*, p.39.

32. Roger Scruton, *The Politics of Culture and Other Essays* (Manchester: Carcanet Press, 1981), p.224.

33. Scruton, 'The Judgment of Beauty'; see n.5.

34. Scruton, *Modern Culture*, p.112.

35. *Ibid.*, p.113.

36. *Ibid.*, p.115.

37. Scruton, *A Political Philosophy*, pp.23–25, and *The Need for Nations* (London: Civitas, 2004), pp.33–38. I shall return to the phenomenon of 'oikophobia' in Chapter 5, below.

38. Scruton, *The Aesthetic Understanding*, pp.264–265.

39. See Scruton's charming account of an afternoon spent with Murdoch and her husband John Bayley in 1989, and his touching tale of their subsequent visit in 1996 to Sunday Hill Farm, in *Gentle Regrets*, pp.186–191.

40. Iris Murdoch, *Metaphysics as a Guide to Morals* (London: Penguin Books, 1992), p.291.

41. Scruton, *The Aesthetic Understanding*, p.272. See also Mark Dooley and Liam Kavanagh, *The Philosophy of Derrida* (London: Acumen, 2007), pp.149–152.

42. Scruton, *The Aesthetic Understanding*, pp.272–273.

43. *Ibid.*, p.273.

44. See Jacques Derrida, *Of Grammatology* (Baltimore: Johns Hopkins University Press, 1974).

45. Rorty, 'The Challenge of Relativism', in *Debating the State of Philosophy*, pp.41–42.

46. Scruton, *The Aesthetic Understanding*, p.283.

47. 'A Conversation with Jacques Derrida' in *Deconstruction in a Nutshell*, John D. Caputo (ed.) (New York: Fordham University Press, 1997), p.8.

48. See Geoffrey Bennington and Jacques Derrida, *Jacques Derrida* (Chicago: The University of Chicago Press, 1991).

49. Derrida, *Of Grammatology*, p.17.
50. *Ibid.*, p.18.
51. Scruton, *The Aesthetic Understanding*, pp.283–284.
52. G. W. F. Hegel, 'The Spirit of Christianity' in *On Christianity: Early Theological Writings*, T. M. Knox (trans.) (Gloucester, Mass.: Peter Smith, 1970), p.186.
53. Scruton, *The Aesthetic Understanding*, p.275.
54. Scruton, *Modern Philosophy*, p.477.
55. Scruton, *The Aesthetic Understanding*, p.253.
56. *Ibid.*, pp.256–257.
57. *Ibid.*, p.257.
58. Scruton, *Culture Counts*, p.29.
59. Roger Scruton, *Untimely Tracts* (London: The Macmillan Press, 1987), p.1.
60. Roger Scruton, 'Two Virtues of Western Culture: Irony, Sacrifice, and the Transmission of Culture' in *Provocations: A Journal from the Trinity Forum*. Available at: *www. ttf. org/index/journal/detail/two-virtues-of-western-culture/*. Elsewhere he writes: 'Education is an end in itself. But it is also a means to social advancement. And there can be social advancement only where there is social hierarchy. In a society of equals there is neither failure nor success, and despair is conquered by the loss of hope. Real societies are not like that: they are shaped by competition, conflict, friendship and love, all of them forces that have distinction rather than equality as their natural outcome, and all of them profoundly antipathetic to the culture of self-esteem. A society of real human beings is quite unlike the society for which children are prepared by a "child-centered" education. It is one in which you can lose or gain; in which talent, skill and hard work are rewarded and arrogance and ignorance deplored … Those elementary truths used to be acknowledged by our education system. When I was awarded a place at our local grammar school, my father, a socialist who jealously guarded his working-class identity, foresaw with a curse that I would "get above my station". And he was right, thank God. Both my father's resentment and my own success testify to the same underlying reality: that you can rise to a higher station in society by getting a good education. Thanks to my grammar school I gained a scholarship to Cambridge, and thanks to Cambridge I gained the kind of education that opened my thoughts, skills and ambitions to a world I never dreamed could be mine. And all this without costing my family a penny. As a result of the culture of self-esteem, however, the helping hand that I received from the state has been withdrawn by the state. Grammar schools have been largely abolished, the curriculum has been vandalized (and also compelled) and the subjects which contain worthwhile knowledge – maths, the hard sciences, Latin, Greek and ancient history – have been driven to the margins of the system. And having destroyed the schools the state would now like to destroy the universities, by forcing them to take the dumbed-down products of its vandalism. All this shows a deep hostility to social hierarchy. But egalitarian dogma does nothing to abolish social hierarchy; it simply ensures that children at the bottom have no chance to rise to the top. The way to make hierarchy acceptable is not to pretend that it can be abolished, but to provide poorer children with the means to rise in it. In other words, it is to replace aristocracy and plutocracy with meritocracy.' All of which goes to prove that Roger Scruton is more of a meritocrat than an elitist. See Scruton, *The Spectator*, 27 November 2004.
61. Scruton, *The Politics of Culture*, p.225.

62. Scruton, *Modern Culture*, p.151.
63. *Ibid.*, p.155.
64. Scruton, *Philosophy: Principles and Problems*, p.55.
65. Scruton, *The Politics of Culture*, p.224.
66. Scruton, *Philosophy: Principles and Problems*, p.55.
67. Scruton, *Modern Philosophy*, p.245.
68. *Ibid.*, p.246.
69. Scruton, *The Philosopher on Dover Beach*, p.108.
70. *Ibid.*, p.109.
71. Ibid., pp.111–112.
72. *Ibid.*, p.106.
73. Scruton, *The Aesthetic Understanding*, p.141.
74. Roger Scruton, *The Aesthetics of Music* (Oxford: Oxford University Press, 1999), p.369.
75. Roger Scruton, *The Aesthetics of Architecture* (Princeton: Princeton University Press, 1979), p.247.
76. Scruton, *The Aesthetics of Music*, p.370.
77. Scruton, 'The Flight from Beauty', see n.80, Chapter 1, p.37.
78. In *Art and Imagination*, Scruton develops this insight as follows: 'The first thing to notice is that the exercise of taste is by no means confined to the experience of art. We exercise taste when we judge what is appropriate in manners and behaviour, and it is precisely here – in regulating our sense not of what is right and wrong, but of what is decent – that taste shows its continuity with moral sentiment. Moral attitudes do not and cannot exist in isolation. On the contrary, they form part of a continuum of normative opinions which mutually sustain one another – as manners and morals sustain one another. Clearly, then, the exercise of taste cannot be described if we confine ourselves to the study of art alone: only in the context of an entire culture can the importance of taste be fully demonstrated.' And further on he insists that the 'notion of the appropriate only makes sense against this background of agreed practice. Without this background it would be pointless to distinguish the exercise of taste from the display of arbitrary preferences (tastes, in the more common meaning of the term). This is not to say that what makes a taste other than arbitrary is its conformity to a rule, but rather that once an established practice exists then the concepts of the normal and of the appropriate can gain a foothold.' Scruton, *Art and Imagination*, p.247.
79. Roger Scruton, *Beauty* (Oxford: Oxford University Press, 2009), pp.134–135.
80. Scruton, *The Aesthetics of Music*, p.378.
81. *Ibid.*, p.379.
82. *Ibid.*
83. Scruton, *Beauty*, p.147.
84. Roger Scruton, 'Real Men Have Manners' in *City Journal*, Winter 2000. I am citing from the online edition which is available at: *www.city-journal.org/html/10_1_urbanities-real_men.html*.
85. *Ibid.*
86. *Ibid.*
87. Scruton, *The Aesthetics of Music*, p.476.
88. Scruton, *Beauty*, p.63.
89. *Ibid.*

90. Scruton, *The Aesthetics of Music*, p.478.
91. *Ibid.*
92. Scruton, *The Aesthetics of Architecture*, p.241.
93. *Ibid.*, p.244.
94. *Ibid.*, p.246.
95. *Ibid.*, pp.248–249.
96. *Ibid.*, p.249.
97. *Ibid.*, p.250.
98. Roger Scruton, 'Classicism Now' in *The Roger Scruton Reader*, Mark Dooley (ed.) (London: Continuum, 2009).
99. Roger Scruton, *The Classical Vernacular: Architectural Principles in an Age of Nihilism* (Manchester: Carcanet, 1994), p.77.
100. Scruton, *The Aesthetics of Architecture*, p.250.
101. Scruton, *The Classical Vernacular*, p.79.
102. Roger Scruton, *Perictione in Colophon: Reflections on the Aesthetic Way of Life* (South Bend: St Augustine's Press, 2000), p.90. This book is a sequel to *Xanthippic Dialogues*.
103. *Ibid.*, p.91.
104. Scruton, 'Classicism Now'.
105. Scruton, *The Classical Vernacular*, p.25.
106. *Ibid.*, p.107.
107. In *Perictione in Colophon*, Plato's former mistress Archeanassa (who also featured in 'Phryne's Symposium' as recorded in *Xanthippic Dialogues*) says that 'when an architect, working in stone, chooses as his unit of construction some particular style of column, then, by a kind of divine logic of which he himself is only half aware, he finds himself compelled to choose ornaments and details which match it and complement its life. There is, if you like, a grammar of ornament, which compels us, if we would build intelligibly, to combine the parts of a building in accordance with its rules. And this does not apply only to sacred architecture, or to the column and its entablature. It applies also to the house and the shop, whose doors and windows speak in muted accents of the same divine idea, and must be ordered accordingly.' P.88.
108. Scruton, *The Classical Vernacular*, p.107.
109. Of the column and its role in the grammar of architecture, Archeanassa says: 'There is, it seems to me, a certain order and logic in the elements of architecture. The temple, surrounded by its peristyle, is permeable to the city, yet sacred and removed from it. This is something that we see: we do not think it explicitly, any more than we think a smile explicitly in order to see it as a smile. And from the permeable temple came the colonnade, and thence the column, as the unit of meaning and the principle of our architectural grammar. In ancient Colophon the buildings conformed to this grammar, but with such variety and humour as befits the members of a peaceful crowd. And in each of them, sensed but not seen, was a column, standing immovably as the spirit stands immovably and invisibly in us. The column was permanent in the midst of change, and endorsed our sense of belonging ... The civility of our buildings was a matter of manners and decency – for these are the virtues of the citizen, of the one who has settled in the land and renounced the habits of the nomad.' Scruton, Perictione in Colophon, pp.90–91.

110. Scruton, *The Classical Vernacular*, p.81.
111. *Ibid.*, p.83.
112. Roger Scruton, 'Cities for Living' in *City Journal*, Vol. 18, No. 2, Spring 2008. I am citing from the online version of this article which is available at: *www.city-journal.org.*
113. *Ibid.*
114. Scruton, *Gentle Regrets*, p.216.
115. Scruton, *The Classical Vernacular*, p.xviii.
116. Scruton, *The Aesthetics of Music*, p.489.
117. Scruton, *Philosophy: Principles and Problems*, p.151.
118. Scruton, *The Aesthetics of Music*, p.92
119. *Ibid.*, p.93.
120. Scruton, *Philosophy: Principles and Problems*, p.145.
121. *Ibid.*, p.149.
122. Scruton, *The Aesthetics of Music*, p.502.
123. Scruton, *Culture Counts*, p.61.
124. Scruton, *Perictione in Colophon*, p.164.
125. *Ibid.*, p.171.
126. Scruton, *The Aesthetics of Music*, pp.390–391.
127. *Ibid.*, p.498.
128. Scruton, *Modern Culture*, p.109.
129. *Ibid.*, p.111.
130. *Ibid.*, pp.110–111.
131. Scruton, *The Aesthetics of Music*, p.499.
132. Scruton, *Culture Counts*, pp.64–65.
133. *Ibid.*, p.94.
134. *Ibid.*, p.95.
135. Scruton, 'Two Virtues of Western Culture'. See n.60.
136. See Scruton's exemplary analysis of 'Avant-garde and Kitsch' in *Modern Culture*, pp.85–95. In that context, he tells us that kitsch is the official art form of the culture of desecration. It reflects, he writes 'our spiritual waywardness, and our failure, not merely to *value* the human spirit, but to perform those sacrificial acts which *create* it. Nor is kitsch a purely aesthetic disease. Every ceremony, every ritual, every public display of emotion can be kitsched – and inevitably will be kitsched, unless controlled by some severe critical discipline, such as [Matthew] Arnold and his followers have conceived to be the social role of high culture. (Think of the Disneyland versions of the monarchical and state occasions which are rapidly replacing the old stately forms.) In one of the few existing studies of the phenomenon the novelist Hermann Broch suggests that we speak not of kitsch art or culture, but of the "Kitschmensch" – the kitschified human type – who lives in this culture and also requires it. This is one reason why you might doubt that [T. S.] Eliot's pilgrimage is still available. It is surely impossible to flee from kitsch by taking refuge in religion, when religion itself is kitsch. The "modernisation" of the Roman Catholic Mass and the Anglican Prayer Book were really a "kitschification": and attempts at liturgical art are now poxed all over with the same disease. The day-to-day services of the Christian churches are embarrassing reminders of the fact the religion is losing its sublime godwardness, and turning instead towards the world of mass production. And surely Eliot was right to imply that we cannot overcome kitsch through art alone: the recovery of

the tradition is also a reorganisation of our lives, and involves a spiritual as well as an aesthetic transformation.' *Modern Culture*, pp.91–92.

137. Roger Scruton, 'Art, Beauty, and Judgment' in *The American Spectator*, July/August 2007. I am citing from the online edition at: *http://spectator.org/archives/2007/08/28/art-beauty-and-judgment*.

138. Scruton, Beauty, p.174.

139. Scruton, 'The Flight from Beauty', see Chapter 1, n.80, p.37.

4

The Meaning of Conservatism

In a world of declining religious conviction, high culture provides a path to membership. By acting on both the individual and his *Lebenswelt*, it presents 'an imaginative picture of man and his fulfilment, of moral motives and their consequences, of situations and meanings defined by a real common culture'. Through Shakespeare's plays, for example, 'we confront the noble, the innocent, the majestic, the pious and the just; and also the vicious, the unseemly, the hellish, the sentimental and the base'. For Roger Scruton, as I noted in Chapter 3, high culture is rooted in 'a core experience of community', one that unites us 'in imagination to the unborn and the dead'. And while it is, as he says, 'valuable to men in every period', it becomes 'irreplaceable once the core experience of membership is lost'. In an age of repudiation and desacralisation, it thus offers 'our last glimpse of the sacred, the last memorial to an experience without which our free and easy manners will bring us face to face with Nothing'. The result, Scruton warns, will not be 'some new and vital community, some new "core experience"; it will be the regimented disorder of the totalitarian state'. [1] What this means in essence is that aesthetics and conservative politics are directly linked, in so far as both seek to fulfil man's primal longing for 'a lost experience of home'.

In contrast to the *oikophobia* of the postmodernists, Scruton follows Hegel in believing that the true task of philosophy is to provide for the 'spiritually homeless, a promise of their proper home'. That is why, to repeat, he believes aesthetics must once again become the 'paradigm of philosophy'. For how else can a person become conscious of who he is and where he belongs, except through building, making and decorating that small patch of earth he calls 'home'? How else, in other words, can he come to see himself reflected in an otherwise objective and alien world? Or, as

Scruton puts it in a discussion of Hegel's thought:

The final end of every rational being is the building of the self – of a recognisable personal entity, which flourishes according to its own autonomous nature, in a world which it partly creates. The means to this end is labour, in the widest sense of that term: the transformation of the raw materials of reality into the living symbols of human intercourse. By engaging in this activity, man imprints on the world, in language and culture as well as in material products, the marks of his own will, and so comes to see himself reflected in the world, an object of contemplation, and not merely a subject whose existence is obscure to everyone including himself. Only in this process of 'imprinting' can man achieve self-consciousness. For only in becoming a publicly recognisable object (an object for others) does a man become an object of knowledge for himself. Only then can he begin to see his own existence as a source of value, for which he takes responsibility in his actions, and which creates the terms upon which he deals with others who are free like himself.[2]

As understood by Scruton and Hegel, aesthetics is a form of cultural labour that rescues man from his temporal isolation. Through the aesthetic endeavour, his alienation gives way to personal identity and human settlement. For it is then that objects are made into 'an expression of ourselves and our common dwelling place'. It is then that we 'endow them with the marks of order, legitimacy and peaceful possession'. In so doing, objects can be said to contain within themselves the subjective *intentionality* of those who made them, an intentionality that 'lingers on after human deaths and departures'. This process is what Scruton refers to as the 'mystification' of the natural order. Through it, 'ordinary things and everyday customs' come to acquire a 'nimbus of authority, a quasi-divine and in any case mysterious *given-ness* …'. It is, moreover, how they come to command the loyalty of those who share a common dwelling-place. And, as he explains, it was how Scruton's beloved England came to be domesticated:

The world of the English was a world of rituals, uniforms, precedents and offices. In any serious business they would spontaneously adopt another and higher tone, borrowing legal and biblical words, addressing their colleagues not directly but through some real or imaginary chairman, and creating a mystical body out of a mere gathering of people. Schools had their uniforms and began their days with an assembly in which hymns were sung, solemn words uttered and the spirit of the school invoked from the dais. Their institutions were marked by ceremonies and offices, and housed in buildings clad in Gothic arches, barbicans and fairy pinnacles. Each defined not just a function but a form of membership. Barristers dined in their Inns and dons in their colleges; each village had its cricket team, its darts club and its Women's Institute. The English accepted titles, coats of arms and insignia of office as endowed with their own special magic, and the College of Arms was kept busy year upon year by their claims for privilege and precedence of a purely symbolic kind. Class, for them, was not an economic but a spiritual fact, and through their tenacious titles of nobility they rendered social differences by and large acceptable, even to the losers. Titles, forms and the mystique of noble birth are costumes, through which the upper classes can display their difference and safeguard their privileges without flaunting their power. The English aristocrat was not a courtier, kowtowing to his sovereign in the city, but the heart and soul of the landscape where he resided, bearing a title that ennobled the country as much as it ennobled himself. Monarchy was, for the English, not a form of political power, but a work of the imagination, an attempt to represent in the here and now all those mysterious ideas of authority and historical right without which no place on earth could be settled as home.[3]

IN PRAISE OF PREJUDICE

The mystification of the natural order is the means by which we humans settle in a specific place and identify it as *ours*. It is therefore the basis of the conservative attitude. Culture matters to the conservative because it involves 'all those activities which endow the world with meaning, so that it bears the mark of appropriate action and appropriate response'.[4] Furthermore, it enables the individual to achieve an appropriate understanding of his 'social nature'. For Scruton, you acquire that understanding, not through individual choice, but through the practices and cultural customs of the 'social organism' to which you belong. Such is what Edmund Burke called 'prejudice', by which he did not mean bias of a bigoted kind, but the 'latent wisdom' contained in the 'general bank and capital of nations and of ages'. Prejudice is, as Scruton writes, 'the set of beliefs and ideas that arise instinctively in social beings, and which reflect the root experience of social life'.[5]

What primarily interests Scruton in Burke's account of prejudice, is that it answers those who would seek to demystify and desacralise the natural order.[6] Broadly speaking, that is the agenda which drives the proponents of liberalism, socialism and their postmodern successors. Each of those 'movements', Scruton asserts, 'proposes a description of our condition, and an ideal solution to it, in terms which are secular, abstract, universal, and egalitarian'. In reality, however, it is no solution at all, for, as he explains in a powerful passage worth citing in full,

... [e]ach sees the world in 'desacralised' terms, in terms which, in truth, correspond to no lasting common human experience, but only to the cold skeletal paradigms that haunt the brains of intellectuals. Each is abstract, even when it pretends to a view of human history. Its history, like its philosophy, is detached from the concrete circumstance of human agency, and, indeed, in the case of Marxism, goes so far as to deny the efficacy of human agency, preferring to see the world as a confluence of impersonal forces. The ideas whereby men live and find their local identity – ideas of allegiance, of country or nation, of religion and obligation – all these are, for the socialist, mere ideology, and for the liberal, matters of 'private' choice, to be respected by the state only because they cannot truly matter to the state. Each system is also universal. An international socialism is the stated ideal of most socialists; an international liberalism is the unstated tendency of the liberal. To neither system is it thinkable that men live, not by universal aspirations but by local attachments; not by a 'solidarity' that stretches across the globe from end to end, but by obligations that are understood in terms which separate men from most of their fellows – in terms such as national history, religion, language, and the customs which provide the basis of legitimacy. Finally – and the importance of this should never be underestimated – both socialism and liberalism are, in the last analysis, egalitarian. They both suppose all men to be equal in every respect relevant to their political advantage. For the socialist, men are equal in their needs, and should therefore be equal in all that is granted to them for the satisfaction of their needs. For the liberal, they are equal in their rights, and should therefore be equal in all that affects their social and political standing.[7]

Statements like that have earned Roger Scruton the lasting enmity of the liberal establishment. Yet, as I see it, Scruton's only sin was to have pointed out that man is instinctually conservative, meaning that he naturally yearns to belong to a community that shares his values and convictions as expressed through the common culture. This means that he is not naturally given to revolutionary politics, which proposes large-scale transformations 'as a remedy for the unhappiness of man'.[8] He is not, generally speaking, a proponent of what Scruton labels 'the malady of agitation'. He looks, rather, to the permanent and concrete facts of communal life as antidotes to social ills. Whereas liberals strive 'to cast away the coat of prejudice, and to leave nothing but the naked reason', the conservative, by relying on inherited customs, 'has a motive to give action to that reason, and an affection which will give it permanence'. That is because, as Burke counsels, prejudice 'engages the mind in a steady course of wisdom and virtue, and does not leave the man hesitating in the moment of decision, sceptical, puzzled, and unresolved'.[9]

And so, according to thinkers like Burke, Hegel and Scruton, politics should be understood as 'living matter'. In contrast to the liberal, for whom 'no particular scheme of values, no particular historical community, no particular custom, circumstance or prejudice, can be incorporated into the abstract statement of basic rights', the conservative believes that we join together not only voluntarily, but also 'naturally and inevitably'. We do so in and through 'institutions of membership', which are, according to Scruton, the '*sine qua non* of social life'.[10] Like traditions, institutions are living entities that are the product of what F. A. Von Hayek calls 'spontaneous order'. They too possess '*inner* life and *inner* purposes' that correspond to a legal and moral personality, one which is the subject of praise and blame. Scruton elaborates:

Institutions can have moral rights and duties; they can invite our respect and consideration, not as means only, but as ends in themselves; and they are rational agents, with their own changing goals and their hopes and fears for the future. This is a strange fact, but it is a fact none the less. Indeed, it is one reason why institutions are so important to us: for they are the objective counterparts of our experience of membership, and can be loved as persons through every change in the persons who compose them. A corporation can be the object of praise, loyalty, pride, as well as of anger and resentment; it can possess habits of mind, virtues and vices. A corporation has even been the central character in a drama (Wagner's Die Meister singer), in which the phenomenon of membership is powerfully vindicated.[11]

CARING FOR INSTITUTIONS

The idea of 'corporate personality' is central to Scruton's conservative outlook.[12] For him, liberalism is mistaken in positing the autonomous individual as the bedrock of political order. That is because, for such an in-dividual, 'the chief political benefit is freedom – freedom from the con-straint and coercion exercised by others'.[13] For the conservative, however, individual liberty is not an absolute, but the result of 'a long process of social evolution, the bequest of institutions without whose protection it could not endure'. Simply put: it is only in and through institutions that genuine freedom can be realised and exercised. That is to say, human free-dom is not something immediately given; it is, like human personality itself, a *social artefact*, and is therefore 'not the precondition but the consequence of an accepted social arrangement'. So what then does it mean for a conservative to value freedom? For Scruton, it means valuing the existing social order, without which the pursuit of freedom would be 'no more than a gesture in a moral vacuum'.[14] Yes, the release of the self from all constraint may indeed appear like 'the fullest flowering of human freedom'. But in reality, it is more akin to 'self-dissipation' than self-realisation.

Scruton's conservatism is, thus, primarily interested in *the preservation and care of institutions.* In so doing, it rejects individual rebellion in favour of what Scruton calls 'congenial authority'. That idea is centred on a repu-diation of the core principle of liberal theory, espoused initially by Thomas Hobbes, and which declares there can be 'no obligation on any man which arises not from some act of his own'.[15] Scruton is here taking aim at the idea of the 'social contract' which has dominated political the-ory in one form or another from the time of Rousseau to that of John Rawls. For the social contract theorist, my obligations, if they are to have any force or meaning, must be grounded in free choice. Hence, those ob-ligations that the self inherits, because not freely or rationally chosen, are considered by him to be illegitimate.

From that standpoint, Burke's appeal to prejudice would be regarded as irrational, as would Hegel's assertion that the pre-contractual order of the family is a necessary stage in political development (see below). That is so because the whole point of social contract theory is to undermine local attachments in favour of *universal citizenship*. It seeks to strip away custom and tradition in order to posit principles which are valid and ac-ceptable to 'all people everywhere, whatever their history and condition'. Indeed, as Scruton points out in various contexts, John Rawls[16] has taken this idea in an absurd direction, by suggesting that we 'discount not only our race and sex, but also our religious values and our "several conceptions of the good" – in short, all that truly makes rational choice conceivable'.[17] In so doing, he pushes 'to the limit – or rather, to one of its limits – the Western idea of a purely political order, in which all bonds of membership are contained within the abstract rights and duties of the citizen'.[18]

The basic liberal contention then is this: institutions are *not* the guarantee of real freedom, but an impediment to it, and only by reordering society so that everyone is party to the contract, will such liberty be ours. However, following Hegel, Scruton believes that the 'We' always precedes the 'I'. For him, to repeat, the individual subject is not the basis of social or political life, but a *gift of culture*. That is what Scruton means when he says that 'human freedom and human personality are social artefacts', and that the person 'has an indefeasible duty to history, and to a culture that he did not choose'.[19] In other words, society precedes the subject, and in so doing supplies it with *concrete* reasons and motives for action. The result is that if we value freedom, then we must 'value something else, which is not the effect of freedom but its precondition – namely the social order from which duties and values spring and upon which the human personality depends for its identity'.[20]

For Hegel, the social order, or *Sittlichkeit*,[21] is composed of all those customs, laws and institutions which 'give reality to our moral scruples, and reconcile in us the contrasting demands of autonomy and community',[22] the most important of which is the family. By 'family' he means 'all those relations of "natural piety" which provide the individual with the core of moral identity and support from which his social nature develops'.[23] The individual does not, in other words, choose his moral or political identity. It too is a gift of culture – a gift of the given social reality which precedes the individual. The upshot is that, for the conservative, the social contract is at best a 'naïve' thought-experiment, in that it presupposes 'the existence of people who are [already] able to communicate, agree, and recognise rights and obligations'.[24] Or, as Scruton puts it in *The Meaning of Conservatism*:

… the very possibility of free and open contract presupposes a sufficient social order, not because it would otherwise be impossible to enforce contracts (although that too is true), but because without social order the very notion of an individual committing himself, through a promise, would not arise.[25]

CIVIL SOCIETY

What Hegel and Scruton both recognise is that good politics is not purely a product of consensual relations. It is, to repeat, a complex process comprised of many layers, one whose legitimacy is rooted in *obligation*: obligation, as Hegel believes, to the family, civil society and the State, each sphere of social existence being dialectically related to the other:

Civil society is the totality of free associations. It depends for its continuation upon institutions which, by defining the obligations of their members, have an inherent tendency to transcend any contractual legitimacy. The principal instance of such an institution is the State, without which there could be no law, and therefore no guarantee of the justice upon which civil society depends for its survival. Our obligation to the State, like our obligation to the family and its members does not arise through a free undertaking, but rather through a slow process of development, during which we acquire obligations long before we can freely answer to their claim on us.[26]

Civil society is the sphere of true freedom, in so far as it is an 'arena of spontaneous institution-building'.[27] It is the sphere of culture – a place where, recalling what I said at the beginning of this chapter, we discover who we are and where we truly belong. For it is there, in the company of others who share our longings and our loves, that we form, in the words of Scruton's Xanthippe, 'our vision of intrinsic value'.[28] Without the freedom that civil society guarantees, human beings would neither have the time nor leisure to contemplate their 'heavenly pleasures'. It follows that,

... free associations are the true source of whatever is ultimately worthwhile, and of the motives – honour and shame – which make it so. It is from our little institutions – and I count the family as the most important among them, along with the brotherhoods and sisterhoods, the groups of kinsmen, the religious guilds and dining clubs – that the meaning of life, or rather the many meanings of life, derive. Without them, deprived of our goals, we can do nothing of value: all our actions then become means, and since nothing has intrinsic purpose, nothing has purpose at all. Our lives become lost in calculation, but the only object of this calculation is to survive the present moment and calculate again.[29]

Worse still, if the State abolishes civil society, which those of a totalitarian complexion are wont to do, the social order becomes *de-personalised*.

In reaction to the Jacobin assault on the old institutions, customs and values of pre-revolutionary France, Burke wrote that society should be viewed as a partnership 'not only between those who are living, but between those who are living, those who are dead, and those who are to be born'.[30] The French revolutionaries sought to peel away the ancient personality of their country, thereby disenfranchising the unborn and silencing the dead. But that is what invariably happens, argued Burke, when the distinction between the State and civil society collapses. For him, as for Scruton, the partnership between those living, dead and unborn, which is guaranteed by the institutions of civil society, should have no 'single or overriding purpose'. To be part of civil society is its own reward – an end in itself. But when society or politics is driven by what Burke called an 'armed doctrine', it will be 'subjected to the State as to a military commander, mobilised about a ruling activity, and directed towards a future goal'.[31]

The best way of understanding what is at issue here, is by returning to the notion of 'corporate personality'. For Scruton, the human person is 'neither identical with his body nor distinct from it, but joined to it in a metaphysical knot that philosophers labour fruitlessly to untie'. Civil society is somewhat similar to the human body, whereas the State is like the human person, it being 'the supreme forum of decision-making, in which reason and responsibility are the only authoritative guides'. The State is, in other words, the sphere of law, in that it affords legal safeguards to the 'little platoons' of civil society. This means that state and society 'are inseparable but nevertheless distinct, and the attempt to absorb one into the other is the sure path to a stunted, crippled and pain-wracked body politic'.[32] For then, the State becomes all-pervasive and all-powerful, dominating every sphere of human activity and forcefully coercing people to its overarching and immediate aims. It is then that we witness the pernicious process of *depersonalisation*, in which the dead and the unborn are summarily elided from the equation. It is then that power is exercised solely 'in a spirit of calculation', being without 'the principle of answerability from which the sanctity of limits derives'. No longer is the State a source of agency, one that can be held accountable for its actions before the law. Neither is it perceived as a 'rational being, responsive to criticism, capable of remorse, shame, pride, honour, self-affirmation and regret'.[33] If anything, it appears as a 'corporate psychopath, respected by none and feared by all'. And in that world of 'thing institutions', there are no obligations 'beyond the lifetime of the individuals who undertake them'.[34]

The remedy for such a malaise, argues Scruton, is to ensure the 'political centrality of the idea of rational agency'. This means prioritising the appearance of the world as the principal source of reason, responsibility and personality. It means recognising the true 'objects of our allegiance, the sources of authority, and the foci of our political concern are corporate agents: institutions, the law, parliaments, churches and schools – all those institutions, in other words, that bear witness to the longings of the dead, and without which the unborn would be denied their rightful bequest. He writes:

The true public spirit – the spirit from which civil society and all its benefits derive – requires just such a projection of our duties beyond the grave. The care for future generations must be entrusted to persons who will exist when they exist; and if there are no such persons surrounding me, how can I have that care, except as a helpless anxiety? I can enter into no personal obligation that will bind me to past and future souls, nor can you. Only a corporate person can enter such an obligation, and only through corporate persons, therefore, can the relation to the unborn and the dead be made articulate and binding … That this relation to the unborn and the dead is necessary for the fulfilment of the rational agent is something that we should not doubt. For it forms the premise of self-justification. The individual is justified by the knowledge that he did right by the knowledge of those who survive him, whom he never knew and promised him nothing; and equally by those who preceded him and bequeathed to him, unknowingly, their store of trust. In the broadest sense, then, the corporate person is necessary to the ecology of rational agency, and without such constructs our aims will be as truncated as our lives.[35]

The important word in that passage is 'ecology'. The institutions of the State and civil society can be said to have a personality, because they concretely express the identity and intentions, not only of those who inaugurated them, but also of subsequent generations who ensured their survival. Institutions, to repeat, testify to the successful settlement of a people and its 'mystification' of the natural order. That is why the manner in which they are built matters: a purely functional building, for example, does not express or symbolise anything, in so far as it merely serves the purposes of the present generation. To possess personality, however, a building must contain and sustain what Hegel called the '*Geist*' (spirit or consciousness) of those who went before. It must bear witness, in other words, to their ideals and values, thereby mediating between absent generations and their surviving counterparts. Hence, it is through institutions that the living converse with the dead, thus preserving the spirit of the past for those who are yet to come. Without the maintenance of institutions, the social, political and moral ecology would simply collapse. The dead would have no means of passing on their wisdom (Burkean 'prejudice'), while the unborn would be severed from their spiritual origins in the common culture. That explains why, for Scruton, the preservation of the given political existence is of paramount significance for the conservative, and what ultimately distinguishes him from the liberal and the socialist:

The task for the conservative is to find the grounds of political existence concretely, and to work toward the re-establishment of legitimate government in a world that has been swept bare by intellectual abstractions. Our ultimate model for a legitimate order is one that is given historically, to people united by their sense of a common destiny, a common culture, and a common source of the values that govern their lives. The liberal intelligentsia in the West, like the erstwhile communist intelligentsia in the East, has persistently refused to accept the givenness of human existence. It has made life, and in particular political life, into a kind of intellectual experiment ...[36]

For Scruton, as we have seen, it is simply impossible to view life as an experiment. We are *of necessity* attached to a place, whose personality and identity is secured through its institutions. This attachment to a people and place is not chosen, but 'is given to us in the very texture of our social existence'. For the liberal, on the other hand, politics is never an end in itself, but always a means to some further goal which Scruton correctly identifies as that of 'equality'. More specifically, it is 'moral equality' or an equality of 'rights' which is rooted in the Kantian idea of pure individual autonomy. But that is to overlook the fact that the political *Lebenswelt* encumbers the individual from birth with obligations 'that are not of my own devising'. Indeed, it is only when I recognise that my principal debt to the world is one of 'piety' and sacrifice (rather than justice and equality), that I will discover the consolations of attachment and homecoming. From that perspective, politics is anything but the sphere of personal experimentation. It is a 'manner of social existence, whose bedrock is the given obligations from which our social identities are formed'. Hence, it is never a means to an end, but always an end in itself.[37]

All this is nicely summarised by the British Hegelian F. H. Bradley, in a piece from the latter's *Ethical Studies* which Scruton excerpts in *Conservative Texts*.[38] Bradley tells us that no child is born 'into a desert'. Rather, he is born 'into a living world, a whole which has a true individuality of its own, and into a system and order which is difficult to look at as anything else than an organism'. And then, directing his pen at liberal 'thinkers' who are wont to dismiss this view of human nature, Bradley asserts that the child,

... does not even think of his separate self; he grows with his world, his mind fills and orders itself; and when he can separate himself from that world, and know himself apart from it, then by that time his self, the object of his self-consciousness, is penetrated, infected, characterised by the existence of others. Its content implies in every fibre relations of community. He learns, or already perhaps has learnt, to speak, and here he appropriates the common heritage of his race, the tongue that he makes his own is his country's language ... and it carries into his mind the ideas and sentiments of the race ..., and stamps them in indelibly. He grows up in an atmosphere of example and general custom, his life widens out from one little world to other and higher worlds, and he apprehends through successive stations the whole in which he lives, and in which he has lived. Is he now to try and develop his 'individuality', his self which is not the same as other selves? Where is it? What is it? Where can he find it? The soul within him is saturated, is filled, is qualified by, it has assimilated, has got its substance, has built itself up from, it *is* one and the same life with the universal life, and if he turns against this he turns against himself; if he thrusts it from him, he tears his own vitals; if he attacks it, he sets his weapon against his own heart.[39]

CONSERVATISM IS NOT COMMUNITARIANISM

This explains why Scruton's brand of conservatism should not be confused with the movement known as 'Communitarianism'. Writing in 1996, at a time when communitarian ideas were gaining currency from the

White House to Downing Street, he says that, ostensibly at least, communitarians 'view themselves as critics of liberalism, defenders of social sentiment against the dispiriting individualism of modern life'. On closer inspection, however, thinkers such as Charles Taylor, Michael Sandel and Michael Walzer are 'just so many made-over liberals, dressed up in a rhetoric of fellow feeling'.[40] In fact, far from forging 'an alternative to the destructive trends unleashed by liberalism, they are the latest incarnation of the old liberal grievance against bourgeois civilisation and its homely virtues'. The reason for that is clear: Scruton contends that communitarians conflate what they call 'community' with the State. Taylor, for example, identifies the welfare state as the antidote to unbridled capitalism.

Likewise, both Sandel and Walzer see the modern welfare state as 'the very symbol of "community"'. But that, Scruton argues, is a serious mistake, for the real 'source of social decline in our day lies in the tendency to mortgage our future for the gratification of those who are living now'. The welfare state, 'with its massive accumulation of power devoted to distributing resources among the living and contemptuous of all limitations contained in custom, tradition, inheritance, and private property', encourages people to prioritise their individual rights over their responsibilities to the dead and the unborn. But as Burke rightly taught, we were not put here to pillage our inheritance. Still less 'have we the right to distribute all goods equally among the living, without regard for who deserves them, who owns them, or who will use them wisely and well'. Rather, we are the living trustees of society, 'bound by the duties of our tenancy. The real duties of social membership are owed not only to the living members. They are owed "transcendentally", to people whom we can never know and whose numbers are uncountable.'[41] Put in simple terms: we have no right to exploit the social and moral ecology for our own short-term purposes.

VIRTUOUS ECONOMICS

As his critique of the excesses of the welfare state suggests, Roger Scruton is a staunch defender of the free market against the planned economy. But his defence is subtle, and one that is entirely consistent with his particular brand of conservatism. Following F. A. Hayek, he contends that the success of economic activity is predicated on 'knowledge of other people's wants, needs and resources'. But how is such knowledge obtained? Like Hayek, Scruton asserts it is through the price mechanism, for prices in a free economy 'offer the solution to countless simultaneous equations mapping individual demand against available supply'.[42] Conversely, when prices are fixed, as they are in a planned economy, they can no longer be used to accurately gauge people's real desires. The result is a black economy, in which the 'spontaneous order of distribution' falls asunder.

The free economy is a piece of social epistemology: it tells you what people want, thereby conferring a correct value on commodities. Any attempt to interfere with the process of free exchange will, however, provide a false picture of what is demanded by consumers. Thus a free economy, like the *given* political reality itself, is one example (perhaps even the best example) of *spontaneous order*. It arises by an 'invisible hand' and bears witness to the phenomenon of 'tacit and collective understanding' which, once again, is what Burke meant by prejudice. Indeed, for Scruton, no tradition can be satisfactorily preserved without the social knowledge conveyed by market relations, for it is on the basis of that knowledge that traditions grow and evolve.

Does this suggest that Scruton subscribes to unbridled capitalism? On the contrary, as can be clearly seen in an unpublished article entitled 'Virtue and Profit: A Critique of Managerial Reasoning'. In that context, he defends what Jim Collins and Jerry Porras[43] describe as the 'visionary company' over the 'profit machine'. A visionary company is one that understands profit 'in the way that a biologist understands oxygen – not as the goal of life, but the thing without which there is no life'. The American giants Wal-Mart and Hewlett Packard are cases in point: such companies do not list profit among their principal goals, but it is 'more often construed as a side-effect of pursuing them'. Consequently, profit becomes a *by-product* of purpose. Following Adam Smith, whose *Theory of Moral Sentiments* he regularly cites with approval, Scruton argues that we often 'achieve our goals by ignoring them, and the most profitable of our actions might be those in which we turn our backs on profit and act for the sake of honour, kindness and compassion'. In so doing, we are led to reject 'the caricature of capitalism that its critics love to reiterate. Private property, private initiative, private risk, and private profit are indeed all essential attributes of the capitalist system. But these things are economically effective only against a background of norms and values, in which profit may be kept in view, but seldom presented as a goal'.

Taking inspiration from Aristotle's theory of virtue, a visionary business will draw on the inherited stock of human capital (prejudice) in order to acquire the moral wisdom necessary to achieve real success and fulfilment. As Aristotle taught, the acquisition of virtue requires that we look for what is 'permanent in human nature, with a view to identifying the qualities that people need in all circumstances of life, if they are to achieve the fulfilment of which they are capable'. This means that, like the virtuous person, the virtuous company will always strive to ensure that it is motivated in the right way and for the right reasons. It will be guided by justice, where justice implies giving each his due. Accordingly, contracts will be upheld, while respect and accountability towards customer and shareholders will become permanent features of the workplace. And so, the just business can be characterised as one which,

... treats others and its employees with respect, that takes responsibility for its faults, honours its agreements, and does not cheat on its rivals. And a business with such a disposition puts honour above profit in any conflict. Studies of virtuous companies have again brought home to us the empirical evidence for the view that justice, seen in this way, is not the enemy of profit, and that honesty remains the best policy ...[44]

THE RULE OF LAW

Now Scruton is well aware that the virtuous business has its enemies, both in the form of the State, and what he calls 'the consultants'. Whereas the latter seek to relegate justice 'to a side-line', the former tends to interfere in the workings of the free market through the pursuit of what has become known as 'social justice'. In order to understand how and why this happens, it is necessary to recognise that for both Hayek and Scruton, the market 'is held in place by other forms of spontaneous order, not all of which are to be simply understood as epistemic devices, but some of which – moral and legal traditions, for example – create the kind of solidarity that the markets, left to themselves, will erode'.[45] Scruton's

Xanthippe describes this phenomenon as 'spontaneous legality', a process she charmingly describes in the following terms:

Out of the strife of the marketplace comes law … People buy and sell by agreement, striking bargains, making contracts, exchanging promises and building thereby a network of trust. Nothing in this is shameful, and if we saw matters rightly, our law of slander would not be required. Suppose then that someone should break his trust, and fail to fulfil his part of the bargain. Surely, he will be at once exposed to blame, not merely from the injured party, but from all those who depend upon the system of mutual trust for their profits. The injured party will seek redress before a judge; and the rest of society will strive to uphold the judgement. An irresistible pressure will exist, for the establishment of impartial courts of law, and for the enforcing of their verdicts against the guilty ones. A kind of spontaneous legality emerges: a legality founded on consent. The law enacted by these impartial courts will therefore strive to uphold agreements, and to ensure that those injured by the breach of them are duly compensated from the goods of the wrongdoer. It will be a law for all, 'extending through the wide air and immense light of heaven'. Its fundamental principles will be recognised and accepted by all men.[46]

For both Xanthippe and Hayek, the spontaneous order of the market emerges in tandem with *the rule of law*. As Hayek teaches, the law is not invented but is rather 'coeval with society'. In the primitive tribe, for example, the individual was accepted as a member only in so far as he adhered to the unspoken rules of the group. Those rules, argues Hayek, were not invented but *discovered* – in as much as they were 'conceived at first as something existing independently of human will'.[47] There is no doubt, therefore, that 'law existed for ages before it occurred to man that he could make or alter it'.[48] This idea that law is discovered rather than being the invention of an individual will is particularly significant for Scruton's understanding of politics. For him, it is nothing less than true legality, and is best exemplified, as one might expect, 'in the English tradition of common law – law made by judges, in response to the concrete problems that come before them, and in which principles emerge only slowly, and already subject to the harsh discipline of the actual'. Common law is founded in judicial precedents, and thus 'bears the stamp of historical order'.[49] That is why Scruton refers to it as 'concrete law', for, as he writes in respect of Hayek:

Its ultimate authorities are embedded in the history and experience of a human community, and although it aims to universalise its judgements, and so to achieve the abstract *form* of law, it is inseparable from a given *content*, which derives from conflicts within a shared historical experience.[50]

We could say, therefore, that the *common law is itself a tradition*, or, better still, the principal means by which a land is settled and the sacred longings of the tribe satisfied. It does this by uniting the 'land and the law in a manner that gives human contours to both'.[51]

For a conservative, the law sustains civil society and protects the personality of institutions by providing for their rights and duties.[52] It does so by standing above the State in the social order of things. Unlike the former communist countries of Eastern Europe, in which the 'impersonal' state spread through society like a cancer, 'cancelling the habit of accounting and replacing legal and moral relations with self-interested calculation as the sole preoccupation of the will',[53] the Western democratic state is a form of personal government founded on, and answerable to the rule of law. It too is a citizen, and is responsible to all other citizens under its care. But in order for it to be effective, the rule of law requires judges who are free of state manipulation. Otherwise there is no restraining hand on the power of the State. It ceases to be a person with rights and obligations, becoming instead an all-pervasive force that strives to occupy every nook and cranny of the civil space. Such, for Scruton, is the aim of the totalitarian system:

In normal societies an association is permitted until it is forbidden, and when permitted its actions are subject to the law, under which it has rights and liabilities. In totalitarian societies associations are forbidden unless expressly permitted – usually by some written dispensation from the party machine. Once permitted, however, their actions lie beyond the law: for the real decisions taken in their name are not taken by the corporations themselves, but by the party, which is immune from prosecution; while the responsibilities which fall on the corporations can never be honoured, unless the party itself requires it. In place of the old forms of civil society, therefore, there is created a new kind of social unity: a conscript unity, foreshadowed in the *levée en masse* of the French Revolution. The people are pulled from the path of compromise and set marching side by side toward the future. Their regimented steps admit of no deviation, and their lingering backward glances are subject to the sternest reproof. Henceforth it is the future that counts, and those who recoil from it betray not the revolutionary vanguard, but the whole of society – indeed, humanity itself.[54]

This explains why judicial independence counts as the bedrock of conservative politics and of an authentically just state. Unlike the liberal, for whom all authority is oppressive, conservatism is rooted in 'the love of existing things, imperfections included, and a willing acceptance of authority, provided it is not blatantly illegitimate'.[55] This is what Scruton calls the 'authority of the actual', and it is the guarantee of legitimate liberty in any political order. In so far as the law responds to concrete problems 'in which principles emerge only slowly', it 'bears the stamp of historical order'.[56] It is the job of the judiciary to protect that historical order from all those who would seek to threaten it, including the State itself. Hence, it must have authority and independence if the voice of tradition is to be heard and if real justice is to be done.

It is, of course, the principal objective of all revolutionaries to abolish the rule of law once in power. That is because they know that the judiciary, as its guardian, effectively limits state power. This makes clear why radicals like Foucault display such hostility towards the law. For them, judicial independence is just one more 'instrument of domination' used to excuse the 'power of the old ruling class'.[57] And so the radical must seek to destroy the judiciary, and thus the authority of existing things. He must replace concrete law with *abstract* justice, or what Scruton labels 'an "equality" of reward – which must inevitably conflict with the concrete circumstances of human existence'. This, in turn, demands the setting up of so-called 'people's courts', in which the will of 'the people' is sacred. Needless to say, the real people are never asked if their will is reflected in the 'decisions' of such 'courts', and have absolutely no way of appealing those decisions in a higher court.

But if Scruton rejects the revolutionary instinct to demote law and politics to 'epiphenomena', he also repudiates the liberal notion of justice as residing 'in some distribution of privilege and property'. For, by equating justice with redistribution, the liberal legislator not only distorts the spontaneous order of the market, but also undermines the spontaneous legality of the social sphere. Hence, following Hayek, Scruton denounces the very idea of 'social justice', saying that in its name 'any amount of injustice can be inflicted'.[58] Why so? Because those who subscribe to that idea refuse to countenance the fact, as Xanthippe puts it, that 'the justice of a state lies in its procedures alone'. In her view, a state is just to the extent 'that justice is done in it; and justice is done when impartial judges give judgment according to natural law', no more, no less. It is simply not the job of the legislator or the judge to use the law as an instrument for social engineering. That would be to impose a planned order on that which has emerged spontaneously, thereby destroying the vital social epistemology upon which civil freedom rests.

The liberal remains convinced, however, that without central planning and control, the cause of justice is doomed, which is why he believes that the law is not an end in itself (something of *intrinsic* worth and value), but the means by which all of society's problems can be solved. Law then becomes an instrument which is used by the legislator 'to impose on the whole of society a common goal which, whatever it may be – health, or virtue or "social justice" – has the immediate effect of destroying the law and putting in the place of it [a] web of unpredictable punishments'.[59] In a personal state, by contrast, goals are not something that can be planned or imposed. As we saw above, they emerge spontaneously and are brought to fruition, as in the market, through a process of mutual compromise and negotiation which it is the function of law to guide and oversee. This leads Xanthippe to declare that the real enemy of society 'is the one with a non-negotiable purpose, the one who wishes to reform the world in his own favoured direction, and who allows the world no right of reply'.[60]

SOCIAL JUSTICE VERSUS CONCRETE JUSTICE

You can see then why, for Scruton, the state-imposed goal of social justice 'distorts the reasoning' of the virtuous business. State-interference which aims towards the forcible redistribution of profit, serves only to make companies cynical. Instead of cultivating real virtue, they engage in politically correct public-relations charades, with a view to keeping the State at arm's length. Such is what the consultants call 'corporate social responsibility'. The disgraced corporate giant Enron, was, for example, 'quite good at corporate social responsibility, giving money to fashionable causes, making the right noises about diversity, equal opportunities, care for the environment, and whatever else the activists were concerned to investigate'. In reality, however, it was all window dressing: Enron wrapped itself 'in a veil of political correctness' merely to avoid getting entangled in what Xanthippe described above as a web of unpredictable punish-ments'. Of course, doing something merely to avoid punishment cannot be counted as virtuous behaviour. Ethics is not, in other words, about conformity to a political agenda. Rather, it is about 'the internal charac-ter, the moral stature, in short the soul of the firm'. For this reason, a virtuous company will seek to fulfil what is, according to St Thomas Aquinas, the 'first principle of the natural law' – namely, 'strive to do good'. And if it does so, it will reject social justice in favour of concrete justice borne of spontaneous legality. In turn, the company will not enter the political realm as 'a craven follower of some political ideology, but as a corporate statesman, taking its place on behalf of its shareholders and workforce in the shaping of our common future'.[61]

But Roger Scruton is anything but naïve. He knows that businesses, like all corporate persons, are oftentimes tempted to sacrifice their souls to greed. In fact, long before the world banking crisis of 2008, he wrote:

What is important to recognise is that banks too have souls, and that, in the nor-mal case, it is by honourable conduct that they earn their place in the economy, and their opportunities for profit. To lend money at a market rate is to offer a service, and a firm can be entirely dependent on this form of business without sacrificing those other and higher goals which earn the trust of its customers and its own place in society. Think of the calamity that befell Barings Bank, in which the old and upright customers of the City of London were exploited from within by one of the new breed of self-centred nihilists. Or think of Lloyd's and its col-lapse, an episode that eloquently illustrates the distinction between honourable and dishonourable ways of using other people's money. Such examples remind us that it is true of money as of any other business, that profit must come sec-ond to virtue, if it is to keep coming for long.[62]

Those prophetic words assumed a new and astonishing urgency in the wake of what we have come to know as the global 'credit crunch'. For, unlike those who used that crisis as an opportunity to call for the over-throw of capitalism, Scruton shows that its root cause lay not in capitalism or the market *per se*, but in the failure of the banking sector to cultivate virtue. In so doing, it unleashed across the money market yet another and more ferocious wave of 'self-centred nihilists', who prostituted their souls for the sake of pure profit. And the result was just as Scruton predicted: their profit very quickly evaporated and the banking system very nearly collapsed.

In short, Scruton does not deny that 'new opportunities for misconduct and vandalism arise every day'. But that does not mean that we should simply replace the market model, for to do so would be to destroy a valuable source of human knowledge and social capital. Instead, we should seek to avoid future banking crises by pursuing an economic model 'which sees profit as the by-product of morally admirable goals'. This means that rather than entertain the current model of business as a 'profit-driven machine', we should recommend the model of the visionary company, as one which cares for its soul 'as we should care for ours, so as to be upright citizens in a realm that we share'.[63]

CONSERVATISM IS CONSERVATIONISM

Conservatives who care for the soul are *conservationists* in every sense. That is why those of Scruton's persuasion cannot be accused of slavishly following free-market ideology. As he says in a cleverly-titled essay on environmentalism, 'A Righter Shade of Green':

Conservatism is about preserving intrinsically valuable things – economic capital, social capital, and natural capital. I use the word 'capital' deliberately, for its opponents say that conservatism is nothing but the apologetics of capitalism. That is absolutely right – provided you understand that capital embraces many things that are not translatable into economic terms.[64]

If your aim is to conserve the social capital, you won't be sanguine in the face of environmental destruction. But such considerations do nothing to placate left-wing hostility towards conservatism. And much of the blame for that, according to Scruton, lies with those conservatives 'in the political context' who are indeed slaves to that form of capitalist ideology which maintains that individual freedom 'means economic freedom and this, in turn, means the freedom to exploit natural resources for financial gain'.[65] But there is a further reason why the Left has sought to seize the moral high ground regarding the environment, and that is 'the cult of the victim'. Scruton explains:

There has been a motivation on the Left, going back to the 19th century and to Marx in particular, of judging every form of human success in terms of its victims. It is assumed that when someone makes a profit, someone else must suffer a loss. This idea of human society as a kind of zero-sum game, in which every benefit is matched by someone else's cost, is dear to a certain kind of left-wing thinking. And in the Earth, we have a wonderful victim – one bigger than any human being, who suffers the results of all our profiteering.[66]

So how should the conservative respond? The Leftist, as you might expect, looks to the State to provide a solution to environmental degradation. But for Scruton, the State is inappropriate to the task. Why, he asks, do environmentalists look for socialist answers to problems that conservatives are best placed to answer? If they studied the issue less ideologically, they would soon realise that it is socialism, 'with its gargantuan, uncorrectable, and state-controlled projects', that is far more damaging to the Earth than its capitalist or conservative counterparts. That is so, as we saw above, because statist solutions are not only 'a threat to individual liberty but also to the process (of which the free market is the paradigm instance) whereby consensual solutions emerge'. Statist solutions are, in other words, the product of a non-negotiable purpose. Observe, says Scruton, how the Dutch and Danish coastal landscapes have been destroyed by 'banks of hideous windmills'. There they stand, 'looming white ranks on every horizon, waving white arms like disconsolate ghosts, blighting the landscape with their nightmare vision of judgment day'. And yet the truth is that they produce hardly any power, 'will never be able to replace the coal-fired power stations that provide the bulk of the country's electricity, and have all kinds of negative environmental effects, not least on the populations of migrating birds'. Despite that, the Danes and the Dutch steadfastly refuse to admit that they were wrong. The official propaganda, declares Scruton, 'continues to speak as though the windmills were the lasting proof of socialist rectitude'.[67]

In sum, large-scale, impersonal and goal-directed solutions are no remedy for the ecological challenges of the age.[68] What you need, argues Scruton, are not universal but *local* solutions. And here I return to the point from which we began this chapter. I said above that aesthetics and conservative politics are directly linked, in so far as both seek to fulfil man's primal longing for membership. In each case, the impulse is to go in search of a lost experience of home. Nowhere is this more obvious than in how the conservative responds to environmental concerns. Conservatism, as defined by Scruton, is distinguished from 'all its phoney libertarian and cosmopolitan substitutes' by two things: the love of beauty and the love of home. Indeed, the love of culture is nothing less than a love of that which spiritually binds one to a particular place. It is, as discussed in the last chapter, 'a way in which we strive to shape the world to our needs, and our needs to the world'. Hence, in despoiling the environment, we are not only looting the landscape in defiance of what Burke called the 'heredity principle'. We are also shattering the aesthetic equilibrium of that place we call 'home'. Scruton writes that,

… when I discuss with my leftist friends about the Dutch and Danish windmills …, we don't just exchange likes and dislikes, as though discussing the rival merits of Cuban and Dominican cigars. We discuss the visual transformation of the countryside, the disruption, as I see it, of a long-established experience of home, and what this means in the life of the farmer, and the presence, as my leftist friends see it, of the real symbols of modern life, which now stand on the horizon of the farmer's world, summoning him to the realities which he has avoided for far too long. By disputing tastes in this way we are not just striving for agreement. We are working our way towards a consensual solution to long-term problems of settlement: we are discovering the terms on which we might live side by side in a shared environment, and how that environment should look in order that we can put down roots in it. Conceived in this way, aesthetic judgment is the primary form of environmental reasoning: it is the way in which human beings incorporate in to their present decisions the long-term impact of what they do.[69]

For Scruton, ecological disasters strike when consensual aesthetic solutions are either ignored or abandoned altogether. It is then that home-building is 'prised free from the constraints contained in aesthetic judgement and surrendered to the utilitarian madness of the bureaucrats'.[70] Consensual solutions matter, because they allow us to accept *what is ours*, while concomitantly 'making common cause with one's neighbours'. Unlike the apocalyptic visions of left wing environmentalists, the consensual solutions of the conservative do not seek to frighten or make

141

people feel insecure. Those 'terrifying scenarios' seem to justify, according to Scruton, the total repudiation of 'existing orders, while encouraging the kind of control from the top that would put enlightened leftists at last in charge of the endarkened middle class'. On his reading of the matter, however, it is the middle class, 'with its plodding adherence to aesthetic norms', that holds the key to environmental sustainability, in so far as it maintains 'a vigilant resistance to the entropic forces that erode our social and ecological inheritance'.[71]

If the Left is dedicated to the destruction of home, if its task is to liberate man from his settled and consoling ways in favour of uprooted universalism, then Scruton's conservatism is an attempt to reclaim that old sense of belonging for the alienated sojourner of modern life. His is a philosophy of homecoming and all the joy that it provides. It is a rejection of existential individualism, liberal liberty and Marxist revolution in favour of Hegelian recollection. It is a repudiation of the culture of repudiation and a denunciation of all forms of *oikophobia*, with the aim of surmounting separation through worship and affirmation of what belongs to us by birth. Ours, he tells us, is a 'condition of dependence. In our "angel infancy" we are at one with the world, protected and embraced by it.'[72] The conservative's vocation is, thus, to follow Hegel's odyssey of selfhood, by restoring the alienated self to his original condition of dependence – albeit one that is now more conscious of its trajectory from individual isolation to the unity and harmony of membership.

As we have seen, Scruton teaches the reader how to take that homeward path through art, architecture, sexual desire, hunting, farming and even wine-drinking. And when it comes to the environment, the quest is exactly the same: to revive and restore the local at the expense of the universal. For, as Scruton tirelessly explains, it is only at the level of the local that ordinary people will find a genuinely motivating force – a motivation, in other words, to preserve what they identify as *theirs*. He reflects that,

... in so far as we have seen any successful attempts to reverse the tide of ecological destruction, these have issued from national or local schemes, to protect territory recognised as 'ours' – defined, in other words, through some inherited entitlement. I am thinking of the recycling initiatives that are gradually freeing Germany from the plague of plastic bottles, the legislation that freed certain states of the United States from polythene bags, the clean-energy initiatives in Sweden and Norway, the Swiss planning laws that have enabled local communities to retain control over their environments and to think of those environments as their shared possession, and so on. These are small-scale achievements, but they are better than nothing. Moreover, they are successful because they make appeal to a natural motive – which is love of country, love of territory, and love of that territory as home.[73]

Once the environmental movement cottons on to the fact that what it ceaselessly repudiates – the home – is paradoxically the most 'effective motive' that it can be relied upon to change people's attitudes regarding the ecosphere, then environmentalism and conservatism will begin to find common cause. For our home is the 'place where we are, the place that defines us, that we hold in trust for our descendents and that we don't want to spoil'.[74]

The best way of describing the difference between Scruton's approach to environmental matters, and the approach of those on the Left, is thus to say that his is a philosophy of love, whereas theirs is one of hatred. In rejecting the local in favour of the global, radical environmentalists embrace Non-Governmental Organisations in their 'war' against 'multinational predators'. But in Scruton's view, NGOs such as Greenpeace are 'as unaccountable and unrepresentative as the predators they oppose'. They are, moreover, driven by hatred of what they euphemistically call 'big business' and capitalist enterprise, which they consider to be the principal cause of ecological desecration. In demonising enterprise, such people stand guilty of putting 'politics on a war footing, in the manner of Saint-Just and Lenin', a position antithetical to what Scruton nicely identifies as 'the conservative desire to found politics in friendship and conversation, and to resolve conflicts wherever possible through dialogue'.[75]

The great irony then is this: throughout his career, Roger Scruton has been consistently attacked by the Left for inspiring hatred against the other. He has been charged with racism, xenophobia and fascism, amongst many other things. And yet, any careful reader of his work will soon discover that the only thing he rejects out of hand, is the same form of dangerous revolutionary fervour that Edmund Burke identified in the French Revolution, and which, as the latter rightly predicted, would eventually lead to social chaos and the loss of France's national inheritance.

Otherwise, Scruton's conservative convictions are inspired by love, conciliation and commitment, unlike those on the Left who persistently revel in a politics of riot and revulsion.

Put simply, if it is a politics of quiet consolation that you seek, turning to the Left will ultimately prove dispiriting. Only by living the gentle conservatism of someone like Roger Scruton will you find such personal peace. But that in turn means bowing 'to the evidence of history, which tells me that human beings are creatures of limited and local affections, the best of which is the territorial loyalty that leads them to live at peace with strangers, to honour their dead and to make provision for those who will one day replace them in their earthly tenancy'.[76]

NOTES

1. Scruton, *The Philosopher on Dover Beach*, p.123.
2. *Ibid.*, p.46.
3. Roger Scruton, *England: An Elegy* (London: Continuum, 2006), pp.11–12.
4. Scruton, *Modern Culture*, p.28.
5. Scruton, *Gentle Regrets*, p.42.
6. See Chapter 3, above.
7. Roger Scruton, 'How to be a Non-Liberal, Anti-Socialist Conservative' in *The Intercollegiate Review: A Journal of Scholarship and Opinion*, Spring 1993, p.18.
8. Scruton, *Conservative Texts*, p.1.
9. Cited in *Conservative Texts*, p.38.
10. Scruton, *Modern Philosophy*, p.436.
11. *Ibid*, pp.471–472.
12. See especially Scruton, 'Gierke and the Corporate Person' in *The Philosopher on Dover Beach*, pp.56–73; 'What is Right?' in *Thinkers of the New Left*, pp.193–211 (reprinted in *The Roger Scruton Reader*, Mark Dooley (ed.) (London: Continuum, 2009); 'Community as Person' in *England: An Elegy*, pp.68–86; 'Reflections on the Revolutions in Eastern Europe' in *The Boston Conversazioni*, 1991; 'Xanthippe's Laws' in *Xanthippic Dialogues*, pp.93–172; Modern Philosophy, pp.471–474. In his *Dictionary of Political Thought*, Scruton defines 'corporate personality' in the following terms: 'In law, a corporate person is an association, such as a firm, a school or a church, which has been incorporated, so as to become a person in law, with rights, duties, privileges and obligations that can be the subject matter of legal dispute. ... Morally speaking, corporate persons exist even if there is no law that recognises them. All reasonable people assume that schools, churches, clubs and societies have moral relations with their members and with other institutions. Not only do they have rights and liabilities in law; they also have duties and rights of a moral kind. You can owe to them debts of gratitude, for example; you can feel bound in duty and allegiance towards them; you can resent and disapprove of them; you can praise them and blame them – and all this in the sense that implies a full personal relationship. It seems, therefore, that our world contains persons who are not human, and not incarnate in any animal organism.

These persons make free choices, and are held responsible for them; they are objects of affection, anger and esteem. And it is partly through our relationships with them that our own personalities are formed.' Roger Scruton, *Dictionary of Political Thought* (London: Palgrave Macmillan, 2007), p.143. I return to the notion of 'corporate personality' later in this chapter.

13. Scruton, *Conservative Texts*, p.8.
14. Scruton, *The Meaning of Conservatism*, p.8.
15. Cited by Scruton in *The Meaning of Conservatism*, p.19; *The West and the Rest: Globalisation and the Terrorist Threat* (London: Continuum, 2002), p.7. See also, 'Objective Spirit' in *Modern Philosophy*, pp.413–437.
16. Rawls is best known for *A Theory of Justice* (Oxford: Oxford University Press, 1971).
17. Scruton, *Modern Philosophy*, p.426. See also Scruton's entry on Rawls in his *Dictionary of Political Thought*, pp.580–581.
18. Scruton, *The West and the Rest*, p.11.
19. Scruton, *Conservative Texts*, p.8.
20. *Ibid.*, pp.8–9.
21. See G. W. F. Hegel, *Philosophy of Right* (Oxford: Oxford University Press, 1967). See also Scruton, *Conservative Texts*, pp.129–163, and for more on Hegel's social ethics see Mark Dooley, *The Politics of Exodus: Kierkegaard's Ethics of Responsibility* (New York: Fordham University Press, 2001), pp.24–42.
22. Scruton, 'Hegel as a Conservative Thinker' in *The Philosopher on Dover Beach*, p.48. This is undoubtedly one of the finest synopses of Hegel's thought available.
23. *Ibid.*, p.49.
24. Scruton, *Modern Philosophy*, p.417.
25. Scruton, *The Meaning of Conservatism*, p.20.
26. Scruton, *Conservative Texts*, p.10.
27. Scruton, *The Philosopher on Dover Beach*, p.50.
28. Scruton, *Xanthippic Dialogues*, p.142.
29. *Ibid.*, pp.142–143.
30. Edmund Burke, *Reflections on the Revolution in France* (reprinted in Scruton, *Conservative Texts*, p.39).
31. Scruton, *Conservative Texts*, p.11.
32. Scruton, *The Philosopher on Dover Beach*, p.52; *Thinkers of the New Left*, p.202.
33. Scruton, *Conservative Texts*, p.12.
34. Scruton, *The Philosopher on Dover Beach*, pp.71–72. Such, of course, was the situation under the Jacobins, but also under the Communists, as Scruton vividly explains: 'Under Communism people were permitted to form families. But any other form of association was regarded with suspicion, and almost all private societies were outlawed. It was not only schools, universities, and medical facilities that were monopolized by the state. Every little platoon, from the symphony orchestra to the local brass band, from the scout movement to the philately club, was either controlled by the party or outlawed. Even the churches came under communist supervision – except in Poland where ... they created a unique space in which civil society endured through the years of darkness. Hence it was in Poland that the overthrow of Communism began.' 'The Limits of Liberty' in *The American Spectator*, December 2008/January 2009, p.49.
35. Scruton, *The Philosopher on Dover Beach*, p.73.

36. Scruton, 'How to be a Non-Liberal, Anti-Socialist Conservative' in *The Intercollegiate Review: A Journal of Scholarship and Opinion*, Spring 1993, pp.19–20.

37. *Ibid.*, p.20.

38. Scruton, *Conservative Texts*, pp.40–58.

39. *Ibid.*, p.43.

40. Communitarianism shares with conservatism the Hegelian assumption that, as Michael Sandel puts it, 'human freedom can only be achieved in a realized *Sittlichkeit*, and ethical political community that expresses the identity of its members'. (*Liberalism and its Critics*, Michael Sandel (ed.) (New York: New York University Press, 1984), p.10.) According to Scruton, however, that is where the comparison ceases.

41. Roger Scruton, 'Communitarian Dreams' in *City Journal*, Vol. 6, No. 4, Autumn 1996. I am citing from the online edition which is available at: *www.city-journal.org/html/6_4_communitarian.html*.

42. Roger Scruton, 'Hayek and Conservatism' in *The Cambridge Companion to Hayek*, Edward Feser (ed.) (Cambridge: Cambridge University Press, 2006), p.210.

43. Jim Collins and Jerry I. Porras, *Built to Last: Successful Habits of Visionary Companies* (10th edn.) (London: Random House, 2005).

44. Scruton, 'Virtue and Profit', unpublished. See also Scruton's fine article on the 'humane economy' of Wilhelm Röpke, 'The Journey Home' in *First Principles: ISI Web Journal*. Available at: *www.firstprinciplesjournal.com/articles.aspx?article=768&theme=home&loc=b*.

45. Scruton, 'Hayek and Conservatism', p.212.

46. Scruton, *Xanthippic Dialogues*, p.133.

47. See Scruton, *Conservative Texts*, p.111.

48. *Ibid.*, p.112.

49. Scruton, 'How to be a Non-Liberal, Anti-Socialist Conservative', p.22.

50. Scruton, 'Hayek and Conservatism', pp.214–215.

51. Scruton, *England: An Elegy*, p.10.

52. It is not surprising that, as a barrister, Scruton makes law the cornerstone of his conservative philosophy. In almost all his publications dealing with politics, he analyses the role of law in human affairs. See especially, *Modern Philosophy*, pp.428–432; *Thinkers of the New Left*, pp.204–205; *The West and the Rest*, Chapters 2 and 3.

53. Scruton, 'Reflections on the Revolutions in Eastern Europe', p.9; see n.12.

54. Scruton, *Modern Philosophy*, pp.473–474.

55. Scruton, 'The Joy of Conservatism: An Interview with Roger Scruton' in *The New Pantagruel*, January 2006. Available at: *www.newpantagruel.com/2006/01/the_joy_of_cons.php*.

56. Scruton, 'How to be a Non-Liberal, Anti-Socialist Conservative', p.22.

57. Scruton, *Thinkers of the New Left*, p.206.

58. Scruton, 'Hayek and Conservatism', p.221. In a 1983 edition of *The Salisbury Review*, entitled 'The Weasel Word "Social"', Hayek observes: 'Only human actions can be just or unjust; the task of government cannot be to create just conditions, but only to prevent unjust actions. To describe as just or unjust a state of affairs that men have not and could not have created, and to which most of them owe their existence, is giving expression to fantasies in socialist baby language. It would indeed be pleasing to our feelings if the world had been made by an almighty spirit whose views about what is desirable were the same as ours. But our present wisdom is not ultimate wisdom and if it had guided evolution, we should never have climbed down from the trees.'

Reprinted in *The Salisbury Review: The Quarterly Magazine for Conservative Thought*, Merrie Cave (ed.), Vol. 26, No. 1, Autumn 2007, p.16.

59. Scruton, *Xanthippic Dialogues*, p.144.

60. *Ibid.*, p.145.

61. See Scruton, 'Virtue and Profit: A Critique of Managerial Reasoning', unpublished.

62. *Ibid.*

63. *Ibid.*

64. Roger Scruton, 'A Righter Shade of Green' in *The American Conservative*, 16 July 2007. I am citing from the online edition which is available at: *www.amconmag.com/article/ 2007/jul/16/00006/*.

65. Scruton, *A Political Philosophy*, p.33.

66. Scruton, 'A Righter Shade of Green'.

67. Scruton, 'Conservatives are Conservationists' in *First Principles: ISI Web Journal*, Autumn 2007. Available at: *www.firstprinciples.com*.

68. The environment is not a new theme in Scruton's thought. In 1987, he wrote in *The Salisbury Review* that the 'ecological catastrophe of the Soviet bloc is caused by two facts: public ownership of the means of production, and the absence of a rule of law. Both are the inevitable consequence of communism. The remedy to pollution exists; but it exists only where there is private ownership of the means of production, under a rule of law – in other words, where the prevailing system is 'capitalist'. In communist countries, those who control the means of production are empowered both to make the law and arbitrarily to evade it. In Czechoslovakia, for example, there are 360 laws dealing with matters of pollution and environmental health. But any enterprise can obtain exemption from them, if the Party officials consider it to be of sufficient economic importance. The result is that all the major polluters remain outside the law. Nothing could be done by a citizen to enforce the law in a country where one party monopolises power, and therefore no force within a communist country can make any lasting difference to the ecological danger. Only outside pressure – our pressure – can do anything to force the communist bloc to comply with internationally settled norms, and outside pressure requires just the kind of military back-up that the Greens would undermine.' 'The Red and the Green' in *The Salisbury Review*, December 1987 (reprinted in Scruton, *The Philosopher on Dover Beach*, pp.234–239).

69. Scruton, 'Conservatives are Conservationists'.

70. *Ibid.*

71. Scruton, *A Political Philosophy*, p.34.

72. Scruton, *Modern Philosophy*, p.465.

73. Scruton, *A Political Philosophy*, p.43. He forgot, of course, to mention Ireland's successful campaign against plastic shopping bags.

74. *Ibid.*

75. *Ibid.*, p.44.

76. *Ibid.*, p.46.

5

In Defence of the Nation

I have argued that Roger Scruton's is a philosophy of love, one dedicated to restoring 'an old experience of home', and all the consolation that it provides. It is an attempt to save the sacred in defiance of pseudo-scientific attacks on the idea of personhood, the self and subjectivity. For Scruton, as for Hegel, identity is a product of cultural consciousness. The self emerges in the context of a common culture, and by dialectically engaging with his surrounds, he acquires a sense of belonging or membership. Hence Scruton's controversial defence of the nation state should not be read as the diatribe of a narrow nationalist, but as the logical outcome of a philosophy that prioritises the appearances, the *Lebenswelt*, the common culture and established authority. His idea of community is rooted in territorial allegiance, the rule of law and national loyalty. It eschews the 'armed doctrine' of nationalism, in favour of a patriotism borne of love for one's ancestral home and its institutions – institutions which are sustained, not through force, but through accommodation, consent and cooperation. They are endowed with the authority of tradition, not as something immovable, but as something revisable and reformable, and always respectful of those 'absent generations' whose bequest to us those institutions are. It is that primal sense of political belonging, which the culture of repudiation repudiates, that Scruton endeavours to revitalise as the only political arrangement suited to a truly free society. Accordingly, his concepts of statehood, national loyalty and membership are not dedicated to exclusion, but to the recovery of a national ideal suited to a society of strangers, who are nonetheless bound by common fidelity to their territorial jurisdiction above religious or tribal attachments.

THE HOUNDING OF HONEYFORD

Put simply, politics, for Scruton, 'deals with the surface of social consciousness'. For him, the appearances matter because political identity requires an understanding 'of tradition, custom and ceremony – of the totality of practices through which citizens are able to perceive their allegiance as an end'.[1] Strip away the appearances in line with the ambition of the social contract theorist, and you are not left with some underlying political *reality*. What you get instead is personal alienation and political dislocation. For without the symbols of membership, authority and allegiance that culture communicates, the individual is deprived of that which enables him to identify with the surrounding social and political milieu.

When he first enunciated those ideas, Roger Scruton was branded a racist and a xenophobe by the British academic Left. As he wrote in *Gentle Regrets*: 'It became a matter of honour among English-speaking intellectuals to disassociate themselves from me, to write, if possible, damning and contemptuous reviews of my books, and to block my chances of promotion'.[2] He tells of how, as editor of *The Salisbury Review* in 1984, he published Ray Honeyford, 'the Bradford headmaster who argued for a policy of integration in our schools as the only way of averting ethnic conflict'.[3] In his article 'Education and Race: An Alternative View', Honeyford had written that it 'is no more than common sense, that if a school contains a disproportionate number of children for whom English is a second language (true of all Asian children, even those born here), or children from homes where educational ambition and the values to support it are conspicuously absent (i.e. the vast majority of West Indian homes – a disproportionate number of which are fatherless) then academic standards are bound to suffer'.[4] Honeyford correctly anticipated that such pronouncements would lead to his vilification, and would certainly make him the object of an 'anti-racist' witch hunt. And so he decided to launch a pre-emptive strike. The term 'racism', he explained,

… functions not as a word with which to create insight, but as a slogan designed to suppress constructive thought. It conflates prejudice and discrimination, and thereby denies a crucial conceptual distinction. It is the icon word of those committed to the race game. And they apply it with the same sort of mindless zeal as the inquisitors voiced 'heretic' or Senator McCarthy spat out 'Commie'. The word 'black' has been perverted. Every non-white is now, officially 'black', be he Indian, Pakistani or Vietnamese. This gross and offensive dichotomy has an obvious purpose: the creation of an atmosphere of anti-white solidarity. To suppress and distort the enormous variations within races which I every day observe by using language in this way is an outrage to all decent people – whatever their skin colour.[5]

The reaction of the left-wing establishment to Honeyford's acute observation was utterly predictable. To begin with, he was hounded out of his job. Scruton, who was then writing a weekly column for *The Times*,[6] took up his cause, arguing that Honeyford,

… is brought into contact with the extensive propaganda against our schools and curriculum produced by people who despise our traditions of understatement, civilised discourse and respect for truth. He must deal with teachers who perceive the professional advantage of supporting multi-cultural education and of making race into a kind of 'high profile' issue that the sowers of discord would like it to be. He is asked to 'respond positively' to suggestions that he censor textbooks, that he give equal weight to Shakespeare and to the works of Linton Kwesi Johnson (author of the immortal *Inglan is a Bitch!*) and that he show no preference for standard English over creole or pidgin … Mr Honeyford's crime was to tell the truth as he saw it. In particular, he told the truth about Pakistani politics – something that the Left will allow when justifying Soviet policy, but not when praising British institutions. For this truth he must be silenced. The ruthless bigotry of those who wish to silence him is matched by their contempt for education. For such people, the dismissal of a headmaster of proven ability is a small price to pay for his replacement by one who spouts the same ignorant rubbish as themselves.[7]

However, even this powerful public intervention on behalf of Honeyford failed to silence the critics. If anything, it simply upped the ante.

In 1985, the British Association for the Advancement of Science accused *The Salisbury Review* of 'scientific racism', both for publishing Honeyford and because of Scruton's ongoing public pronouncements in support of the national idea.[8] It did not matter that Scruton had courageously written in defence of those benighted Lebanese Christians, who were then struggling to preserve their country from Syrian tyranny.[9] It did not matter that the contributors to the *Review* 'included Jews, Asians, Africans, Arabs, and Turks'.[10] Neither did it matter that the journal was considered a beacon of hope by many across Eastern Europe, a *samizdat* edition appearing in Prague during 1986. All that mattered to his enemies was that Scruton and his wretched *Review* be put out of business as soon as possible. The result was that in response to a threat from 'one socialist author – a Mr Abbs, whose educational books were a lucrative source of income to our former publisher', Longmans terminated the periodical's contract.[11] But there was also a heavy personal price to be paid by Scruton himself:

One academic philosopher wrote to Longmans, who had published one of my books, saying that 'I may tell you with dismay that many colleagues here [i.e. in Oxford] feel that the Longman imprint – a respected one – has been tarnished by association with Scruton's work'. He went on to express the hope that 'the negative reactions generated by this particular publishing venture may make Longman think more carefully about its policy in the future'. Even more curious was the letter sent to my head of department by another colleague, who acted as external assessor for academic promotions. He would have had no difficulty in recommending me, he wrote, before my articles began to appear in *The Times*, and on the strength of my academic work. But those articles, with their un-remitting conservative message, were the real proof of my intellectual powers, and the conclusive demonstration that I was unfit to hold a university chair.[12]

THE FASCISM OF THE NEW LEFT

The book in question was *Thinkers of the New Left*, which I consider one of Scruton's finest. It comprises 16 essays, 13 of which originally appeared in *The Salisbury Review*, and which focus on left-wing intellectuals such as Ronald Dworkin, Michel Foucault, Louis Althusser, Perry Anderson and Jean-Paul Sartre. The essays are insightful and penetrating critiques of the liberal and Marxist assumptions at the heart of each author. But what most irritated the leftist intelligentsia about this particular book was Scruton's ability to highlight the ideological hypocrisy at the heart of the leftwing agenda. Hence, of Antonio Gramsci (who Eric Hobsbawm ludicrously crowned 'the most original communist thinker of the twen-tieth century'[13]) Scruton says that he borrowed all the classic features of Italian fascism against which his writings ostensibly railed. The underly-ing theory of Gramsci's celebrated *Prison Notebooks*[14] is, therefore, 'the true theory of fascism: of the power which had pre-empted Gramsci's ambition, by realising it in other hands. When, in an early article, Gramsci described the proletariat as making up an ideal unity, a *fascio*, he antici-pated in his hopes precisely the form of social order which was later to be achieved by his rival. The philosophy of praxis – so like the philosophical "dynamism" of Mussolini ... retains its charm for the intellectual precisely because it promises him both power over the masses and a mystic unity with them.' Scruton concludes by arguing that the reason the left-wing establishment 'needs to identify the fascist as the single enemy' is because 'what better way to conceal one's intentions than to describe them as the intentions of one's enemies?'[15]

In revealing the fascist tendencies of the New Left, Scruton hit a raw nerve. He had exposed how intolerant the so-called paragons of tolerance, justice and equality were in practice. This enabled him to shed light on why both he and Ray Honeyford were the targets of such vehement abuse. In an essay entitled 'The Left Establishment', he recalls how, when 'attempting to give a public lecture on the theme of "Toleration" at the University of York', he was 'threatened and shouted down'. Likewise, Honeyford was 'lucky to escape from Liverpool University with his life'.[16] And the reason for that was not because their arguments lacked intellectual force or objective truth, but simply because people like Scruton and Honeyford were considered an 'existential threat' to the ideological dominance of the liberal establishment. Consequently, they needed to be condemned as heretics, racists or xenophobes, and put on trial. The result was that Roger Scruton was systematically showered with calumny for no good reason, other than having summoned up the courage to expose the moral, intellectual and political incoherence of left-wing ideology.

This phenomenon came into focus once again in 2006, when he agreed to address the Belgian Eurosceptic party – the Vlaams Belang. Here is Scruton's account of what happened next:

I had heard of Vlaams Belang, and its predecessor, the Vlaams Blok, as a controversial party, with widespread support among the Flemish population of Belgium. I knew that the party had been targeted by the liberal establishment, and had been accused of 'racism and xenophobia', and had been disbanded, in its previous incarnation, by a Belgian court. On the other hand, there were plenty of explanations of the accusations apart from their truth, and it seemed to me that the true offence of the Vlaams Belang had been to threaten the vested interests of the European Union. That suspicion was to a certain measure confirmed when emails began to arrive from concerned 'colleagues' in Belgium – people who had never before shown any interest in my views, but who were now beseeching me to cancel this engagement, asking me not to give credibility to a dangerous right-wing party, and warning me of the damage to my reputation, should I be associated with a party of extremists. It became immediately clear that the controversy surrounding the Vlaams Belang is one that goes to the heart of Belgian politics, and that the opponents of the Vlaams Belang do not wish merely to defeat it in fair and free elections, but to destroy it as a political force. And because they cannot destroy it by democratic means, since it has the habit of receiving the largest number of votes in Parliamentary elections, they wish instead to destroy it through the courts, and to silence and intimidate those who might otherwise confer legitimacy on its efforts. The very suggestion that, by addressing the Vlaams Belang – whether in tones of agreement or tones of rebuke – I have somehow associated myself with it, indicates the intention of the Party's opponents, which is to put it beyond the pale of dialogue.[17]

The attacks on the Vlaams Belang reminded Scruton of what he had endured 20 years previously, when he and Honeyford advanced the commonsense view that 'the official policy of "multiculturalism" was a mistake, and that the future of Britain depends not on encouraging immigrants to live apart in cultural ghettoes, but on integrating them into a common culture of nationhood'.[18] Race was consequently never an issue for Scruton, for what he has consistently argued is that it is not *blood* which binds a people together, but their *shared values, customs and institutions*. Those are specifically *cultural* features which are inscribed across the surface of a nation. They are the *appearances* that give life and meaning to the *Lebenswelt*; they give it its *personality*, as it were. Hence, a prerequisite of political harmony is that all those dwelling in a particular place, pledge allegiance to its institutions and values. That is why, even at the political level, the aesthetic (*qua* the appearances) is pivotal for the consolidation of membership and national loyalty.

Still, even when that is clearly elucidated, it is hard for someone like Scruton to fend off the accusation that, beneath it all, he is still a racist and a xenophobe. In a number of pronouncements, including his speech to the Vlaams Belang, he suggests why this is so. Scruton believes, despite having lately conceded the truth of his assertions regarding the dangers of multiculturalism, the liberal establishment is still in a state of denial regarding the need for comprehensive integration policies for immigrants. However, by denying that something is wrong, you prevent debate around the issue until it is too late:

... one of the weapons that the elite has used, in order to ensure that it is never troubled by the truths that it denies, is to accuse those who wish to discuss the problem of 'racism and xenophobia'. People of my generation have been brought up in fear of this charge, just as the people of Salem were brought up in fear of being denounced as witches. We saw what happened to Enoch Powell, as a result of a public speech that warned against the dangers ... That was virtually the last time that a British politician dared to warn against the effect of large-scale immigration. Since then an uneasy silence has prevailed at the political level, while discussion at every other level has been hampered by the periodic show-trials of those judged to be guilty of 'racism' – for example, because they have argued that immigrant communities must integrate, and that separatism is intrinsically dangerous: the position adopted by *The Salisbury Review* under my editorship, and which was the cause of my own castigation.[19]

ENOCH POWELL: AN HONEST PATRIOT

The mention of Enoch Powell here is significant for many reasons, not least of which is the fact that, although they are very different in tone and temperament, Scruton has often been identified in the public's perception with the old Tory. Powell was, of course, a leading contributor to *The Salisbury Review,*[20] and, more recently, Scruton came to his defence in a BBC documentary marking the thirtieth anniversary of the latter's notorious 'Rivers of Blood' speech, in which he warned of the dangers to the British state of unlimited immigration.[21] So why does Scruton publicly associate himself with a man so reviled by so many? The answer can be found in a glorious little vignette published in *On Hunting*, which is well worth reproducing here in full:

The [Salisbury] Review celebrated its fifth anniversary [in 1987] with a dinner, at which Enoch Powell was the guest of honour, and since I had to introduce the Right Honourable gentleman, I sat next to him. Intimidating people are not many, but Enoch Powell was one of them. The constant sideways glances from his steely eyes seemed to express a suspicion that he had turned up at the wrong dinner, and that I was trying to make a fool of him. At the same time he radiated a deep and absolutist conviction on every topic that I touched on, leaving a short silence in the wake of his robust paragraphs, into which, it was implied, I was free to stuff my disagreement. His speech, with its level of intonation, Victorian syntax and biblical turns of phrase, belonged with those ancestral voices of Coleridge, prophesying war even while welcoming the pudding. And he gave a distinct impression that present company was no more than temporary – that he might at any moment be lifted by divine intervention from this world of fools to take his former place among the angels. Matters were made worse by the fact that I admired him. He was one of the few politicians for whom England was still the centre of the world. Even if there was something mournful and valedictory in his vision of our country, there was also a wilful, Nelsonian scorn – the kind of scorn of the timid and the ordinary that had saved us in the past and might save us again. He was free of small-talk. Whenever an escape-route appeared in the wall of trivia, his conversation would veer away into sublimities, and the components of British politics – the crown, the common law, the lords and commons – appeared in his discourse not as humdrum collections of modern people but as radiant and transfiguring ideas, which shone above the course of history and cast their great light along the centuries. Long before the pudding appeared, my inability to say anything new on Wagner, Nietzsche or Aeschylus had been conclusively established. As the time for speeches neared, I decided to make one last sally, and to speak about what really interested me. At the mention of fox-hunting, Enoch laid down his fork, and looked at me long and hard, with eyes which had lost their glassy remoteness, and burned with a living fire. He seemed to be noticing me for the first time, as he poured out a confiding flow of memories. Enoch had been a keen follower in his day, and hunting with hounds was for him not only integral to the identity of our kingdom, but also something of profound, almost metaphysical, significance. He spoke of Homer and Xenophon, of Swinburne and Trollope, and painted a romantic picture of Northern Ireland from which I gathered that the Unionist cause is in some mystical way continuous with the survival of classical civilisation and that the connecting link is to be found in hunting. Seeming convinced by now that I was neither a spoof nor an imposter but an apprentice member of the very angelic host that had dispatched him on his mission to the English, Enoch finally addressed me with a question: 'Are you not the same basic size, physically, if not mentally, as I?' – such was its gist. Without waiting for an answer, he offered to sell, at rock bottom price, the hunting costume which lay unused in his chest of drawers at home. The offer was irresistible. A week later I emerged from a small but elegant house near Sloane Square, carrying a pair of hunting boots with mahogany-coloured tops and spurs, and a black coat which – though somewhat tight at the chest, notwithstanding the indignation which had once so magnificently swelled in it – compared favourably to the coats I had seen at the VWH [Vale of White Horse Hunt].[22]

In Powell, Scruton identified the quintessential patriot, someone who passionately loved England, its symbols, ceremonies and customs. Powell was not, for him, as he was for the rest of the left-wing media and its political cheerleaders, a firebrand racist, but someone who had the courage to express the truth, even when it was deeply uncomfortable for many to accept it. The so-called 'Rivers of Blood' speech, which Powell delivered to a meeting of the Birmingham Conservatives in 1968, was for Scruton, 'a speech that raises in its acutest form the question of truth: what place is there for truth in public life, and what should a politician do when comfortable falsehoods have settled down in government, and their uncomfortable negation seeks forlornly for a voice?'[23] As the hysterical reaction to that speech proved, there was little place for truth in the political life of 1960's Britain. Moreover, enshrining 'comfortable falsehoods' at the heart of political policy has had catastrophic consequences. Indeed, Scruton goes so far as to suggest that 'the silencing of Enoch Powell has proved more costly than any other post-war domestic policy in Britain, since it has ensured that immigration can be discussed only now, when it is too late to do anything about it or to confine it to those who come in a spirit of obedience towards the indigenous law'.[24]

Had politicians listened seriously to Powell instead of trying to silence him with charges of racism, they might have understood that what he was really defending was that experience of home to which Scruton has devoted so much of his intellectual energy. It is true, as Scruton himself admits, that Powell's image of 'the Tiber foaming with much blood' was unhelpful. It was 'all too easy to accuse him of scaremongering, and his quotation from the Cumean Sibyl in *Aeneid* Bk VI – which of course nobody recognised – was instantly re-written as "rivers of blood", and he himself dismissed as a dangerous madman'.[25] But underlying Powell's rhetoric was an idea of England as a *place*, one that is 'consecrated by custom'. This, argues Scruton, was a particular conception of patriotism akin to that forged by the Romans, 'in which the homeland, rather than race, was the focus of loyalty'.[26] And when looked at in that way, one can clearly see that the disquiet over immigration was the result, not of racism,

... but of an old experience of home, and a loss of the enchantment which made a home a place of safety and consolation. Until this fatal disenchantment, immigrants were regarded by the English as newcomers to the home, entitled to hospitality while they found their feet. It was thus, for example, that the Huguenots were received, following the revocation of the Edict of Nantes in 1685; likewise the Dutch and German immigrants, who came in such numbers when the English borrowed foreign princes and recycled them as kings. And to this day the right of asylum is an untouchable provision of the English law, and one that survives despite widespread and criminal abuse of it.[27]

TERRITORIAL LOYALTY

As defended by Roger Scruton, patriotism manifests itself in 'a natural love of country, countrymen and the culture that unites them'.[28] The patriot, unlike the nationalist, looks upon his homeland as a place of solace and refuge at day's end. It is there, in that place of settlement, that identity is nourished and the heart consoled. That is why the charge of narrow nationalism is so unfounded in the case of Scruton. For him, the nation state 'has proved to be a stable foundation of democratic government and secular jurisdiction'.[29] Hence, it cannot be equated with those particular nations which were responsible for the genocidal wars of the 20th century. For that is simply to identify 'the normality of the nation state through its pathological versions', such as France in the age of the Revolution or Germany in the age of Hitler. As he rightly argues, 'those were nations gone mad, in which the sources of civil peace had been poisoned and the social organism colonised by anger, resentment and fear'.

But who, on the other hand, has ever felt threatened 'by the Spanish, Italian, Norwegian, Czech or Polish forms of national identity, and who would begrudge those people their right to a territory, a jurisdiction and a sovereignty of their own?'[30] Such nation states are models of democratic order. And that is so because they consist of a 'society of citizens', one in which 'strangers can trust one another, since everybody is bound by a common set of rules'.[31] It is for this reason that they differ fundamentally from their tribal and creedal counterparts, in which individuals do not see themselves as *citizens* subject to a common rule of law, but as 'members of an extended family', or as brothers and sisters in the Faith. Membership in those circumstances is, in other words, characterised exclusively by fidelity to one's own people or to one's own Gods.

In Western society, however, people are bound by their sense of belonging to a common *territory*. Allegiance to the *land* supersedes tribal or religious attachments. That is not to say, of course, that national loyalty relies on the State succumbing to secularism. As Scruton argues:

National loyalty does not rule out religious obedience. The nations of Europe began life as Christian communities, and the boundaries between them often mark out long-standing religious divides ... Nevertheless, once the national idea gains ascendancy, religion is gradually reshaped in terms of it – which is why we distinguish Greek from Russian Orthodox, for example, or the Anglican from the Scandinavian forms of Protestant Christianity. The English experience is particularly important, since it involved the wholesale subordination of the priesthood to the head of state, himself regarded as bound by a territorial law that preceded his accession and also confirmed it.[32]

That said, the problem we face today in the West, and one which people like Ray Honeyford and Enoch Powell prophesied would become a serious threat to social cohesion, is that badly coordinated immigration policies have resulted in migrant communities refusing to give primary allegiance to their host community. Consequently, they cannot be integrated 'into a form of life that perceives exclusion, militancy, and public displays of religious apartness as threats to the experience of membership'.[33] Observe, for example, the dilemmas faced by those wishing to integrate people of the Islamic faith seeking to settle in the West. Whereas Westerners, even those of a devout religious disposition, recognise that the State should be free from religious control, many Muslims do not. The idea that citizens should owe their primary loyalty to the secular constitution, and the rule of law that enforces it, is steadfastly resisted by the Islamic mindset. That is so because, as Scruton correctly writes:

Islamic jurisprudence does not recognise secular, still less territorial, jurisdiction as a genuine source of law. It proposes a universal law that is the single path (*shari'*) to salvation. And the *shari'a* is not understood as setting limits to what can be commanded, but rather as a fully comprehensive system of commands – which can serve a military just as well as a civilian function. Nor does Islam recognise the State as an independent object of loyalty. Obedience is owed first to God, and then, below him, to those situated at greater or lesser remove in the web of personal obligations. Nor is there any trace in Islamic law of the secular conception of government that Christianity inherited (via St Paul) from Roman law.[34]

Of course, St Paul's idea of the Church as something separate from the secular legal order, was presaged by Christ himself in his parable of the tribute money. That parable, in which Christ famously declares: 'Render therefore to Caesar the things that are Caesar's, and unto God the things that are God's', is one that Scruton often cites in defence of his belief that the contemporary Western conception of citizenship has been gifted to us by Christianity. If Islam is founded on the law of God, a law that looks on those who disbelieve as heretics, the Western model of jurisprudence looks upon all those belonging to a given territory as free subjects entitled to their beliefs, so long as those beliefs do not compromise their loyalty to the State. Enlightenment citizenship has, in essence, a specifically *Christian* provenance. Our common culture and the high culture that emerged from it were nourished by the underlying religious conviction that redemption and peace can only be obtained through *forgiveness*. And that is so because forgiveness vanquishes revenge and violence in favour of negotiation and consent. It permits one to live in peace with one's neighbour, in as much as you 'accept his otherness', thus granting him 'in your heart, the freedom to be'. The striking political consequence of this is that a society founded on forgiveness 'tends automatically in a democratic direction, since it is a society in which the voice of the other is heard in all decisions that affect him'. This means that in a democratic society strangers are forgiven their faults and failings by those with whom they share the social space.

Under Sharia Law, however, there is no room for deviation, irony or forgiveness. In the presence of Islam, Scruton writes, 'you have to tread carefully, as though humouring a dangerous animal. The Koran must never be questioned; Islam must be described as a religion of peace ..., and jokes about the Prophet are an absolute no-no. If religion comes up in conversation, best to slip quietly away, accompanying your departure with abject apologies for the Crusades.'[35] Irony, on the other hand, means 'accepting "the other", as someone other than you'. It means tolerating others with whom you might disagree on the basis that they are, first and foremost, *fellow-citizens* prepared to make sacrifices to defend the common home. It means rejecting the idea, espoused by extremist groups such as al-Muhajiroun ('exiles') or the Muslim Brotherhood, that territorial loyalty must take second place to the law of Allah. It means privatising religion and publicly endorsing the secular rule of law. It means 'living with strangers on terms that may be, in the short term, disadvantageous; it means being prepared to fight battles and suffer loses on behalf of people whom you neither know nor particularly want to know'. It means, in sum, 'appropriating the policies that are made in your name and endorsing them as "ours", even when you disagree with them'. [36]

Such is the experience of the 'first-person plural', or the pre-political experience of the 'we'. If the creed community demands obedience to a common object of worship, the first-person plural requires loyalty to the *law of the land*. That, in essence, is what belonging to a nation means: living peacefully with one's neighbours on the basis of a shared history, language and legal norms. Neighbours in a democratic order are not bound together by blood, but by a deep affection for the land and the way that it has been 'mystified', 'personalised' or 'settled'. You will recall that for Scruton, as for Hegel, the individual discovers his identity through the aesthetic symbols that bear witness to the longings of the tribe. The appearances are, in other words, 'endowed with a soul' or a 'subjectivity'. [37] They give a particular place its personality, and in so doing serve as a basis of membership.

Put otherwise: through the appearances the 'I' finds its place among the 'we'. Central to that process is, of course, the law. For, as we saw in the last chapter, the law is also a means by which the land is settled. It transforms a 'shared territory into a shared identity' – the identity of the nation state. Through the law the surface of the *Lebenswelt* is personalised, thus imbuing the territory with a character that commands allegiance and sacrifice. We might say that the law is the 'skin of significance' that attaches to the land, thereby making true national loyalty possible. Peel that skin away, as liberalism recommends, and you won't get justice, but only 'social disintegration'.

The upshot of this is that the form of membership which the nation makes possible is founded 'in the love of place, of the customs and traditions that have been inscribed in the landscape and of the desire to protect these good things through a common law and common loyalty'. And that is why, even at the political level, *culture counts*. For it is in the art and literature of a nation, that you encounter 'a celebration of all that attaches the place to the people and the people to the place'. Indeed, for

Scruton, it is this which marks the real achievement of European civilisation:

Europe owes its greatness to the fact that the primary loyalties of the European people have been detached from religion and re-attached to the land. Those who believe that the division of Europe into nations has been the primary cause of European wars should remember the devastating wars of religion that national loyalties finally brought to an end. And they should study our art and literature for its inner meaning. In almost every case, they will discover, it is an art and literature not of war but of peace, an invocation of home and the routines of home, of gentleness, everydayness and enduring settlement. Its quarrels are domestic quarrels, its protests are pleas for neighbours, its goal is homecoming and contentment with the place that is ours. Even the popular culture of the modern world is a covert re-affirmation of a territorial form of loyalty. *The Archers, Neighbours, EastEnders*: all such comforting mirrors of ordinary existence are in the business of showing settlement and neighbourhood, rather than tribe or religion, as the primary social facts.[38]

This, once again, helps explain why national loyalty should not be confused with nationalism, for nationalism is a corruption of the symbols of peace and homeliness that form the identity of a people. As in the case of the Nazis, those symbols were not used to inspire love of the homeland, but 'to conscript the people to war'. Consequently, the German nation was 'deified, and used to intimidate its members, to purge the common home of those who are thought to pollute it'.[39]

Nationalists of the belligerent variety are, therefore, the very antithesis of what Roger Scruton represents. His has always been a Burkean defence of settled things in the face of those who would wantonly pillage them. That is why, from his earliest political pronouncements, he has consistently underscored the importance of the rule of law and an independent judiciary as that which consolidates and guarantees the 'we' of membership. Conversely, as a 'quasi-religious call to re-create the world', nationalism violently undermines the 'we' feeling of membership. Such, as we have seen, is the reason why, for Burke, the French Revolution was anything but an exercise in liberty. In essence, it was a spectacular triumph for tyranny. Scruton agrees, but he goes further by suggesting that the abolition of the rule of law is the fundamental goal of *all* revolutionary politics. Here is how he describes this terrifying process in his magisterial account of the ideological basis of the French Revolution, 'Man's Second Disobedience':

Tocqueville remarked that there is the greatest difference between a 'revolution' (such as that of 1688, or that which founded the United States of America) through which law and adjudication continue undisturbed and which has the maintenance of law as one of its objects, and a revolution, such as the French, in which legal continuity is cast aside as an obstacle and an irrelevance ... Armed with his Rousseauist doctrines of popular sovereignty, or his Marxist ideas of power and ideology, the revolutionary can de-legitimize any existing institution, and find quite imperceivable the distinction between law aimed at justice, and law aimed at power. His own power is sustained by the promise to abolish it; he is therefore impatient with all institutions which use existing powers, in order not to abolish but to limit them ... Under revolutionary justice you are tried, in the end, not for what you do but for what you are: émigré or kulak, Jew or anti-socialist, enemy of the people or running dog of capitalism – in each case the crime is not an action, but a state of being.[40]

THE DANGERS OF INTERNATIONALISM

The benefits of the nation state are then as follows: it inspires loyalty to the land and the law, above fidelity to tribe or faith. In so doing, it 'confirms our common destiny and attracts our common obedience'. This means that national loyalty is fundamentally 'assumed' by democratic government, for when people are bound by a national 'we' they will place their individual interests below that of the common good. They will peacefully tolerate a government 'whose opinions and decisions they disagree with; they will have no difficulty in accepting the legitimacy of opposition, or the expression of outrageous-seeming views'.[41] That is why, as Scruton argues, 'every attempt to replace national loyalty with some internationalist ideal threatens the historical balance of power and the local forms of equilibrium that depend on it'.[42] For the objective of transnational government, such as the European Union, is precisely the same as that of the revolutionary, if somewhat more benign in form and content: it is to scrape away the cultural topsoil from which territorial loyalty grows. Look back at recent history, urges Scruton, and you will see that it was not nationalism, but *internationalism* which brought the most misery to people. The Communists, for example, sought to institute 'the most comprehensive form of internationalism that has ever been devised'. And they did so by repudiating loyalty to place and people in favour of attachment to a class. Once again, the primary purpose was to destroy the law, which for Marx and Lenin was 'merely an instrument of class oppression, a means to secure the property rights of the bourgeoisie'. Hence by liquidating the bourgeoisie, the need for law would then, as Lenin put it, simply 'wither away', and with it that form of national loyalty which is its precondition.[43]

Now look at what is happening across Europe today, and you will notice the similarities between the bureaucrats of Brussels and their communist forebears. In both cases, there is an 'attempt to make the law and impose it without any reference to any focus of loyalty that could be recognised by the people'. The bureaucrats of the European Union issue diktats and decrees 'without respect for national differences or existing sentiments of legitimacy …'. The result is that law is diminished in the eyes of the ordinary people of Europe. There is moreover 'the growth of a new kind of corruption – a bureaucratised mafia which shields its actions by passing laws which no one is expected to obey, least of all the bureaucrats'.[44] How, inquires Scruton, could such a body ever command the *pre-political loyalty* of its citizens? It could not, simply because all 'the factors that formed the loyalties of the European peoples – shared language, shared religion, shared customs, shared legal systems, and shared ways of life – are absent'.[45]

Bodies like the EU and the UN[46] are, in other words, destroying the territorial loyalties which once 'formed the basis of European legitimacy'. They ignore the fact that the ordinary people of Europe do not consider themselves citizens of the world, but are 'creatures of flesh and blood, with finite attachments and territorial instincts, whose primary loyalties are shaped by family, religion and homeland …'.[47] The attempt to subsume the European nation states into a federal body is, thus, a flawed project. But that does nothing to prevent European *oikophobes* from continuing to declare war on the nation, as witnessed in their insistence that Ireland hold a second referendum after it resoundingly rejected the Lisbon Treaty in 2008. It does nothing to stop them from striking at the heart of the culture of old Europe, as enshrined in the educational curricula of individual member nations. It does nothing to stop them peddling the well-worn line that European-Western civilisation is illegitimate, nothing but an ideological construct 'manufactured by the ruling classes in order to serve their interests and bolster their power'.[48]

That is why, for Scruton, the EU is but a political version of the culture of repudiation. And therein is the great difference between it and the United States of America. Both are federations, and yet American federalism does not aim at empire. When it undertakes foreign adventures, it does not do so in order to colonise other nations, but rather to restore their sense of nationhood. Sometimes, that ambition may be misguided, as in the case of Iraq – an artificial entity that never has been and never will be, as Scruton rightly observes, a nation state. It has never been 'a *country*, a place defined as *ours*, where *our* way of doing things prevails, and which must be defended at all costs if *our* way of life and web of affections is to survive'.[49] Still, even if President George W. Bush did not fully appreciate the fact that democracy is not the default mode of people the world over, that it 'depends upon a pre-existing rule of law and established customs upholding the freedom of individuals and the rights of minorities', he did not invade Iraq in order to conquer but to liberate it from the manacles of a vicious tyrant.[50] And he did so, despite what the cynics claim to the contrary, to defend the national interest.

Defending the national interest is something that America takes seriously because, despite its vast size and federal system, it is a proud nation state. It is, Scruton writes, 'nearly unique among the states that have a seat at the United Nations in being both united and a nation. It is the last integrated nation state in a world of imperial, tribal and religious powers'.[51] That is why, he suggests, anti-Americanism has become so fashionable amongst Europeans: for Europe has failed where America, despite its many problems, has succeeded. In America, Europeans catch a glimpse 'of their own past, in the days before cynicism and nihilism wiped away their sense of home. They observe a country trusting its own people, as they once trusted theirs, to rise in the common defence. They see a country that can still confess to its faults and repent of its mistakes, because it is confident in its good intentions'.[52]

America is, in other words, a proud and patriot nation state, one that is not embarrassed to rehearse, on a daily basis, its founding myths. A nation's myth of origin is, of course, essential to its sense of identity. It tells of how the land was settled and mystified – how it acquired its distinct personality. In the case of America, however, the founding myth is unique, for 'it focuses on a precise moment, the moment of the Founding Fathers, heroes who stand higher in the narrative of history than ever they stood in reality, and who bequeathed to their countrymen a text every bit as sacred as the Hebrew Bible or the Holy Koran'. This text, explains Scruton, is both 'sacred in its origins and secular in its effect', in as much as it enshrines the 'Enlightenment conception of citizenship, purged of all belligerence and defiance'. It thus commits people to a shared destiny in defiance of all that 'might otherwise drive them apart'.[53]

In Europe, however, American patriotism is condemned as little more than jumped-up jingoism. Its founding myth is derided as a threatening example of that racism and xenophobia 'which is lurking under every bed'. Indeed, *all* national myths of origin are now looked upon by the political elite of Europe as unsophisticated fairytales unsuited to the modern world. Scruton explains:

Some of our national narratives have been scribbled over and cancelled out, like that of the Germans. Others have become stories of class-conflict and oppression, like that now told in English schools, or records of belligerent episodes that never paid off – like the national stories that no longer appeal to the French. Everywhere we find a kind of repudiation of those fortifying legends on which nations have always depended for their sense of identity. Whether this is the cause of our loss of sovereignty or an effect of it is hard to tell. Maybe it is a bit of both. But it is certain that the European Union does its best to encourage the debunking of national narratives. The EU-sponsored history textbook, which is now proposed as a basic text for both French and German schools, says little about France and Germany as nation states, representing their history as a series of unfortunate conflicts on the way to a Union where conflicts can no longer occur. The textbook is consistently anti-American and equates America with the Soviet Union as joint causes of the Cold War and of the tensions that divided Europe.

And why is this happening? For Scruton, the answer is very clear:

The EU cannot create a rival identity to the nation state, unless it can identify itself as something superior to the nation states. It must become a project of release from the errors and crimes of nationhood. And this means identifying the nation state as a symptom of the adolescence of mankind, a stage on the way to transnational maturity. And it also involves identifying the last great nation state in the modern world – the United States of America – as an example of what must be overcome, if mankind is to enter a secure and peaceful possession of patrimony.[54]

Put simply: America constantly serves to remind Europe that it is impossible to have a community 'based in repudiation'. Destroy the political *Lebenswelt* by peeling away one's founding narratives, and you won't reveal the 'really real'. You will simply create a culture of alienation, in which people drift without any sense of home, settlement or belonging. It is then, 'when loyalties no longer stretch across generations or define themselves in territorial terms', that democratic societies fracture. It is then that the young, having no sense of domestic security, are forced to 'confront a moral void'. And what follows is that which we are currently witnessing: 'Either they reach for some new form of loyalty, like the members of al-Muhajiroun, or they obliterate the demands of society entirely, through a collective dissipation of the will to inherit – a dissipation that is both cause and effect of the sex-and-drugs lifestyle of the modern teenager'.[55] In other words, the culture of repudiation has sought to undermine the only thing that could possibly ensure the successful integration of newcomers. By denouncing Western civilisation and the nation state, it deprives people of those 'rites of passage and forms of submission that grant, at the end of the long hard road of adolescence, the transition to a higher form of membership'.[56] In so doing, immigrants have nothing to join except those tribal and religious forms of membership which they carry with them into the West. As Scruton puts it in *The West and the Rest*:

Entering this new and bewildering political labyrinth the Muslim immigrant will certainly find a freedom and a prosperity that are unfamiliar in his country of origin. He will also enjoy welfare benefits, free education – or at any rate 'education' – for his children, and free medical services. He will find plenty of work on the illegal market, since the states of the European Union have raised the cost of employing people to the point where small enterprises can no longer afford to offer work in the official economy. What the Muslim immigrant will not find, however, is any process of nation-building that might serve to recruit him to membership in the surrounding social order. He will live in strict isolation, and regard the world in which he earns his living as of no independent concern to him. Such membership as he enjoys will come to him from his family and the immigrant community to which his family belongs. And it will depend upon their shared obedience to the rituals of prayer and fasting and to the revealed will of God.[57]

IN SEARCH OF SOMEWHERE

So what is the solution to the political version of the culture of desacralisation? According to Scruton, we must reinforce the nation state as a bulwark against internationalism. That would mean rejecting global government in favour of those 'negotiated solutions, consensual institutions and legal precedents on which our democracies depend'.[58] In saying that, however, one must insist on the distinction between internationalism and *cosmopolitanism*. Whereas the internationalist is someone who sets out to destroy local loyalties and attachments, 'and who does not feel at home in any city because he is an alien in all', the cosmopolitan takes pride in his own nation. That said, he is also someone 'who appreciates human life in all its peaceful forms, and is emotionally in touch with the customs, languages, and culture of many different peoples'. He is, as Scruton nicely phrases it, 'a patriot of one country, but a nationalist of many'.[59] We can, in other words, be cosmopolitans without being internationalists.

If the internationalist trades in alienation by seeing the world 'as one vast system in which everyone is equally a customer, a consumer, a creature of wants and needs', the cosmopolitan endeavours to reinforce settled things. He looks with deep suspicion on what we now call 'globalization', not because he rejects the free market, but because he believes that by pursuing free trade at all costs, we threaten the very 'thing that makes international trade into a durable and beneficial feature of the human condition – namely national sovereignty'. Look at anti-globalization protests by farmers and local communities in that light and you will see that these are not only 'protests on behalf of a poor way of life against what may prove to be a wealthier one'. They are, much more importantly, 'a protest on behalf of the way of life that they can call *ours*, against a way of life from elsewhere – indeed from nowhere'. They are the defiant shouts of patriots from *somewhere*, in the face of a 'presumptuous force that roams the world like a tempest, vandalising everything in its path'.[60]

Restoring that old sense of somewhere, that peaceful paradise we know as home, is the ultimate aim of Roger Scruton's political philosophy. It is a celebration of the soil 'as an object of worship and a source of moral strength'. In Scruton's account, the soil becomes that source of such strength when it surpasses tribal and religious attachments as a primary source of loyalty. It is then that it takes on a 'quasi-theological character' in the minds of all those who seek settlement. As he says, 'nowhere becomes somewhere when we settle there'.[61] Alienation is then surmounted as people fulfil their instinctual need to be rooted to a particular place, living on peaceful terms with their neighbours, and striving 'to make that place more agreeable to all'.

Internationalism is, however, the glorification of *nowhere* and of *nothingness*. It produces rootless and ruthless beings who whizz 'around from one place to another without any sense of belonging to any of them'. It desecrates once-beautiful cities like Brussels, rendering them desolate 'except for the cars and taxis which take the stuffed suits from meeting to meeting'.[62] In such ghost towns, only an 'outline of the city remains', the old *Lebenswelt* having long-since been repudiated in favour of a postmodern paradise. No settlement, no belonging, no dwelling – *nothing*.

If, therefore, Roger Scruton has one central political message for this age, it is this: let us put 'something in place of nothing, and love in place of denial'. Let us rediscover, as he has done through farming and fox hunting, communities founded in 'love and affirmation'. Let us, in short, start living and caring for one another as people did in the old world. But that, in turn, means retreating from the global back to the local and being clear 'as to who we are'.[63] It means learning once more the value of 'patience and sacrifice, of rooted loves and settled customs'.[64] And being thus deflected from 'our self-centred projects', we are offered 'a guarantee of national survival'.[65]

Such is the true lesson of conservative politics. And it is not one to be found in the despair-ridden tomes of Michel Foucault, Karl Marx or Jean-Paul Sartre – thinkers for whom the human world (*Lebenswelt*) is a mere construct. All those features of human existence which make it worthwhile – the person, the sacred and the aesthetic are, they tell us, just artefacts that may be dispensed with 'whenever the better functioning of the whole requires it'. When the conservative looks at the human form, he sees a portal to the divine. He encounters the 'incarnation of reason' and the principal source of the sacred on earth. For him, the other is a font of freedom and subjectivity in the midst of a mute world of objects. But for the high priests of the culture of repudiation, the human subject, and all those institutions which preserve and protect it, 'can be placed in the balance of calculation and discarded for the sake of the "liberation" of mankind'. And that is because nothing is sacred or divine for the liberator.

Whereas the conservative sees the 'little platoons' of civil society as enshrining the personality of their members, the liberator views them as centres of oppression. He looks upon them with contempt because they speak to him of somewhere – a settled sphere in which people 'combine in a spirit of conciliation, willing to renounce even their dearest ambitions for the sake of agreement with their fellows'. There is no room in such a place for the individual ego, or the culture of rights on which it thrives. Those who dwell somewhere are guided by the spirit of cooperation, duty and obligation. Theirs is a culture of responsibility in which the needs of the entire community are factored into all decisions. Hence the will of the 'we' becomes that of the 'I'. And from this experience of membership, argues Scruton, great emotions arise in us:

… our sense of duty is spread more widely than the circle which inspired it, to embrace other places and other times. We come at last to respect the dead and the unborn, and this is the experience on which free and stable government is founded.[66]

In contrast to the revolutionary who wishes to tear everything down in pursuit of an 'idealised freedom', and to extirpate all 'humble forms of human life', Scruton seeks to restore a society rooted in obedience: obedience to one's family, one's neighbours, to the community and the State. His is a philosophy which recognises that without obedience, authority and sacrifice, we end up with a 'peculiar society, devoid of counsel, in which decisions have the impersonality of a machine'. But when you view the surrounding world as endowed with sanctity, you will willingly respond to the claims of those individuals and institutions that constitute the homeland. You will sacrifice on their behalf, and work to ensure that future generations can claim what is rightfully theirs.

Scruton's is, therefore, a philosophy that repudiates abstract right as a 'phantom' which 'poisons our attachment to the realities through which we might, in our fallen condition, live and find fulfilment'.[67] As we have seen, the fundamental reality for the conservative is the nation, defined as 'a sphere of local duties and loyalties'. But it is also the sphere of freedom – not freedom from constraint, but liberty that is realised through negotiation, compromise and cooperation. Hence, a truly free society is not one which repudiates the law and squanders the sacred in the name of revolution, rights, excess or equality. It is, rather, 'a community of free beings, bound by the laws of sympathy and by the obligations of family love'. Conservative constraint is, therefore, *moral* constraint. That is why liberals are so committed to the notion that morality, especially that surrounding sexuality, is none of our business. For in the liberal mind, at least as it is shaped by John Stuart Mill, everything is permitted so long as no one is harmed in the process. Liberty is thus confused with licence in the culture of rights.

Scruton responds to this by simply pointing out that without moral constraint, 'there can be no cooperation, no family commitment, no long-term prospects, no hope of economic, let alone social, order'. Indeed, in a society devoid of moral constraint, it is the State which rushes in to fill the moral vacuum. For when people are no longer prepared to take responsibility for their own lives, when they refuse 'to commit themselves to others or to social networks', or when they prefer to enrich the ego rather than perform acts of self-sacrifice, it is then that the State must assume the role of the parent or guardian of licentious children. The result, warns Scruton, is not a gain, but a loss of political liberty. Why so? Because the State, he says, always comes with an agenda: 'it is less interested in freeing people than in equalising them, less interested in upholding responsible choice than in extending its relief to the irresponsible.'[68]

And so, in the end, Roger Scruton urges his readers to eschew the lust for transgression which characterises the philosophies of liberalism and liberation. For they are nothing but 'lies and delusions, products of sentimentality which has veiled the facts of human nature'. We should instead go in search of somewhere, recognising that what we have is a precious gift which no one has any 'God-given right to destroy'. It is then that we shall finally understand that we are members of 'something greater than ourselves', and that all religious, aesthetic and political experience is nothing other than a search for community, which is 'at the same time a search for home'.

NOTES

1. Scruton, *The Meaning of Conservatism*, p.29.
2. Scruton, *Gentle Regrets*, p.55.
3. *Ibid.*, p.52.
4. Ray Honeyford, 'Education and Race' in *The Salisbury Review*, Roger Scruton (ed.), Vol. 2, No. 2, Winter 1984, p.20. Reprinted in *Conservative Thoughts: Essays from The Salisbury Review*, Roger Scruton (ed.) (London: The Claridge Press, 1988), pp.91–99, and in *The Salisbury Review*, Vol. 26, No. 1, Autumn 2007, pp.17–20.
5. Honeyford, *The Salisbury Review*, Autumn 2007, p.17.
6. Scruton wrote for *The Times* from 1983–1986. His columns are collected in *Untimely Tracts* (London: The Macmillan Press, 1987).
7. *Ibid.*, pp.137–139.
8. See Scruton, *Gentle Regrets*, p.52.
9. See Scruton, *Untimely Tracts*, p.234, and his stunning little book on *Lebanon, A Land Held Hostage: Lebanon and the West* (London: The Claridge Press, 1987). As a journalist who has had the dubious honour of publicly debating Robert Fisk in recent years (especially regarding his stance on Iraq), I view *A Land Held Hostage* as a landmark text. In it, Scruton courageously rows against the tide of pro-Fisk adulation and questions the real motivation behind the latter's anti-Western diatribes. As an example, here is one fine passage worth quoting in full: 'On February 3rd of this year [1987], returning from Beirut, I happened to pick up a copy of the previous day's *Times* at Larnaca airport. The Terry Waite affair was engaging the attention of the press, American citizens had just been forbidden to set foot in Lebanon, and the newspapers were more than normally attentive to the situation there. Sure enough, there was the routine article by Robert Fisk, prominently displayed, describing the poor Shi'ite communities, "driven in their tens of thousands by Israeli raids to the slums of the capital", and ignored by the "predominantly Christian government". I read again of the West's preference for a "Christian-controlled" order in the Lebanon; of the Palestinian victims in their squalid camps, who were so brutally massacred by the Christian militia in the wake of Israel's invasion; of the "friendly thoughtful Shi'as" whose patience had been driven to breaking point by the "foreigners", and who had adopted the Iranian flag – as sure a symbol of "the struggle against oppression" in West Beirut as was the tricolour in Eighteenth-Century Europe. The article continued by a process of free association to its foreseeable conclusion. An American woman complains to one of the marines who came in 1984 to "rescue her from terrorists", that "it is you who have turned my friends into my enemies and forced me to go". Fisk signed off with the remark that the Americans in Beirut were "saying that again this weekend". I read the article with some interest, since that same edition of *The Times* carried another, and more up-to-date article by Fisk, concerning Iranian matters and sent from Tehran. In fact he had not been seen in Beirut for some weeks (at least, by those to whom I spoke during my visit). Nor did the article show any awareness of the actual situation in

Lebanon. It might have been written two years ago; and it seemed to have no other purpose than to black in for the hundredth time the contours of a caricature whose credibility derives nothing more than Fisk's habit of repeating it. But then, I reflected, suppose Robert Fisk had written the *truth* about the Islamic militancy which is now at work in Lebanon: would he have been able to reside comfortably in the Iranian capital? Suppose he had, over the years, written the truth about the Syrian occupation: would he have been able to claim that special expertise which attaches – he hastens to inform us – to those who can travel freely "North of Baalbek" (i.e. into the zone occupied for the past ten years by Syria)? Or suppose he had written the truth about the Palestinians, whose lawless cohorts roamed the countryside of Lebanon, tormenting the Shi'ite and Christians alike, and driving thousands from their homes, long before the Israeli invasion: would he have been able to enjoy the comfort, along with so many other Western correspondents, of a West Beirut hotel owned by the Palestinians? And would he have been able to travel freely in countries whose leaders depend for their legitimacy on a united opposition to the "Zionist enemy", and on a selfless championship of the Palestinian cause (a championship which has invariably stopped short of offering the Palestinians a home)?' Pp.12–13.

It was also Fisk that Scruton had in mind when he penned that truly great column in *The Times*, 'In Memory of Iran' (6 November 1984), a piece which begins with the following astonishing lines: 'Who remembers Iran? Who remembers, that is, the shameful stampede of Western journalists and intellectuals to the cause of the Iranian revolution? Who remembers the hysterical propaganda campaign waged against the Shah, the lurid press reports of corruption, police oppression, palace decadence, constitutional crisis? Who remembers the thousands of Iranian students in Western universities enthusiastically absorbing the fashionable Marxist nonsense purveyed to them by armchair radicals, so as one day to lead the campaign of riot and mendacity which preceded the Shah's downfall?' Scruton concludes by observing that 'it is difficult now for a Western correspondent to enter Iran, and if he did so it would not be fun. He would not, like the ghouls who send their dispatches from Beirut, adopt a public posture of the front-line hero. He would have to witness, quietly and in terror of his life, things which beggar description: the spontaneous "justice" of the revolutionary guards, the appalling scenes of violence, torture and demonic frenzy, the public humiliation of women, the daily sacrifice of lives too young to be conscious of the meaning for which they are condemned to destruction. He would also have to confront the truth which has been staring him in the face for years, and which he could still recognize had the habit of confessing to his errors been preserved: the truth that limited monarchy is the right form of government for Iran, which can be saved only by the restoration of the Shah's legitimate successor. But such a result would be in the interests not only of the Iranian people, but also of the West. Hence few Western journalists are likely to entertain it'. *Untimely Tracts*, pp.190–191.

During a heated debate on Irish television in 2005, Fisk told me that just before departing Baghdad Airport en route to Dublin, a rocket had missed his head by inches (yet more public posturing of the front-line hero). His point was that Al-Qaeda was by then so strong in Iraq that they were on the verge of taking the airport. I replied: 'They probably knew you were coming here tonight, Robert, and wanted some free publicity'. Fisk responded in anger: 'Very funny, Mark, very funny indeed!'

10. Scruton, *Gentle Regrets*, p.53.

11. Scruton, 'Sense and Censorship: The Case of *The Salisbury Review*' in *The Salisbury Review*, Vol. 26, No. 1, Autumn 2007, p.22 (first published in *The Salisbury Review*, 1986).

12. Scruton, *Gentle Regrets*, p.55.

13. Cited in Scruton, *Thinkers of the New Left*, p.76.

14. Antonio Gramsci, *Prison Notebooks: Selections* (London: Lawrence and Wishart Limited, 2005).

15. Scruton, *Thinkers of the New Left*, p.85.

16. Scruton, 'The Left Establishment' in *The Philosopher on Dover Beach*, p.287.

17. Scruton, 'Immigration, Multiculturalism and the Need to Defend the Nation State', Speech given to the Vlaams Belang, Antwerp, 23 June 2006, and reproduced on *The Brussels Journal* at *www.brusselsjournal.com*.

18. *Ibid.*

19. *Ibid.*

20. Powell's 1988 contribution to *The Salisbury Review*: 'By Our Consent: Britain and Europe', was reproduced for the periodical's twenty-fifth anniversary edition. See Vol. 26, No. 1, Autumn 2007, pp.24–26.

21. See 'Rivers of Blood', *White Season*, BBC2, 8 March 2008.

22. Scruton, *On Hunting*, pp.54–56.

23. Scruton, 'Should He have Spoken?' in *The New Criterion*, September 2006. I am citing from the online edition, which is available at: *www.newcriterion.com/articles.cfm/have-spoken-2450*. It is also included in *The Roger Scruton Reader*, Mark Dooley (ed.) (London: Continuum, 2009).

24. *Ibid.*

25. Scruton, 'Immigration, Multiculturalism and the Need to Defend the Nation State'.

26. Scruton, *England: An Elegy*, p.7.

27. *Ibid.*, pp.7–8.

28. Scruton, *A Political Philosophy*, p.3.

29. *Ibid.*, p.2.

30. *Ibid.*, p.3.

31. *Ibid.*, p.7.

32. Scruton, *The West and the Rest*, p.47. It is important to note that although Scruton perceives the separation of Church and State as a precondition for political harmony, he does not subscribe to the liberal interpretation of the 'no establishment' clause. As he writes, religious people 'are by nature hostile to license, strive to control their sexual lives, and are usually first in the exercise of those conservative virtues that get up the liberal nose. They are eager to teach children the norms of restraint and decency; they are in favour of discipline and respect and on the whole support the adult against the adolescent in all matters where the two conflict. Hence the advocates of self-expression and moral anarchy would like to marginalise religious people, and to remove their influence from the public space of our culture. To this end, they have reinterpreted the "no establishment" clause not as *permitting* religion but as *forbidding* it. Religion, they argue, is excluded from every office, activity, or social arena governed (however indirectly) by the State – so there cannot be prayers or Bible classes in public schools, there cannot be any acknowledgement of God, the Ten Commandments, or the ascendancy of the Christian religion in any legal or political institution, and those who receive state support for their charitable work among the poor and the broken-hearted cannot use the Bible as their guide. Never has a more effective means

been discovered, of cutting off a whole people from its inheritance of moral and spiritual capital than this one, whereby the constitution devised to permit religious beliefs is used as an instrument for suppressing them.' Scruton, 'The Limits of Liberty', p.52. See also, Scruton, 'Religious Freedom in America' in *The American Spectator*, 13 February 2007. This article is available at: *www.spectator.org.*

33. *Ibid.*, p.51.
34. *Ibid.*, p.66.
35. Roger Scruton, 'Islamofascism: Beware of a Religion without Irony' in *The Wall Street Journal*, 20 August 2006. I am citing from the online edition, which is available at: *www.opinionjournal.com/editorial.* I can personally testify to the truth of Scruton's assertion regarding having to tread carefully in the presence of Islam. Writing in the *Sunday Independent* in 2005, I called for Irish Islamic leaders to show good authority by encouraging moderation among the faithful. In the same article, I revealed that certain elements within the Irish Islamic community were actively engaged with militant groups. I also cited an interview with Ireland's leading Imam, in which he refused to say that Irish constitutional law is the only law that counts in Ireland. The day after the article was published I received threatening phone calls from senior members of the Islamic community. And one week later, as I was appearing on television, the police got wind of yet another threat. That prompted them to place surveillance on my home. But as Roger Scruton wryly remarked when I told him that story: 'Instead of putting surveillance on people like you, why don't the police put their resources into tracking down those responsible for the threats?'

In a similar vein, he cites the case of a French schoolteacher Robert Redeker who, in 2006, 'published an article in *Le Figaro* arguing that Christians, when incited to violence in the name of *their* religion, can find no authority for this in the life and words of Christ as recorded in the Gospel, while Muslims, incited to violence in the name of their religion, can find plenty of support for their belligerence in the Koran'. For his troubles, Mr Redeker received death-threats, forcing him and his family into hiding under police protection. Scruton considers this as a typical example of European cowardice in the face of fascism: 'The reaction of the French authorities typifies the European response. Critics of Islam are not defended, but marginalised, by removing them from society and keeping them under house arrest. Instead of going after those who threatened Mr Redeker with every weapon available to the law, instead of passing legislation of whatever severity might be required to restore the freedoms that have been gratuitously removed by the newcomers, the European authorities try to bluff their way to peace through appeasement, while pushing Islam's critics off the stage. It is now increasingly rare for public discussion of Islam and its stance to proceed with the open-minded concern for truth that is necessary if the discussion is to get us anywhere. Europe has seen private enterprise censorship of the Islamist kind before: notably when the fascists worked to take power in Italy and the Nazis in Germany. But Europe has not learned the lesson. People living under secular government, and enjoying the comforts of a modern economy, easily become blind to the deep religious need of our species. They readily assume that religious passions can be quelled by a dose of Enlightenment, and that a sprinkling of skepticism will suffice to quell those perverted passions, like Nazism and fascism, that arise in religion's place. And when the truth suddenly displays itself, they stare aghast, utter abject apologies, and quickly retreat from the field.' Scruton, 'Religious Freedom in America'.

36. Roger Scruton, 'Friends, Muslims countrymen, lend us your ears' in *The Sunday Times*, 15 February 2004. I am citing from the online edition, which is available at: *www. timesonline.co.uk/tol/news/article1020161.ece*. One should not, however, give the impression that Scruton is in any way 'Islamophobic'. In many contexts, he has expressed a deep admiration for the 'natural piety' of Islam, and the way of life that it encourages. For example, in *The West and the Rest* he writes that Islam 'is less a theological doctrine than a system of *piety*'. It is, he argues, a 'system that safeguards the family as the primary object of loyalty and trust; that clarifies and disciplines sexual conduct; that sanctifies ordinary obligations of friendship and kinship; and that lays down rules for business that have a power to exonerate as well as to blame'. We should, moreover, 'recognise the immense importance of the *madrasah* in providing young people with a loyalty and a rite of passage that they can no longer easily obtain from our own secular schools. Backward though Islamic education may seem, when judged in terms of free inquiry and scientific rigour, it is vastly superior, from the moral and cultural point of view, to the education now available to a great many young people in Western cities. It teaches piety, consideration, and respect for age; it offers a clear rite of passage into the adult world; it presents the student at every point with certainties rather than doubts, and consolation rather than anxiety. It also promotes the study of classical Arabic, and leads the student to commit vast amounts of a great and dignified text to memory, so providing what most modern people lack to their detriment – namely, a repertoire of quotations, maxims, and well-crafted sayings upon which to draw in one's daily life and relationships ... In short, it is an education that provides what the liberal systems of education in Western states have, disastrously despised – authority'. *The West and the Rest*, pp.104–106.

   It should also be noted that in the wake of the Mohammed cartoon controversy in 2006, Scruton was the sole member of the conservative commentariat to call for accommodation between Christianity and Islam. In a sensitively written piece for the *Daily Mail*, he wrote that we need to understand 'that icons and rituals are holy things, and that it is our duty to respect them, even when – especially when – we regard them as ridiculous. This discipline is hard, and I confess that I have often strayed from it. But it is the precondition of peaceful co-existence. This does not mean that we should not criticise another's religion or mention the unpalatable truths about its followers. On the contrary, there can be no accommodation between Muslim and Christian culture if we surround all points of disagreement with a veil of frightened silence. I'm ashamed that Christians established the Inquisition, pillaged Constantinople and the Holy Land, and imposed colonial systems of government in Muslim lands. I expect Muslims to challenge me about these things, and I know that I must be prepared to discuss them and to show, if I can, that they are deviations from the Christian message. But then, Muslims should reciprocate. Murder, pillage and conquest have been part of their legacy too, and we urgently need to hear them acknowledge these crimes and also repudiate them as violations of their faith. The purpose of this debate is not to score points, but to remind each other of our shared humanity and its imperfections, and of the need for courtesy and respect if we are to live together as citizens.' Roger Scruton, 'Decent debate mustn't be the victim' in the *Daily Mail*, 3 February 2006, p.6.
37. Scruton, *England: An Elegy*, p.12.
38. Roger Scruton, *The Need for Nations* (London: Civitas, 2004), pp.16–17; *A Political Philosophy*, p.14.

39. Scruton, *The Need for Nations*, p.18.

40. Scruton, *The Philosopher on Dover Beach*, pp.212–213.

41. Scruton, *The Need for Nations*, p.23.

42. Scruton, *The West and the Rest*, p.61.

43. See Roger Scruton, 'The Dangers of Internationalism' in *The Intercollegiate Review*, Fall/Winter, 2005, p.30.

44. *Ibid.*, p.33.

45. Scruton, *The West and the Rest*, p.154.

46. See Scruton, 'The United States, the United Nations, and the Future of the Nation-State' in *The Heritage Foundation: Heritage Lectures*, No. 794. Available at: *www.heritage.org/research/internationalorganisations/hI794.cfm*. See also *A Political Philosophy*, where Scruton observes that a 'national parliament is accountable to the people who elected it, and must serve their interests ... A transnational assembly need obey – and can obey – no such constraints. Normally, it has just one legislative goal – in the case of the World Trade Organisation the advancement of free trade – and no duty to reconcile that goal with all other goods and needs of a real human society. That is why its rulings are so dangerous. They are made on the strength of reasoning that ignores the real database from which rational political choices must be made. The UN Convention on Asylum and Refugees was proposed as an answer to one problem only – and a problem whose scale and gravity have since immeasurably increased. The UN assembly has no duty to reconcile its ruling with the many interests which will inevitably conflict with it, and no duty to return the matter when conditions have changed. The ruling is therefore irrational, in the true sense of ignoring almost all the data that are relevant to its justification'. P.29.

47. Scruton, *The Need for Nations*, p.31.

48. Scruton, *The West and the Rest*, p.79.

49. Roger Scruton, 'The Nation-State and Democracy' in *The American Spectator*, 14 February 2007. Available at: *http://spectator.org/archives/2007/02/14/the-nation-state-and-democracy*. Reproduced in *The Roger Scruton Reader*, Mark Dooley (ed.) (London: Continuum, 2009).

50. Scruton gives a philosophical justification for the decision to invade Iraq in 'Immanuel Kant and the Iraq War' on *www.openDemocracy.net*, 19 February 2004. The article can be found at: *www.opendemocracy.net/faith-iraqwarphiloshophy/article_1749.jsp*.

51. Scruton, 'The Nation-State and Democracy'.

52. *Ibid.*

53. *Ibid.*

54. *Ibid.*

55. Scruton, *The West and the Rest*, p.82.

56. *Ibid.*, pp.81–82.

57. *Ibid.*, p.155.

58. Scruton, *The Need for Nations*, p.41.

59. Scruton, 'The Dangers of Internationalism', p.35.

60. Scruton, *The Need for Nations*, p.45.

61. Scruton, *News from Somewhere*, p.3.

62. Scruton, *On Hunting*, p.159.

63. Scruton, *A Political Philosophy*, p.46.

64. Scruton, *News from Somewhere*, p.174.
65. Scruton, *Gentle Regrets*, p.56.
66. Scruton, *Modern Philosophy*, p.475.
67. Scruton, *The Philosopher on Dover Beach*, p.327.
68. Scruton, 'The Limits of Liberty', p.54.

Afterword

It was just before Christmas in 2019 when I travelled to Sunday Hill Farm, Scruton's fabled home in Wiltshire. I was there to chat about his health and some future collaborations that we had planned. When he was diagnosed with cancer earlier that year, he had written asking me to visit so that we could, as he put it, 'chat about the future'.

'Scrutopia', as he liked to call it, looked the same as it always had: a quaint oasis in the heart of Wiltshire that gives food for thought and much thought to food. It is a genuine settlement that roots you to the past, to culture and to the land. On my previous visits, Roger invariably cooked, blending purchased produce with that grown on the farm. In everything, he practised what he preached. Hence, he lived as a farmer, yet wrote like an angel. And, in his mind, the two were perfectly compatible. For through writing, he could richly convey a sense of what it meant to belong somewhere rather than nowhere. In his mind, we each yearn to belong to that little patch of earth that we call 'home'. A true home is one that binds us to the soil as much as to the soul, for in this is to be found our lasting identity as human beings. In Wagner and wine, in Hegel and hunting, we discover redemption from loneliness, alienation and that tragic sense of life that has become the default mode of modern existence.

In all my writings on Roger Scruton, I have consistently identified him as a philosopher of love. Against those who, in the name of 'progress', wish to 'liberate' us from our past, our traditions and cultural heritage, Scruton showed us why it is important to love and cherish such things. We love them because they reveal to us who we are and where we came from. In them, we discover the roots of our common home and the story of how we came to settle there. To denounce them as 'oppressive', 'patriarchal' or 'exclusionary', is to deny absent generations a say in how we live now. It is to silence our dead and to disenfranchise future generations from the inherited wisdom which is rightfully theirs. Restoring the love of existing things – of 'community, home and settlement' – was the central theme of Roger Scruton's social, cultural and political outlook. As such, his was a philosophy of consolation for people tired of repudiation and rejection, of nihilism and naysaying.

After two days, I left Sunday Hill Farm, not with a sense of foreboding, but grateful for having had the chance to spend more time with a truly great man. In *Conversations with Roger Scruton*, I suggested that he was best defined as a 'man of letters.' He loved that description, for it best summed up the extraordinary life that he lived. In my career as a philosopher and journalist, I have met and known some remarkable minds. None, however, could hold a flame to Roger Scruton. He was a genius of the first rank, someone who could master any subject and make it his own. He was not born to privilege, but to a modest home with socialist values and an aversion to culture. And yet, through sheer hard work, he rose to become the most articulate defender of high culture in the contemporary era. In Wagner and Wittgenstein, in Kant and Kierkegaard, he saw an answer to postmodern nihilism. Like Hegel, he believed that human fulfilment requires art, religion and philosophy. For only in these things can be found the meaning of who we are as subjects. And that is because they offer redemption from time by giving us a vision of what lies beyond it.

I cannot say that Scruton was a deeply religious man, in the sense that he was devoutly observant. As he once said to me, however, it is in the religious experience that 'the opposition between the aesthetic and the ethical is transcended and reconciled, since that is what the encounter with the sacred ultimately is – a fusing of the experience of beauty with the moral order'. We have lost touch with beauty, just as we no longer affirm the moral sense. As such, the modern world is more profane than sacred. If we need Roger Scruton, it is because he shows us a way to reconcile beauty with the moral order. He shows why our deepest longings will remain unsatisfied once we deny truth, goodness and the beautiful. And, in so doing, he rescues the sacred from the decline of religion.

I was celebrating my fiftieth birthday when I received the news that Roger Scruton had died. During our last weekend together, I watched in silent grief as he began to rise 'above the wind of contingency that blows through the natural world'. In a way, he had already passed through the window of our empirical world to that 'other sphere' about which he had so often written so beautifully and persuasively. He was dying, yet he was also rising to assume the transcendental standpoint which, he believed, was the answer and the solution to every form of pseudoscience. Whether it was aiding dissidents in Communist Czechoslovakia or abandoning the academy for a life of farming and writing, Scruton had always given concrete expression to his ideals. In his own life, he had always given witness to what he believed in and resolutely fought for. And now, as he approached the end, he was showing us how to transcend suffering by finding meaning in it. 'I not only learned things about the world, but I absorbed them to the point where they became part of who I am,' he said. One of those things was the deep mystery at the heart of each person – the fact that we are in the world but not of it. The fact that we can somehow stand back from our natural condition and question it from a perspective seemingly beyond time and space. Could we say, therefore, that his whole life was a rehearsal for death – a rehearsal for that moment 'when death shines a light back across life and ennobles the love that led up to it'?

In a poignant essay from 2005, entitled 'Dying Quietly', Scruton wrote that 'My death is not simply, for me, the death of RS, the event about which you might read in an obituary. It is a vast crisis, standing athwart my life and commanding me to prepare for it…Every death prompts the search for meaning – especially the death of someone loved. But my death challenges me in another way; its inevitability is like a command – namely, live your life so that this will be part of it and not just an end to it. St Paul reminds us that "in the midst of life we are in death" meaning that our normal ways of living forbid us to plan either the time or the manner of our extinction. Yet we need to live in such a way that death, when it comes, is not a catastrophe but (if possible) a culmination – a conclusion to our actions that can be read back into all that preceded it and show it to be worthwhile'.

In the quiet and dignified way in which he died Roger Scruton testified to the truth of his own words. For many people, his death was, indeed, a catastrophe – the loss of someone who had given them hope in dark times. And yet, as I glanced at him for the last time, I saw a smiling man whose end was the conclusion he had always hoped for and richly deserved. It was a fitting conclusion that rendered his brave and beautiful life profoundly worthwhile.

A Bibliography of Roger Scruton's Books, 1974–2022

Art and Imagination: A Study in the Philosophy of Mind, South Bend: St. Augustine's Press, 1998 (first published in 1974).

The Aesthetics of Architecture, Princeton, NJ: Princeton University Press, 1979.

The Meaning of Conservatism, South Bend: St. Augustine's Press, 2002 (first published in 1980).

The Politics of Culture and Other Essays, Manchester: Carcanet Press, 1981.

Fortnight's Anger, Manchester: Carcanet Press, 1981.

A Short History of Modern Philosophy: From Descartes to Wittgenstein, London & New York: Routledge, 2006 (first published in 1981).

The Palgrave Macmillan Dictionary of Political Thought, London: Palgrave Macmillan, 2007 (first published in 1982).

Kant: A Very Short Introduction, Oxford: Oxford University Press, 2001 (first published in 1982).

The Aesthetic Understanding: Essays in the Philosophy of Art and Culture, South Bend: St. Augustine's Press, 1998 (first published 1983).

Thinkers of the New Left, Harlow: Longman (subsequently London: The Claridge Press) 1985.

Sexual Desire: A Philosophical Investigation, London: Continuum, 2006 (first published in 1986).

Spinoza: A Very Short Introduction, Oxford: Oxford University Press, 2002 (first published in 1986).

A Land Held Hostage: Lebanon and the West, London: The Claridge Press, 1987.

Untimely Tracts, London: The Macmillan Press, 1987.

Conservative Thinkers: Essays from 'The Salisbury Review' (Ed.), London: The Claridge Press, 1988.

Conservative Thoughts: Essays from 'The Salisbury Review' (Ed.), London: The Claridge Press, 1988.

The Philosopher on Dover Beach: Essays, Manchester: Carcanet, 1990 (subsequently reprinted by St. Augustine's Press in 1997).

Francesca: A Novel, London: Sinclair-Stevenson, 1991.

A Dove Descending and Other Stories, London: Sinclair-Stevenson, 1991.

Conservative Texts: An Anthology (Ed.), London: Macmillan, 1991.

Xanthippic Dialogues, London: Sinclair-Stevenson, 1993 (subsequently reprinted by St. Augustine's Press in 1998).

Modern Philosophy: An Introduction and Survey, London: Pimlico, 2004 (first published in 1994).

The Classical Vernacular: Architectural Principles in an Age of Nihilism, Manchester: Carcanet, 1994.

Animal Rights and Wrongs, London: Continuum, 2000 (first published in 1996).

Philosophy: Principles and Problems, London: Continuum, 2005 (first published as *An Intelligent Person's Guide to Philosophy*, 1996).

The Aesthetics of Music, Oxford: Oxford University Press, 1997.

On Hunting, London: Yellow Jersey Press, 1998.

Modern Culture, London: Continuum, 2005 (first published as *An Intelligent Person's Guide to Modern Culture* in 1998).

Perictione in Colophon: Reflections on the Aesthetic Way of Life, South Bend: St. Augustine's Press, 2000.

England; An Elegy, London: Continuum, 2006 (first published in 2000).

The West and the Rest, London: Continuum, 2003 (first published in 2002).

Death-Devoted Heart: Sex and the Sacred in Wagner's Tristan and Isolde, Oxford: Oxford University Press, 2004.

News From Somewhere: On Settling, London: Continuum, 2004.

The Need for Nations, London: Civitas, 2004 (an abridged version of this pamphlet appears as 'Conserving Nations' in *A Political Philosophy*, 2006).

Gentle Regrets: Thoughts from a Life, London: Continuum, 2005.

A Political Philosophy: Arguments for Conservatism, London: Continuum, 2006.

Culture Counts: Faith and Feeling in a World Besieged, New York: Encounter Books, 2007.

Beauty, Oxford: Oxford University Press, 2009 (Published as *Beauty: A Very Short Introduction*, 2011).

Understanding Music, London: Continuum, 2009.

I Drink Therefore I Am, London: Continuum, 2009.

The Uses of Pessimism: And the Danger of False Hope, London: Atlantic Books, 2010; Oxford: Oxford University Press, 2013.

Green Philosophy, London: Atlantic Books, 2011 (Published as *How to Think Seriously About the Planet: The Case for Environmental Conservatism*, Oxford: Oxford University Press, 2012).

The Face of God, London: Continuum, 2012.

Our Church: A Personal History of the Church of England, London: Atlantic Books, 2012.

Notes From Underground, New York City, NY: Beaufort Books, 2014.

The Soul of the World, Princeton, NJ: Princeton University Press, 2014.

How to Be a Conservative, London: Bloomsbury Continuum, 2014.

The Disappeared, London: Bloomsbury Reader, 2015.

Fools, Frauds, and Firebrands: Thinkers of the New Left, London: Bloomsbury Continuum, 2015.

Confessions of a Heretic, London: Notting Hill Editions, 2016.

Conversations with Roger Scruton (Roger Scruton & Mark Dooley), London: Bloomsbury Continuum, 2016.

The Ring of Truth: The Wisdom of Wagner's Ring of Nibelung, New York City, NY: Harry N. Abrams, 2017.

On Human Nature, Princeton, NJ: Princeton University Press, 2017.

Conservatism: Ideas in Profile, London: Profile Books, 2017.

Where We Are: The State of Britain Now, London: Bloomsbury Continuum, 2018.

Conservatism: An Invitation to a Great Tradition, New York City, NY: St. Martin's Press, 2018.

Music as an Art, London: Bloomsbury Continuum, 2018.

Souls in the Twilight, New York City, NY: Beaufort Books, 2018.

Wagner's Parsifal: The Music of Redemption, London: Allen Lane, 2020.

Against the Tide: The Best of Roger Scruton's Columns, Commentaries and Criticism (Mark Dooley ed.), London: Bloomsbury Continuum 2022.

Index

183